Consecrated Spirits

Consecrated Spirits

*A thousand years of spiritual writings
by women religious*

Compiled by

Felicity Leng

Paulist Press
New York / Mahwah, NJ

Originally published in the UK under the title
Consecrated Spirits
by the Canterbury Press of
13A Hellesdon Park Road,
Norwich, Norfolk NR6 5DR

Library of Congress Control Number: 2012946058

Published by Paulist Press
997 Macarthur Bouelvard
Mahwah, New Jersey 07430

www.paulistpress.com

Printed and bound in the
United States of America

Contents

In memory of Sister Pia Buxton CJ
(1932–2010)

I think the communion of saints is stronger than we realize. You haven't got to meet a person in the flesh really to get to know them, to affect one another very deeply at a spiritual level.

Dame Felicitas Corrigan, OSB

Introduction

This is an anthology of spiritual writings by women religious from the earliest times to the present day. To ensure the basic coherence of the pieces included, all the writers lived or expressed themselves within the Judaeo-Christian, and for the most part the Western, tradition. They come mainly from the Roman, Anglican (Episcopalian) and Orthodox churches, but with some input from what might be called dissenting traditions. The book includes prayers, meditations, expositions, divine psychology, autobiography, spiritual advice, and comments on and recommendations for the appropriate pursuit of a religious life. Some extracts describe or reveal attitudes and experiences that typify certain important periods of convent life but also show how nuns related to each other and to their families.

Many of these passages are taken from journals and other autobiographical writings in which women engage in a dialogue with God or the Absolute. They may be analytical, testify to God's action in their minds and spirits; seek clarity, reassurance, courage, support and so on; but as often, after relating experiences of spiritual emptiness and then refreshment, seek to strengthen and encourage the faith and self-confidence of others. They may record the emptying of ego as a preparation for a mystical encounter with God, or for an entry into a communion with the natural world that liberates from rule, order and role-playing, but as often celebrate moments of self-realization in a world that seems to deny the God-given uniqueness of being this woman now. They range from the life-saving conviction of election to a hope, in the midst of doubt, in its possibility against all the odds.

The main structure is not chronological and the book does not advance towards some final enlightened clarification of thought and practice, since I do not hold that the understanding and vision of religious women of previous centuries, however constricted by the roles assigned them, were necessarily more 'primitive' and less privileged than those of our age. The longing of religious women of the past for self-expression and celebration, and for social, political and sexual emancipation appropriate to their individual and communal spiritual purpose, carries an exemplary power to strengthen our own resolve in seemingly very different circumstances, in which similarly inimical forces try to deny the individual her chance to create, define, realize her charisms, and discover and communicate with her ultimate significance.

I am sure that many of these passages manage to convey what the contemplative nun Sister Wendy Beckett has admired in one of her chosen women artists, Martha Alf, who drew four pears yet created 'contemplative formal equivalents to mystical experiences', speaking 'to us of the human heart and its hunger for spiritual wisdom', and in another, Maria Chevska, whose 'faith in the enormous inner strength a woman can command' is evident when we see a figure in a painting 'refusing to be quenched by many waters' and instead 'riding the waters, yielding to their force and thereby taking into herself potential death – but transforming it . . . Her desire is more inward, a desire that depends on no outward rescue for its fulfilment'.[1]

* * *

All things are done with mystery and because of love
(St Catherine of Siena).

Everything God makes is produced in love, humility and peace. That is why humans are able to love and find peace in true humility. If people live in love, avoid pride and maintain a state of peace, they will not ruin the world. Love, humility and

---

1 Wendy Beckett, *Contemporary Women Artists* (Oxford, 1988), pp. 18, 32

peace are the divine powers of healing by which God restores
our pristine state of being
(St Hildegard of Bingen).

Similar sentiments are to be found in the writings of women
religious throughout the ages. Although there have been many
changes in the religious life as its characteristic forms and interests developed over the Christian centuries, Catherine's and
Hildegard's statements can scarcely be bettered as taut summa-
ries of the main themes in this book, however varied the local
interests referred to and however nuanced the chosen forms of
expression may be.

The qualities of religious communities

Ideally, religious communities incarnate many things that people
of any political persuasion no longer find in society: nobility of
spirit, a sense of sacrifice, freedom within the bounds of chosen
restrictions, sincerity, an ecologically responsible environment,
time and space for silence and meditation, and reflection on
ultimate experiences, such as death, that most contemporary
societies sentimentalize or ignore.

A successful religious community is a microcosm of the
Church, which itself is modelled on the family, and its associa-
tions with love, affection, generosity and compassion, the prime
qualities of an effective successful religious society.

Now, as often in the past, the religious life can offer a stable
yet, compared with secular society, radical form of human
community and relations, and an emphatic image of the 2000-
year-old community to which its particular tradition tries to give
a new emphasis. The life of women religious has always been
radical in that sense, however long-lasting and unchanged any
specific form of Rule has been. A woman living in a community
of women (even in a community of one) echoes, yet exists at a
critically valuable distance from, the society she has not rejected
but is a distinctive part of. The social nature of Christian faith
is far from lost to the thinking and contemplation of religious

women. The religious conscience is not cut off from society but is potentially one of its essential shaping forces.

Throughout the ages their distance from society has enabled women religious – paradoxically it might seem – to take or to prompt major steps in the emancipation of women, and therefore of society as a whole. The seventeenth-century education of women outside the home initiated mainly by the Visitandines and Ursulines was an immense social change that fed back into the religious life itself as the range of women's possible knowledge was extended by instruction and discussion (in fact, the Ursulines had already founded a girls' school at Avignon in 1574). The spread of an essential set of Renaissance ideas and ideals, in the form of the Catholic Counter-Reformation, depended to a considerable extent on the access to culture and the beginnings of an actual rather than Utopian equality of education for men and women. Of course it also relied on the extraordinary impulse furnished by the organizational abilities and writings of individual women religious, such as the incomparable Teresa of Avila. The Protestant Reformation (with certain rare exceptions) suppressed monasteries, convents and religious vows and redefined the cultural life of women in many ways in the vast number of priests' and pastors' families that now came into being throughout Reformed Europe. But the opportunities for concentrated devotion and thinking provided by, say, the whole gamut of Teresa's production, from the burgeoning new understanding of psychology and introspection, of the relationship between the transcendent and humanity, of practical community direction through letter-writing and an intense exploration of the humanity of Jesus, relied on the religious community and on avoiding the risks of marriage and child-bearing.

Madeleine Sophie Barat, who founded the more modern Society of the Sacred Heart of Jesus after the French Revolution (and with the constant threat of similar upheavals ahead), still looked to Teresa of Avila as a model for her nuns because: 'I love this Saint, her Christlike spirit, her love for him, and her inward life which we ought to imitate. I am pleased to find souls among my daughters who thought of becoming Carmelites at one time, because they enjoy the basis of the inward life, and that makes them first-class religious when it is joined to the apostolic spirit. Our Society is intended for both aims: to cultivate prayer and to save souls and its strength must come from the power of contemplation. It is all the more important to do that now because we live in times that are much more difficult than St Teresa's.'[2]

Silence and contemplation are major themes in nuns' writings, for silence is an important means of apprehending the divine. For instance, as Sœur Marie-Aimée de Jésus (Dorothée Quoniam, 1839–74) wrote in her The twelve degrees of Silence: '. . . the interior life could consist of one word: silence!'; and Mother Maribel of Wantage (Mary Isabella Rough, 1887–1970), remarked: 'Silence is not a thing we make; it is something into which we enter'.

On many occasions, the religious life has been seen as a morally rigorous area, and even as one opposed to the secular, extra-monastic world, which permitted a more relaxed, and less legalistic practice of Christianity. Latin Catholicism inherited a highly rational legalism from ancient Rome, but its 'pervasive sacramental system' offered 'innumerable "escape hatches" from the kind of total rationalization of life demanded by Old Testament prophecy . . . Ethical absolutism of the prophetic variety was more or less safely segregated in the institutions of monasticism, thus kept from "contaminating" the body of Christendom as a whole'.[3] This conviction of greater purity of contemplation and endeavour has persisted over the centuries. It has emerged not only in strict Catholic communities but among those Evangelical sodalities that have hankered after and, in spite of repression and even persecution, even achieved a religious life apart, and the greater degree of consecration to the authentic Christ they imagined it would provide. The austerity of the Cistercians and Port Royal, but also their contemplative enthusiasm, was echoed when the brilliant Anna van Schurman took Ignatius of Loyola's motto as the watchword of her doubly

2 cf., Margaret Ward, The Life of St Madeleine Sophie (Roehampton, 1925)
3 Peter L. Berger, The Social Reality of Religion (London, 1969), p. 127

reformed life in this new 'garden of souls' (*Amor meus crucifixus est*: 'My love is nailed to the cross') and joined a Labadist community in the Netherlands of the late seventeenth century. She remarked: 'Amongst all mortals I have never found any that has expressed so truly and vividly the spirit and manner of living of the early Church or the calling of the first Christians . . . How can anyone blame me for following the best teacher and leader, for accompanying other believers, for looking to Jesus, author and perfecter of faith, for hurrying towards my heavenly Fatherland, and pursuing the highest and only goal, the glory of God and the honour of Christ'.[4]

Anna von Schurman, together with a surprisingly large number of women religious in past centuries, such as the Mexican Sor Juana Inés de la Cruz, was a passionate defender not only of the right of women to choose their religious community but of women's intellectual rights. Of course, for centuries the roles of women in Christian society were subordinated to those of men, with various degrees of emphasis, especially when, as so often happened, military prowess and conquest were conceived of as prime virtues. Woman's supposed part in the origin of sin and the expulsion of humanity from Paradise constantly reinforced her material and intellectual inferiority. The novel stress on the Virgin Mary as the new Eve in devotion from the twelfth and thirteenth centuries onwards helped to correct the image of women to some extent, and strong devotion to Mary in women's Orders was understandable. Another outcome, which has persisted to our own times, was the recurrent inclination of religious women, and particularly of women religious, to play a major role in heretical movements such as Catharism, and to a certain extent Albigensianism, and scarcely tolerated and perhaps quasi-heretical movements such as Beguinism in Germany and the Low Countries, the highly intellectual Jansenism and near-Jansenism of the nuns of Port Royal in seventeenth-century France, or the English Catholic Mary Ward's courageous attempt to found a

---

4 Una Birch, *Anna van Schurman: Artist, Scholar, Saint* (London, 1909), p. 180

female equivalent of the Society of Jesus, and certainly the many socio-political versions of the Missions inspired by Vatican II and the theology of liberation. The last-mentioned efforts even led to a new kind of martyrdom on behalf of the poor, marginalized and disenfranchised, as with the Maryknoll Sisters and members of similar Orders working in Latin America, whose solidarity with the greater community of the impoverished and repressed masses was rewarded with torture and death.

The religious life in the post-war age

The thinking of Dietrich Bonhoeffer, German theologian and martyr under Nazism, has proved to be relevant to many aspects and areas of Christianity long after his lifetime, and the life of women religious is no exception. In 1935, two years after Hitler came to power, the necessarily unaccommodating Bonhoeffer wrote: 'The restoration of the Church will surely come only from a new kind of monasticism which has nothing in common with the old but a life of uncompromising adherence to the sermon on the Mount in imitation of Christ.'

The new Rules and Constitutions devised by most religious orders and congregations during the immense rethinking of purpose and practice initiated by the Roman Catholic Church in the 1960s–70s, after the Second Vatican Council, might well have taken Bonhoeffer's statement as their watchword. But some were slow or unwilling to put their revised guidelines into practice. In his equally critical yet optimistic comments on the contemplative life in the modern age (in *Contemplation in a World of Action*, London, 1984), the American Trappist Thomas Merton was sure that this return to basics meant that certain structures of the religious life needed to be shaken and others to fall, and that the real problem of monastic renewal was not surrender to the 'secular city' but a 'recovery of the deep desire of God that draws' a person to seek a 'totally new way of being in the world'. The contemplative life has to be a real challenge, but one that 'tones us up to meet new possibilities, the unexpected, for which we have not been previously capable, for which we have not been previously ready.' Religious now must choose the world, in the sense that 'to choose the world is to choose to do the work I am capable of doing', in collaboration with my sister or brother, 'to make the world better, more free. More just, more liveable, more human.' Yet he also reminds us: 'Contemplatives have a special slant on the theological and spiritual problems of the Church and the world . . . In the contemplative life, action exists for the sake of contemplation and vice versa.' The openness of contemplatives is justified in so far as it enables them to be better contemplatives, and to share with others the fruit of their individual contemplation. But: 'We can have a certain personal fullness even when the changing institution is provisional, and we have to learn to be able to be contemplatives in the midst of the dynamic, in the midst of movement.'

Contemplation is the heart of what it means to be a monk, or nun, for the Greek word *monos* means 'alone'. Inspired by the European Taizé and Iona communities, there is a growing movement to revive evangelism in the United States by reclaiming part of the Catholic monastic tradition. Numbers of Christian communities practising this 'New Monasticism' are springing up in blighted urban settings all over America.

Some religious communities have responded to the challenges of twenty-first-century conditions and are pioneering new ways of living. For instance, the Caldwell Dominican Sisters, who run Genesis Farm, an ecological learning centre in the USA; the Dominican Sisters in Wicklow in Ireland, who set up *An Tairseach*, an ecological farm and education centre; and the Benedictine nuns of the Conventus of Our Lady of Consolation, Stanbrook, who have downsized and relocated from their magisterial building in Worcestershire to the environmentally friendly nunnery in the North York moors National Park in England.

Such efforts are real expressions of the thinking behind the joint declaration of the Pope and the Ecumenical Patriarch, which said: 'It is God's will that his design and our hope for it will be realized through our co-operation in restoring its original harmony. In our own times we are witnessing a growth of an ecological awareness which needs to be encouraged, so that it will lead to practical programmes and initiatives'.

* * *

This volume is offered in its own right but also complements my *Invincible Spirits: a thousand years of women's spiritual writings*, which itself contained many extracts from the spiritual and practical writings of women religious. The widespread and encouraging reactions to that book show that there is a call for an anthology that reveals more of the whys, wherefores, advantages, assurances and achievements, but also of the difficulties and puzzles peculiar to the lives of women religious as revealed by some of their most illustrious but also some of their valuably obscure representatives. I hope that the passages selected will send readers to the original works and to go on to make their own discoveries of the many other brilliant historical and contemporary woman religious not included in this book. The best result would be that they would help to re-create them by adding their own adaptations and embarking on their own inspirational records and enactments of the same and similar experiences.

Felicity Leng
Lisieux, France, 2011

I

Visionaries, Mystics & Contemplatives

❧

JULIAN OF NORWICH

One constant of mystical visions is the ability to demonstrate how the infinitely small or insignificant reveals the infinitely great, the consummation of all good. Julian of Norwich cultivated the intensity and clarity that made such revelations possible.

This little thing

In my vision he showed me something very small. It was only as big as a hazel nut as it lay there, it seemed, in the palm of my hand. It was as round as any ball. I looked at it and tried to work out what it might be and what it might mean. 'What on earth can it be?' I asked myself. The same answer came back however I put the question: 'It is all that is made' was what I heard again and again. I was quite astonished to think that it could last, because it was so very small that it could easily have faded away entirely. But then came the explanation: 'It lasts and will always last because God loves it.' After all, everything originates in God's love.

I could see that this little thing had three qualities: God made it, God loves it, and God looks after it. But I cannot say what it should mean to me that God makes, looks after and loves me since I shall never find true rest or joy until I am joined to him essentially. Indeed, I shall never know that rest and joy until I am so united with God that nothing created can come between him and me.

It seemed to me that this tiny thing was creation, and might have disappeared because it was so small. If we are to come to love the uncreated God, we have to realize that everything that is made is like nothing. That is why our hearts and souls are not entirely peaceful. Instead we try to discover peace in this tiny thing. Then we find that it is so very small that it offers us no peace whatsoever; yet we cannot acknowledge our Lord, who is entirely powerful, wise and good. He is peace indeed, perfect peace. He wants to be acknowledged and is glad when we find our peace in him. Everything that is below him is inadequate for us. That is why no soul can find peace until it is without everything created. When a soul has decided to become nothing for love's sake, in order to possess God who is everything, it will be able to know and enjoy spiritual peace and rest.

Our Lord showed me that he is overjoyed when a simple soul approaches him without complication, simply and genuinely. I think this means that the Holy Spirit inspires the soul to long for God, as if it asked God of his goodness to give himself to that soul, declaring that God is sufficient for it and that it cannot ask him for anything less than that if it is to be truly worthy of him. It tells its Lord that if it asks for anything less, it will always be lacking, for it can find everything only in God.

A soul loves to say the words 'God, in your goodness', and to come close to God's good will. All God's creatures and all his blessed works are wrapped in his goodness, eternally and supremely. God is eternity and made us only for himself. He has restored us by his precious passion and keeps us always in his loving-kindness. God does all this because he is goodness.

This revelation was intended to show us how wise it is to cling to the goodness of God.

Composite translation from surviving versions of the Middle English of Julian of Norwich. Cf. *A Showing of God's Love*, Sr A.M. Reynolds, CP, ed. (London, 1958); *A Book of Showings to the Anchoress Julian of Norwich*, vols I & II (Toronto, 1978); with reference to the extracts in the Westminster Cathedral *Florilegium*, ed. J. Walsh & E. Colledge as: *The Knowledge of Ourselves and of God* (London, 1961).

BD BEATRICE OF NAZARETH

Beatrice's thirteenth-century description of the seven modes of ascent to absolute love is one of the most lyrical yet consistently developed examples of the Cistercian tradition of contemplation. It is a marvellously sustained exposition of the truth that 'visible things are transitory: it is the invisible things that are really permanent' and therefore: 'We want our transitory life to be absorbed into the life that is eternal' (2 Cor. 4.15–8). Because she writes from her own experience, she offers a 'potency that far surpasses our own limits', for 'ancient authors were more aware of some aspects of truth than we are ... They help us move towards a more integral wisdom by challenging many of our presuppositions ... about the nature of reality' and show us that the 'true meaning of life is not immediately accessible, but has to be sought in transcendence' (Michael Casey, Sacred Reading, Liguori, Miss., 1996, pp. 108–9).

The sixth and seventh ways of holy love

Almighty God offers the soul seven ways of loving that enable it to reach him.

When our Lord's bride has made considerable progress in the ascent towards perfect love, has passed through five initial stages and is closer to salvation, she experiences a sixth way that brings her closer to her Lord and gives her more profound knowledge of him. She feels that love has completely overcome all resistance in her; that she has mastered all her inadequacies; and that she is now able to use all her capacities. Because she no longer holds back in any way, she knows that all her strength is available to her. She is sure that her heart is secure and untrammelled, for it can act in peace and she is free to express herself fully.

Now everything seems uncomplicated and easily managed or abandoned, as she wishes. She can allow herself to do anything and illumine what seemed obscure, for everything is seen in the noble light of love. Now loving is joyous and she experiences God's own power operating in her, clear and pure, sweet in spirit, as free as she might wish, truly wise, and calmly accepting God who loves her.

Now she is like a housewife who has looked after her home. She has furnished it astutely and has made it neat and orderly. She has made sure that it is well protected and guarded. What she does is intelligently planned and is inwardly and outwardly assured. She does this or leaves that as seems due and right.

So it is with the soul. She is guided by love alone and love alone empowers her. Love is in her, doing things or leaving them aside, and love is in her and outside her, as she wishes. Like a fish that swims the length and breadth of the sea, and takes its rest in its depths; like a bird that flies the width and height of the air, and knows its freedom, so she feels her thoughts are unrestrained as her mind moves in the breadth, height and depth of love.

This higher power of love has guided the soul, and has guarded and protected her during her ascent. Love has given her the intellect, wisdom and the kindly strength of love. Yet love has also waited for her to reach greater heights, to be liberated from her personal restraints, and to rule her more intensely, before disclosing any hint of the violent passion that lies at the heart of love itself. But then love releases the soul and makes her so strong that in her actions she is indifferent to man, woman or devil, angel or saint, and even God himself, whether at work or at rest.

Then she realizes fully that love is quite alive in her, ready to operate as effectively in every part of her body as in everything she does. Yet she is well aware, for she can clearly see, that love is never found in the heavy labour and sweaty drudgery of those whom it chooses as its own.

All who want to unite with love must look for it reverently and faithfully. They must desire it so much that they keep to the road and surmount all obstacles before they find it. They cannot search out love if they want an easy time, with no effort, and with nothing irksome or inconvenient. They must treat every little thing as equally important before they are one with love supreme within them: with love that pays all debts, and makes everything simple, labour welcome, and all effort a pleasure. It rises through and above mere clarity of conscience, purity of heart, nobility and harmony of spirit, and sublimity of mind, and transcends all as the very principle of eternal life, so that the soul, already living an angelic life on this earth, is ready to pass into the everlasting life which God of his goodness offers to us all and every one.

Yet the soul has an even more sublime path of love to take, involving her in immense inward travel. Then love of eternity itself draws her relentlessly above all human notions of love, above senses and reason, up there above all the capabilities of the human heart in and of itself, so that the soul is raised by sheer love of eternity into the ultimate forever of love, into the unassailable wisdom of its silent heights, and simultaneously down into the ultimately profound abyss of God, down through and into everything in everything, into indestructibility itself, there above and in everything, everlastingly, almightily, all-embracingly supreme in all that is and all that exists and all that is all.

Now the soul is so profoundly immersed in love, and so driven by intense desire, that her heart is wrenched within, and grows restless, forcing her soul to pour out and melt in love, and her mind to become one with a great and irresistible longing. From this point her senses know that she may enjoy the pleasure of love for ever. Yet she must persevere and attune her desire to what awaits her, so that with all her heart she asks this and no more than this of God.

She cannot relax her longing, for love will not allow her to calm her spirit or just breathe quietly to recover her strength. Love keeps her at a point between encouragement and disappointment, suddenly testing her, even tormenting her, bringing death and giving life, making whole and wounding once again, rendering insane and then restoring peace and clarity of mind. Thus love raises the soul to a higher state of awareness. And so the soul ascends spiritually, progressing beyond this world until she reaches the timeless eternity of love. Then the soul moves above human forms of love as her desire to rise and transcend lifts her above the bounds of her own nature . . . She has reached a place where there is no room for fear, for she has entered a state of mutual love that lasts for ever. She knows the joy of the Lord, and there is no better way to know and possess him . . . Lord, may we all know you thus. Amen.

From the Latin and Old Dutch versions of: [Beatrijs van Nazareth] L. Reypens, ed., *Vita Beatricis: De autobiografie van de z. Beatrijs van Tienen O. Cist., 1200–68* (Antwerp, 1964), *passim*.

MARGUERITE PORETE

Marguerite Porete, one of many female martyrs to ecclesiastical fundamentalism and exclusivism, describes an aspect of the way to live in the love of God and reach perfect illumination of the spirit. She writes from personal knowledge not only of the vagaries and joys of contemplation, but of the everyday experiences of unpretentious souls wishing to clarify and intensify their prayer-life and experience of God.

The life of love

When a soul comes to love God as he is, she is made conscious of her own nothingness – being nothing, having nothing, whether from herself, from her fellow-Christians, or even from God himself. The soul is then so small she cannot see herself. All created things are so far from her she cannot feel them. God is so infinitely greater she cannot grasp him. Through this nothingness she has the assurance of knowing nothing, being able to do nothing by herself, and willing nothing. And this nothingness brings her everything which otherwise she would not have.

She is afloat on a sea of peace, drifting without any impulse from inside herself or any breeze from outside – both of which can undo peace, but not for her, because she is in full command and beyond interference or care. If she did anything through her outer senses, this would remain *outside* her, and if God did anything in her, this would be him working in her, for his own purpose, and so also *outside* her. What she does no more burdens her than what she does not do. She has no more being in herself, having given it all freely without asking 'Why?'. She no longer feels doubt or trust. Reason asks what she does feel then, and Love replies: Absolute certainty and total acceptance of the divine will. This is what makes her completely free.

The free soul lost in love

Being completely free, and in command on her sea of peace, the soul is nonetheless drowned and loses herself through God, with him and in him. She loses her identity as does the water from a river – like the Ouse or the Meuse – when it flows into the sea. It has done its work and can relax in the arms of the sea, and the same is true of the soul. Her work is over and she can lose herself in what she has totally become: Love. Love is the bridegroom of her happiness, enveloping her wholly in his love and making her part of that which is. This is a wonder to her and she has become a wonder. Love is her only delight and pleasure.

The soul now has no name but Union in Love. As the water that flows into the sea becomes sea, so the soul becomes Love. Love and the soul are no longer two things but one. She is then ready for the next stage. Reason asks if there can be another stage, and Love answers: Yes, once she has become totally free, she falls into a trance of nothingness, and this is the next highest stage. Then she lives no longer in the life of grace, or in the life of the spirit, but in the glorious life of divinity. God has conferred this special favour on her, and nothing except his goodness can now touch her . . . What this means is being in God without being oneself, since to be in God is indeed being . . . Her way to God is no longer through penances, or the sacraments of the Church, or thoughts or words or deeds. She is not helped on her way by creatures of this earth or by those of heaven. She is beyond justice, mercy, glory, the knowledge and love of God, and beyond praising his name . . . Those who have been truly caught up and captured and completely taken over by love have no heart for anything but love, even if they have to suffer love's pangs and torments for ever, even though their sufferings are as great as God is good. Those who doubt this have not loved truly.

A French mystic of the thirteenth century [Marguerite Porete], *A Mirror for Simple Souls*, Charles Crawford, tr. (Dublin & New York, 1981), pp. 120–22.

BD YVETTE OF HUY

Yvette of Huy, mother and recluse, relates (as recorded by Hugh of Floreffe) the occasions of intense rapture in the Lord when she was granted an extraordinary ability to read the thoughts, misdeeds, temptations and trials hidden in the hearts of novices, nuns, priests and others, and to predict their actions, so that she could detect and if possible correct their behaviour, deflect them from danger and even confound certain evil designs.

What I saw when I contemplated divine mysteries

Whenever I was enraptured in spirit, I was accompanied by two angels from each of the nine orders, so that there were nine angels to the right of me and nine angels to the left of me. Each single angel was dressed entirely in golden garments interwoven with strings of a vast range of multicoloured jewels as described in the Book of the Prophet. When I was enraptured in contemplation, I could understand, recognize and mark out clearly what each gem signified. I saw the angels' names and their various orders and their tasks as precisely as we humans can ever mark such things out. My spiritual rapture made this possible for me although, being a simple woman without education, I had never learned anything about such matters before this point.

I saw myself clothed in various garments and most extraordinarily honoured by being allowed to appear before the throne of God and the Lamb dressed like an angel and adorned as if I were a bride prepared for the wedding ceremony. I was vouchsafed certain knowledge of a number of divine mysteries, but I have never revealed these to other mortals even though they have so often pressed me to do so, for such things are forbidden to humans unless enraptured . . .

When I am lost in profound contemplation of eternity and the three Persons of the Blessed Trinity, I cannot be brought back from meditation on the unseen world without a dire threat to my mental and bodily health. My senses are as if numbed, and I suffer severely, for I am torn between my desire to live normally and the glory of my enraptured state.

When I feel that I am sunk in the Lord's presence and immersed in the vision granted me of everlasting life, God's grace is extended to me and to all those whom I know, so that his intentions for us are fulfilled. If you are steeped in God and the more you enter into the glory of the unseen world, the more you are cleansed of any desire for the visible world. Then my mind is replete with love for him who made me, so that I persist only in him and I am indifferent to everything that lies outside him, and even to my own body, for attending to it takes away from the joy of contemplating God, and recalling that supreme happiness is my only pleasure. Thus the maintenance of my very life seems like a form of death when compared with concentration on different aspects of the divine . . .

When I had to leave my Lord for any considerable stretch of time, I did not forget but focussed on the human nature of Jesus Christ, who chose to be born of Mary within the confines of earthly time. But I could not long bear the distress of my absence from Jesus my Beloved, and I began to twist and shake, to shout and scream as if I were in the throes of childbirth. I would sigh as if I were a girl enamoured of a lover and refused to eat the earthly food they put before me, for, strange to say, I had no desire for human sustenance. Yet my body received a certain strength that kept me alive, even though my mind was set on heavenly things, and I was only partly separated from my Beloved . . .

The Lord gave me the grace of understanding and knowledge through the Holy Spirit residing in me, so that I knew the secret intentions of everyone living in my house. If they tried to keep secret from me all manner of things which they believed only they and God were aware of, when they came before me I would immediately relate everything in their hearts in minute detail, as if their innermost conscience had been turned inside out and I could look at everything in it. As a result, people who had done wrong secretly would try to avoid me in case I scrutinized them relentlessly and openly described, for all to hear, whatever lurked within them.

Translated and adapted from: Hugh of Floreffe, 'De Beata Yvetta vidua reclusa Hui in Belgio', *Acta Sanctorum* (1642), vol. xiii, Jan., cc 863–86, *passim*.

HADEWIJCH II

Hadewijch describes the mysterious luminosity of love in terms developed from traditional mystical sources by the medieval Beguines of the Low Countries.

The spark

God's everlasting light
Shines within,
An ever-pure spark,
A beam intensely bright;
The core of inner truth,
One with the divine Spring.

It is our deepest truth:
Love overflowing
Beyond all mind and sense;
The divine spark of being
And supernatural truth of
God's transforming power.

The one that is many,
The inward way to truth;
Calling on infinite light,
Banishing all mystery;
Never dimmed
By difficulty or darkness.

We must face this clarity
Without prejudice or conceit,
Free from received ideas,
And follow the beam
Through infinite depths
To find light in our own light.

We must forget the years
Of wanting all those things
That bind our souls in iron,
And, without care or shame,
Pierce through nothingness
To the essence of the light.

How foolish to look here and there
For traces of the wholesome light
That lives within us infinitely strong,
Offering freedom from all struggle,
From desires to impose and rule,
And all objects or vain dreams of self.

How glorious to exist
In infinite space by love bereft
Of all but love's own freedom to exist,
Where love is everlasting life
In sheer delight of knowing
God's eternal love and power.

Translated from Hadewijch II, *Mengeldichten* 27 (Hadewijch, J. Van
Mierlo, SJ, ed., *Mengeldichten* [Antwerp, 1952]; cf. *Hadewijch d'Anvers*,
J.B. Porion, ed., [Brussels, n.d.]).

ST GERTRUDE THE GREAT OF HELFTA

Dom Gueranger's comments on the seventh of St Gertrude's exercises for her nuns also apply to the sixth: 'To make this exercise more dramatic to some extent, she has impersonated the divine perfections which act more directly on people in this life: Mercy, Truth, Peace, Wisdom, Self-oblation, Compassion, and Constancy. She takes the seven canonical hours, which pious practice has associated with our Lord's Passion from his agony in the garden to his burial, and she cites the soul, with Love as its advocate and defender, before these seven divine perfections successively. She tells the soul how to plead its cause; a cause the soul cannot lose, because it is humble and penitent. This kind of drama, in which abstract perfections are treated as living persons, was at that time in great favour in Germany.' The following is a summary combination of the sixth and seventh exercises.

Fixed where Jesus wishes it to be fixed

You are like a bereaved and lonely turtle-dove, saddened because of the weariness of this life and of your longing to see the face of your Beloved, so fold the wings of your restless desires like living creatures before God's throne. Tell him that your heart is wholly where your treasure is, and beg him to grant you a happy death:

'My heart is fixed where Jesus wishes it to be fixed. Jesus, supremely beloved above all, you are the undying life of my soul. My heart longs for you and thirsts after you. A wound of rapture has torn and pierced it, and the light of this world is torment and anguish, because I know your beauty and greatness, your love and the blessedness in you.

'Waiting disappoints my heart. How long, my well-beloved, must I wait for the moment when I know you and see your glorious face? My thirsting soul finds heaven and earth and everything in them apart from you, as chill and dreary as a winter's day. You are my glad spring-time, and my only consolation will be to see you at long last.

'My love, when will you tell my body to return to dust, so that my liberated soul can soar on high to you, her God and living source? The divine rays streaming from your throne reach me and fill my whole being with the pure light of your loving kindness. So why do you leave this poor and helpless leaf so long on the tree, to be shaken and buffeted by the fierce storms of this world?

'My love, watch over me at the hour of my death. Mark me out now so that I know you will be with me then, and your goodness, my only support during that time which we must all endure, will exclude anything that might harm my soul.'

* * *

Take Compassion and Love with you, and present yourself before God in their company, charging them with the duty of answering to God at the end of your life for all your debts and all your imperfections. Then say this prayer:

'Charity is thrice blessed, for she can quench her thirst in you, Fountain of life, and the eyes allowed to see you face to face are thrice blessed. Show your great goodness, God, and blot out all my sins with your unfailing mercy and forgiveness. Although I am quite unworthy to look up at you, hear my prayer; satisfy my soul with the sight of you at the hour of my death; and grant me the sure hope of eternal rest in you.

'Divine Compassion, how exquisite you are! Merciful God, how dear you are to me! You open your arms to all; for you are the father of the fatherless, and the refuge of the poor.

'What shall I do, divine Compassion? Where shall I find refuge from this intolerable cold? My heart was always tepid and now it is overcome by a frost affecting every furrow of my soul. Let me find a shelter near you where I can recover from my soul's cold and confusion. Then I shall know warmth and life beneath your wings, and my hope will be fulfilled for ever in their shade. Make me entirely what you want me to be, so that, when I quit this life, the cloud of my body is dissolved and I behold your loving face.'

The Exercises of St Gertrude Virgin and Abbess, of the Order of St Benedict (London, 1863) (adapted), pp. 161–6; 199–204.

BD ANGELA OF FOLIGNO

Angela of Foligno offers a classic definition of love resulting from her visionary and intuitive, but also her practical, experience. The love she describes is the love that 'all love of other sights controls' (John Donne).

A reflection of God's own love

The vision of the Supreme Being awakens a love corresponding to God's own love. He inspires us to love everything that owes its existence to him, to love all good things and well-made things, and teaches us to love all creatures, rational and irrational, for love of him; and also inspires us to love everything, whatsoever it may be, which owes its existence to him and which he loves, especially those creatures in which we can see he delights particularly; for when our soul finds that God is particularly loving towards his creatures, then it also yearns for them in particular.

The clear sign of those who live as friends of God is that they are true followers of his only Son, keep their mind's eyes always fixed on him, and are ready to love and be with him, and always follow the will of their Beloved, the only Son of Almighty God . . .

The way to find the love of God is by constant, untiring, devout and ardent prayer, and by reading the Book of Life, from which we obtain the knowledge of God which we need if we also want his love.

Take comfort, my beloved, and see how we should love God and transform ourselves entirely in him; for this Christ, God uncreated and God incarnate, is all love, and therefore loves all and desires to be loved completely. Therefore he wants his children to be wholly transformed in him through love.

You are spiritual children, chosen through love, who live in the grace and charity of the good and perfect God. I pray you to transform yourselves by the perfection of love. Of course, we are all sons and daughters of God by creation, but his elect spiritual children are those in whom the God of love has planted his love, and in whom he delights because he finds his own likeness in them. This image in the soul of each child of God is formed there only through the grace of God and through perfect divine love. Those are perfect who have already transformed their behaviour and life in accordance with the life of Christ, who lived in this world poor and despised and full of suffering.

God, whose nature is noble, wishes to possess his children's hearts whole and entire, and not only a part of them, and longs for them directly, and without hindrance or anything contrary whatsoever. But he is so merciful to the soul that if it gives him its whole heart he accepts it willingly, and if it gives him only a part he also accepts the part, even though his perfect love naturally longs for the whole and not only a part.

We know that a bridegroom who loves his bride cannot endure her having any other companion either openly or in secret. Similarly, God cannot endure that. But I am quite certain that if people were to understand and taste the divine love of God who was made man and crucified for us, and who is the supreme Good, they would give themselves wholly to him, and take themselves away not only from other creatures, but from their own selves, and would love this loving God with their whole heart, and transform themselves entirely in God, the supreme Love.

Therefore, if the soul wishes to achieve this perfection of perfect love, which gives itself wholly and does not serve God for the sake of the reward which it hopes to receive from him, or because of the future life, but gives itself to God and serves him for his own sake, who is essentially good in himself and worthy of being loved for himself, then the soul must enter by the straight way and must walk along it on the feet of pure love, and remain upright, fervent, and orderly . . .

The characteristics of lovers

There are three properties peculiar to lovers which we must be aware of. There are also certain signs of love which show each of us whether he or she is a true lover or not.

The first property is to be truly transformed as the will of the Beloved decides. It seems to me that the will of the Beloved is his life as he demonstrates it in his own self. He shows us his poverty, suffering, and contempt, which we must all certainly experience, and when the soul is strengthened and practised in these things it is quite proof against all vice and temptation.

The second property is to be transformed in the qualities of the Beloved, of which I shall mention only three here. The first is love; that is, to love all creatures as is due and seemly. The second is to be humble and gentle. The third (which God gives to his true children) is steadfastness; for the closer the soul is to God, the less it changes in its own self . . .

The third property is to be wholly transformed in God, when we are beyond all temptation. Then we no longer live in ourselves, but in him; yet when we fall back again into our misery we must beware of too great concentration on any other creature and on our own selves.

Keep control over yourselves. Do not surrender to any creature, or lend yourselves to anything whatsoever; but give yourselves wholly to the one who says: 'You shall love the Lord with all your heart, and with all your mind, and with all your soul, and with all the strength that you have.'

The signs of love

The first sign of true love is that lovers submit their own will to the will of the beloved.

The second is that they forsake all other friendships that might be contrary to their love, even forsaking father and mother, brother and sister, and any other affection which is contrary to the will of the beloved.

The third is that there is nothing hidden in one which is not revealed to the other; and this (as I see it) is the sum and complement of all the other signs and effects of love.

The fourth and last is that lovers strive to make themselves like the beloved. If the beloved is poor, they strive to be poor; if the beloved is reputed to be untrustworthy, then they try to be untrustworthy too; if the beloved is grieving, then they try to share that distress, so that the state of one is like that of the other.

True and perfect love cannot exist between rich and poor, honourable and untrustworthy, sorrowful and joyous, because these states are quite different, and there can be no perfect love between them because one does not share the nature of the other. Love is a true virtue, which not only makes things like each other but unites them, and it always leads the soul to its like and not to its opposite.

Jesus Christ, who is Everlasting Love, certainly exhibited all these signs.

The Book of Divine Consolations of the Blessed Angela of Foligno, Mary G. Steegman, tr., Algar Thorold, intro. (London & New York, 1909), p. 124 *et passim.*

ST TERESA OF AVILA

Marina Tsvetaeva, one of the most perceptive Russian writers of the twentieth century, summarized the importance of the condition of rapture thus: 'Human beings see the world as it should be seen only in a state of absolute exaltation. After all, God created the world in a state of exaltation (although we might think that he created humankind in a somewhat less exalted condition . . .) and anyone who is not in a state of exaltation cannot see things as they really are' (Marina Tsvetaeva, Vivre dans le Feu: Confessions, *ed. Tzvetan Todorov, tr., Nadine Dubourvieux [Paris,*

2005], p. 91). Julia Kristeva has summarized the special physicality of Teresa's writing about this state of rapture: 'Your writing transcends your own historical period . . . it reaches us like water, that liquid matter you adore . . . and this water is more than a metaphor as it presents the metamorphoses of your supposed identity in the very act of writing, as you run like water from one state to another, from spasm to rejoicing, from your feelings to understanding them . . ."everything is nothing" [todo nada] . . . but you say Yes to this everything that is nothing, to this nothing that is everything . . . You say Yes to your visionary endeavour that is not an obra, *not an object, thing or product, but a continual process of transformation, as your writing infiltrates words into things and things into words, yet preserves their differences . . .' (Julia Kristeva,* Thérèse mon amour: Sainte Thérèse d'Avila *[Paris, 2008], pp. 87–8.*

The state of rapture

I happened to be at Mass on a feast of St Paul when suddenly the divinely human Jesus stood there before me in all the beauty and majesty with which painters portray him after his resurrection . . . This was an imaginary vision. I didn't see it with my physical eyes, or any other kind of eyes but the eyes of the soul. People who know much more than I about this kind of thing say that the intellectual vision is perfect compared with this way of seeing things, although this imaginary vision is certainly more proficient than images available to your physical eyes. These experts think that physical vision is the lowest form of seeing, and the most open to demonic deceit. I was not aware of this at the time, for when I saw the vision of Jesus I wished it had appeared in such a way that I could see it physically, for then my confessor could not have told me later that I was just being fanciful.

When the vision had gone, I started thinking immediately that I had fancied all this . . . but then Jesus gave me his grace and banished any suspicion that what I saw was just fanciful. Since then I have realized how silly I was to think otherwise. Even if I spent years and years trying to work out how to see something so beautiful, I would never be able or know how to do so, because what I saw was and remains beyond the scope of any human capabilities. Its whiteness and brilliancy alone are inconceivable. It isn't a dazzling brilliancy, but a delicate whiteness and an infused brilliancy which delights your sight more than anything else. Your eyes never grow tired of looking at it, and the visible brightness that makes this divine beauty apparent never strains them. This light is so different from any earthly light that even the brightness of the sun itself, compared with the brightness and light before our eyes, seems so obscure that we would never want to open our eyes again.

All descriptions fail, but the closest I can manage is that it is like transparently clear water running in a bed of crystal and reflecting the sun's rays compared with the muddiest water on a cloudy day flowing on the ordinary earth. Of course there is nothing like the sun present here, and the light I see isn't like sunlight. This light seems quite natural. Indeed, all other forms of light are artificial when compared with it. It never turns to night, and so, because it's always light, nothing ever changes it. No human beings, however talented, and however long they live and try to fathom it, could ever have the least idea of what it is. God puts this vision before us so instantaneously that we would never have time to open our eyes in time to see it, if it was necessary to open them at all. But it doesn't matter whether our eyes are open or shut. When Jesus want us to see this vision, we have to look at it, even if we don't want to. No distraction can blank it out, no force can resist it, and we can never see it by hard work or any efforts of our own. I have discovered this from experience, quite unmistakably . . .

If what I saw was an image, it was what I can only describe as a living image. I didn't see a dead man, but the living Christ. When this happens, he makes me see that he is God and man: not as he was in the tomb, but as he was when he had left it and had risen from the dead. Sometimes he is present in such great majesty that no one could ever doubt that this is our Lord himself, especially after communion. We know that he is present then because faith tells us so. He shows himself so clearly as the Lord of that tiny space that the soul seems to be dissolved and lost in Christ.

Jesus, who can describe your majesty when you show yourself? Then you are entirely the Lord of the whole world and of heaven, and of a thousand other and innumerable worlds and heavens which you can create. The majesty of your appearance shows the soul that you are naturally, effortlessly, Lord of all this and all that is . . .

Even afterwards, when the vision is forgotten, there is so deep an impression of God's majesty and beauty, that it is impossible to forget it (unless our Lord allows the soul to suffer from aridity and desolation . . . for then it seems to forget God himself). The after-effect of the vision is so overwhelming that the soul is no longer itself. It is always inebriated as if a living love of God of the highest kind were beginning all over again within it. Although the former vision, which represented God without any image of him, is of a higher kind, because we are so weak and so that the memory of the vision can last and occupy our thoughts, it is essential for it to remain and dwell in our imagination. These two kinds of vision almost always come together, for we see the supremacy, beauty and glory of God's most holy humanity with the eyes of the soul. In the other way, that of intellectual vision, we learn how he is God, is powerful, can do all things, govern all things, and fill all things with his love.

Santa Teresa de Jesús, 'Libro de la Vida . . .', *Obras Completas* (nueva revision del texto, Biblioteca de Autores Cristianos), vol. 2 (Madrid, 1951), pp. 762–70 [*The Life of St Teresa*, ch. 28, i–xviii].

BD ANNA KATHARINA EMMERICK
(Anne Catherine Emmerich)

The stigmatic visionary Anna Emmerick, aided by the transcriptive power of Clemens Brentano, a German Romantic master of lyrical fantasy, conveyed in extraordinary detail scenes only sug-

gested in the Gospels but worked on in her creative imagination over years of reclusive concentration. It is not surprising that her descriptions have provided instructions for more than one cinematic shooting script in the twentieth and twenty-first centuries. This account of and meditation on Pilate's palace (low-key in comparison with her sometimes horrific set-pieces, and devoid of her and Brentano's often time-bound and theologically inept prejudices) is an excellent example of Anna's ability to show the contemporary and intensely-felt personal relevance of the Passion. The enforced closure of her Augustinian convent and the expulsion of the nuns under a petty monarch, which disappointed her childhood hopes of a lifetime spent in the Order, are shown not only to echo but to continue divine events with which she is thereby directly associated.

The lessons of buildings

The palace of the Roman governor, Pilate, was built on the north-west side of the mountain where the Temple stood. To reach it people had to ascend a flight of marble steps. It overlooked a large square surrounded by a colonnade, under which the merchants sat to sell their various goods. A parapet, and an entrance at the north, south, east, and west sides alone broke the uniformity of this part of the market-place, which was called the forum, and built on higher ground than the adjacent streets, which sloped down from it. The palace of Pilate was not quite close, but separated by a large court, the entrance to which at the eastern side was through a high arch facing a street leading to the door called the 'Probatica,' on the road to the Mount of Olives. The southern entrance was through another arch, which leads to Sion, in the neighbourhood of the fortress of Acre. From the top of the marble steps of Pilate's palace, you could see across the court as far as the forum, at the entrance of which a few columns and stone seats were placed. The Jewish priests stopped at these seats, in order not to defile themselves by entering the tribunal of Pilate, a line traced on the pavement of the court indicating the precise boundary beyond which they could not pass without incurring defilement. There was a large parapet near the western entrance, supported by the sides of Pilate's Praetorium, which formed a kind of porch between it and the square. The Praetorium was the part of Pilate's palace which he made use of when acting as a judge. A number of columns surrounded this parapet, and in the centre was an uncovered portion, containing an underground part, where the two thieves condemned to be crucified with our Lord were confined; this part was filled with Roman soldiers. The pillar upon which our Lord was scourged was placed on the forum itself, not far from this parapet and the colonnade. There were many other columns in this place; those nearest to the palace were used to inflict various physical punishments, and the others served as posts to which were fastened the beasts brought for sale. Upon the forum itself, opposite this building, was a platform filled with seats made of stone; and from this platform, which was called Gabbatha, Pilate was accustomed to pronounce sentence on great criminals. The marble staircase ascended by persons going to the governor's palace also led to an uncovered terrace, and from this terrace Pilate gave audience to the priests and Pharisees, when they brought their accusations against Jesus to him. They all stood before him in the forum, and refused to advance further than the stone seats before mentioned. A person speaking in a loud tone of voice from the terrace could be easily heard by those in the forum.

Behind Pilate's palace there were many other terraces, and also gardens, and a country house. The gardens were laid out between the palace of the governor and the residence of his wife, Claudia Procles. A large moat separated these buildings from the mountain where the Temple stood, and on this side you could see the houses where the people who served in the Temple lived. The palace of Herod the elder was located on the eastern side of Pilate's palace; and numbers of the Innocents were massacred in its inner court. At present the appearance of these two buildings is a little altered, as their entrances have changed. Four of the main streets started at this part of the town, and ran in a southerly direction, three leading to the forum and Pilate's palace, and the fourth to the gate through which people passed on their way to Bethsur. The beautiful house which belonged to Lazarus, like that of Martha, were in a prominent part of this street.

One of these streets was very near to the Temple, and began at the gate called Probatica. The pool of Probatica was close to this gate on the right-hand side, and in this pool the sheep were washed for the first time, before being taken to the Temple; while the second and more solemn washing took place in the pool of Bethsaida, which is near the south entrance to the Temple. The second of the above-mentioned streets contained a house belonging to St Anna, the mother of the Blessed Virgin, which she usually stayed in when she came up to Jerusalem with her family to offer sacrifice in the Temple. I believe that the betrothal of St Joseph and the Blessed Virgin was celebrated in this house.

The forum, as I have already explained, was built on higher ground than the neighbouring streets, and the aqueducts which ran through these streets flowed into the Probatica pool. On Mount Sion, directly opposite to the old castle of King David, stood a building very similar to the forum, while to the south-east might be seen the Cenacle, and a little towards the north the tribunals of Annas and Caiphas. King David's castle was a deserted fortress, filled with courts, empty rooms, and stables, generally let to travellers. It had long been in this state of ruin, certainly before the time of our Lord's nativity. I saw the Magi with their numerous retinue enter it before going into Jerusalem.

When I am in meditation and see the ruins of old castles and temples, realize their neglected and forlorn state, and reflect on the uses to which they are now put, which are so different from the intentions of those who built them, my mind always reverts to the events of our own days, when so many of the beautiful buildings erected by our pious and zealous ancestors have either been destroyed or defaced, or are used for worldly, if not wicked purposes. The little church of our convent, in which our Lord deigned to dwell, in spite of our unworthiness, and which was a paradise on earth for me, is now without either roof or windows, and all the monuments have been effaced or carried away.

Our beloved convent, too, what will be done with it in a short time? That convent, where I was happier in my little cell with my broken chair, than a king could be on his throne, for from its window I beheld that part of the church which contained the Blessed Sacrament. In a few years, perhaps, no one will know that it ever existed – no one will know that it once contained hundreds of souls consecrated to God, who spent their days in imploring his mercy upon sinners. But God will know all, he never forgets – the past and the future are equally present to him. He it is who reveals to me events which took place so long ago, and on the day of judgment, when all must be accounted for, and every debt paid, even to the farthing, he will remember both the good and the evil deeds performed in places long since forgotten. With God there is no exception of persons or places, his eyes see all, even the way in which they put out this small talent to interest, and the large harvest which they reaped and presented to him. It is often said that poor souls remain in purgatory in punishment for what appears to us so small a crime as not having made restitution of a few low-value coins which they had obtained unlawfully. May God therefore have mercy upon those who have seized the property of the poor, or of the Church.

[Clemens Brentano] *Das bittere Leiden unseres Herrn Jesu Christi. Nach den Betrachtungen der gottseligen Anna Katharina Emmerich* (Regensburg, 1833), ch. xvi; Anna Catherine Emmerich, *The Dolorous Passion of Our Lord Jesus Christ* (New York, 1904) (adapted in accordance with the original German).

SR MARIE DE LA TRINITE
(Paule de Mulatier)

Paule de Mulatier's contemplative encounters often took the traditional form of sacred conversations: with God, with our Lady or with another saint. Originally, she had wanted to become a Carmelite, and throughout her life thought of its saintly patron, St Joseph, as a major partner in her spiritual conversations: 'When

I consider the silence of St Joseph, I long to be entirely wrapped in it to make sure that grace grows within me and fortifies me.' Joseph, who 'lived in very deep solitude with God,' was her special comfort during her long depression and when she underwent surgery as part of her cancer treatment: 'The best form of preparation for spiritual motherhood (which is divine motherhood), and the best way of ensuring its protection, is surely to follow Jesus and Mary in trusting oneself to St Joseph, to his personal grace, and to his silence of adoration, obedience, humility and his fatherly heart . . .'. The following passages from her writings come, first, from her notes of encounters with the divine, and, second, from her thoughts on St Joseph.

I need you near me

If you seek me, you will lose yourself, but you will find me.

Think of that longing for identification which I placed in your soul. But you have to make a choice: Do you want to identify with me, or me to identify with you?

Your soul is one. There is no room for you and for me.

My night of graces granted. The mystery of identification.
God, may what you have enabled me to understand be realized in me.
(19 August 1929)

I must put what I know into practice. and before all else make sure that love and humility are at the centre of my soul.
I must desire perfect love ardently, truly and sincerely: I must want to identify with Jesus Christ.

I shall place your intellect in total silence, so that it is one with your soul.
Sunday
(3 August 1930)

I shall plunge you whole and entire into a deep silence, for it is in silence that I shall be one with you.

I created the soul that is silence because I am silence. My only utterance in eternity, my only movement, is the Word. And you are well aware what the Word says and that it is like me.

Give way to the Holy Spirit, for he will take it all upon himself and stay there within you.'

Paule de Mulatier (known as Marie de la Trinité), Dominique Sterckx, OCD, ed., *Je te veux auprès de Moi: Agenda, 1927–1930* (Orbey, 2005).

* * *

Joseph's silence

Please pass your silence on to me, so that Jesus can grow in me. (23 August 1941)

This is intense contemplation wholly concentrated on the Father, never referring to any detail of the mysteries of his public life and his Passion, but only to his most holy Humanity as the very bosom of the Father.

I entrust myself entirely to you, St Joseph. Although you were not actually a father, you shared in the mystery of divine fatherhood more than any other human being. Although I am not a priest, may God, in whatever way and to whatever extent he wishes, allow me to share personally in the mystery of Christ's own priesthood.

St Joseph, hide me in creation as you hid Jesus in the world! (20 September 1941)

Although the grace that was granted to Joseph is more hidden, it is very profound. His life was entirely a hidden life, for it was a life of expiation and adoration and nothing else. The Angel's

revelation of the mystery of the Incarnation showed him how to forget his own personal purpose when compared with the unique glory of God.
(22 November 1941)

Agree to be nothing, like St Joseph.
(23 November 1941)

There are many 'things which eye saw not, and ear heard not, and which entered into the heart of humankind: whatsoever things God prepared for them that love him' [1 Cor 2.9]. For what degree of love was the pure, chaste and humble heart of Joseph prepared, and for what kind of love for the Father? In comparison, I should say, no one before him could be said to have loved, contemplated or served the Father at all – but what about after him?
(30 August 1942)

The confusion of St Joseph was intense natural suffering and humiliation, but without any admixture of pride, egotism or jealousy. It was a form of confusion appropriate to a soul aligned in priestly mode with what is of God and has to do with God. It was intensely felt, yet free of worry and fear. It was the permissible puzzlement of a son of God.
(4 September 1942)

Paule de Mulatier (known as Marie de la Trinité), Dominique Sterckx, OCD, *Le Silence de Joseph* (Paris).

ANNA VAN SCHURMAN

Preparing for her eventual dedication to the religious life, the hitherto exceptionally erudite Anna van Schurman, famous for her learning throughout the length and breadth of the Continent, and admired by monarchs, scholars and eminent churchmen, began an in-depth exploration of her own spirit in search of the spirit of Christ. She began to neglect the mere accumulation of knowledge, the pursuit of self-culture and book-religion. She began to see that, although 'the soap-bubbles of learning glint prettily, the crystal sphere of Christian truth alone irradiates the world, alone shows people in every station how to conduct their lives,' and reached the point where she felt that created things were manifestations of the divine energy, that 'from every blade of grass streamed ever-present God', and that the 'Dazzling Example' of Christ and the continuity of holiness were to be found in the company of those in whom the apostolic succession was manifest. This prepared her for entry to the community of brothers and sisters founded by Labadie, a 'garden of souls planted at Amsterdam, watered at Herford, and fruiting at Altona,' which she herself, after Labadie's death, animated with illumination and piety. 'I never found any', she wrote, 'that has expressed so truly and vividly the spirit and manner of living of the early Church or the calling of the first Christians . . . How can anyone blame me for following the best teacher and leader, for accompanying other believers, for looking to Jesus, author and perfecter of faith, for hurrying towards my heavenly Fatherland, and pursuing the highest and only goal, the glory of God and the honour of Christ?'

A Christian woman's intellect

Above all, the knowledge of things past, which is acquired by the reading of history, does minimize the danger which those inevitably run who conduct their lives by experience alone. In these books, as in a clear mirror, all past centuries are reflected, and by reading them we are enabled to make the most likely conjectures on those which are to come, and in consequence may attain to that state of perfection in which we admire nothing as new upon earth . . . The essence of things remains in spite of the fact that appearances and circumstances change . . .

I will content myself with expressing myself in clear terms upon the desirability of women's not only desiring higher things, but doing their utmost to attain them. The higher minds among us may not be cramped within such narrow confines; nor should the peak of soaring intelligence be crushed down against nature. I should not wonder indeed, if such Draconian rule came to be enforced, to see some women lured away to evil courses by flattery on account of their distaste for allotted tasks. For it has come to this, that no hope is left us of enjoying honour nor dignity, nor reward of merit such as lures the soul to higher flights.

Vain is our boasting of such nobility as we owe to descent, if we ourselves must for ever languish in obscurity. Hence it comes that in after time the reader of history finds no more record of our names throughout a long period than a ship leaves traces of her course through the waves. But, say some, 'What renown have you ever won? What claim have you to undying fame? Surely you don't expect to derive glory from leisure?' And why not? So the leisure be lit up with learning? For indeed we women should invoke the aid of Pallas, not in arms but in robes. Where true philosophy has been allowed to occupy our minds, no vain and empty anxieties can gain admission, a fact which that distinguished patron of letters, Erasmus, has commented on when writing about the education of Thomas More's daughters. 'Nothing,' he writes, 'so takes up a girl's mind as study.' Again, with regard to nature: to what purpose are we endowed with that which the Philosophers tell us is common to man: the desire to know? To what purpose have we been given an erect stature unless we are to raise at once our eyes and mind in contemplation. It were better to be logs than human beings; strangers, not dwellers on earth, if our souls be not quickened and our hearts kindled for love of matters so august and beautiful in which the Majesty of God has revealed itself from all eternity. Nor do we hold our duty done, if we have gazed awhile as through a glass darkly at these things . . . Nothing is more worthy study than man himself, nothing is more beautiful than the soul's dwelling place.

The Life of Christ

Walk where thou wilt, seek what thou wilt, and thou wilt find no higher way above, no safer way below, than the way of the holy cross. The cross is always ready and everywhere awaits thee. Thou canst not escape it, whithersoever thou runnest; for whithersoever thou goest, thou carriest thyself with thee, and always shalt thou find thyself . . .

I found that the best and truest picture of the life of Christ was the life of Christians, and I grieved that it was so seldom to be found nowadays. I thought myself obliged to put all works of art on one side for these living pattern portraits. I wrote to a leading man in the world of art and knowledge (who had asked my opinion on certain excellent pictures), saying: A quite other art floats now before my soul, and I am only concerned how I am to transcribe the heavenly picture of godly virtues of our highest and most beautiful Master and Saviour Jesus, not as I have heretofore endeavoured to do with a pen on paper, but in some fashion in my soul. More and more do I perceive how long is this art, and how short is life, and how easily opportunities are missed. Notwithstanding there is no one to whom the Kingdom of God is not open, if he has but a few of these traits, and whoever has learnt to delineate any of these features in himself, infinitely surpasses those most celebrated artists of antiquity, Protagoras and Apelles. I resolve to end my life in this studio, and I end with the wish that God, the only teacher of this art, may teach you, me, and all that are his.

* * *

Contemplatives who believe that exclusion from the world is a necessary condition of effective meditation must remember the advice of St Francis of Assisi: 'Meditate as much while on this journey as if you were shut up in a hermitage or in your cell, for wherever we are, wherever we go, we carry our cell with us. Brother Body is our cell.'

Anna van Schurman, *The Learned Maid* or *Whether the Study of Letters is Fitting for a Christian Woman. A logick exercise* (London, 1641, 2nd ed. 1659); Constance Pope-Hennessy [Una Birch], *Anna van Schurman: Artist, Scholar, Saint* (London, 1909), *passim.*

LUCIE CHRISTINE

Lucie Christine is a highly-nuanced introspective mystic who already belongs to the era of Franz Kafka (for they both knew they were 'in the midst of a wide solitude'). She reports her spiritual insights as an encounter between herself and the transcendental and, as a mystic of the modern age, interprets this experience in the form of a dialogue between an as yet unresolved self and a very personal God. Although she agonizes over the impropriety of feeling adrift in her environment, her condition is redressed by her meeting with God, whom she conceives as a distinct individual with characteristics which she describes with precision.

My soul meets God

Suddenly, I saw the words 'God alone' before my inward eyes . . . It sounds very odd for someone to say she sees words. But I certainly did perceive them in my inner self, though not in the way in which one usually sees and hears things. I am well aware how inadequately the expressions available to me convey what I felt, even though I can recall what I saw then just as clearly now. These words afforded light, attraction and power at one and the same time. The light showed me how I could belong completely to God alone in this world, and I realized that I had not really understood what this meant until then. It was an attraction that took hold of my heart entirely and delightfully, and a power that made me generous and resolute, and somehow, I knew, made it possible for me to reach my goal. The nature of divine words that you can see like this is to enact what they enunciate. These were the very first such words that God of his goodness allowed my soul to see, and to enter the new life that began with them . . .

One day I was engrossed in the life of St Françoise Chantal de Bougaud. At the end of the seventeenth chapter, I came across this statement: 'A profound sense of inner union overcame her as soon as she started to pray . . .' My inner self was deeply affected by these words, and I recognized the mysterious yet now familiar state that my soul had so often experienced over the last two years. The following pages were even more emphatic, and a few lines from them will give an especially exact description of my spiritual state: 'I dwell in quite simple union with God in the innermost reaches of my spirit . . .' When I read this I experienced the joy that the spirit knows when it is certain of the truth and of an immense, overwhelming love, and feels most profoundly thankful for the occasion.

I saw within myself God the ground of all that is and perceived how he possesses everything and is the source of everything true, beautiful and good. In fact, I saw God as ultimate truth, goodness and beauty and realized how all things are only something through him, and how all created things are as nothing compared with their uncreated Source. This way of knowing God can be described as sight, but of course it is a very imperfect way of seeing him. Here God seems to exclude any form of mediation and to show himself to the soul. And then the soul is like someone emerging from darkness into intense daylight. It begins to feel that its weak vision is unable to take in what God is revealing, and cannot fully grasp it. It is quite overcome with amazement.

At that time God favoured me with the gift of a profound awareness of his presence in the most holy Sacrament. He would leave me free to pray orally or deprive me of that ability, as he might decide. In faith we are certain of the true presence of Christ by virtue, as it were, of a witness once removed, whereas in the form of grace which I am thinking of we feel God's irresistible presence with the same absolute assurance that we enjoy when we sense the undoubted presence of another person standing next to us and talking to us, although our eyes are tight shut . . .

And now I was allowed to look at him for some time. I could only dimly perceive the outline of our Lord's radiant eyes, but

I was able to appreciate the extraordinarily expressive force and intense beauty flowing from them. I could never properly describe the nature of this sublime and totally enchanting gaze. I can only say that the more I try to find appropriate language for it, the further I tend to drift away from what I actually saw. I have often had this experience . . .

Sometimes I am surrounded by other people, or I am deep in conversation, and suddenly remember my Lord. At first I hear only the faintest trace of his voice . . . and then, without warning, I am totally beset: I feel my cheeks go white, my body shake, my hands and feet are like ice, and my heart is beating terribly fast yet softly glowing in the way I have grown used to in passive prayer. I now know that this is how we physically acknowledge the approach of our Creator when he descends into inward union with a humble soul . . .

I began to examine his robe with the eyes of my inward vision. I followed its outline, then its folds (I cannot find a more appropriate term) began to coalesce and I became aware of a lambent whiteness that did not merely shine, for it was composed of pure light. It did not consist of anything like cloud, mist, woven cloth or even flame. It was something other than that. I had never come across anything like this before. I tried to puzzle it out, unsuccessfully. This shining was different to the brightness of daylight or the stars in the night sky, or any other kind of light we experience. The rays of this light filled my eyes, but did not dazzle them and my spirit was immersed in a sea of divine light . . .

Dear Lord, you showed me your divinity when, like a glowing substance, it enveloped my entire existence and simultaneously permeated and inspired my whole being. Then my soul was cut off from the world and was enclosed in you alone, for then I was at peace and drew my life from you as you really are . . .

Lucie Christine, *Journal Spirituel*, A. Poulain SJ, ed. (Paris, 1910), *passim*; cf. *The Spiritual Journal of Lucie Christine*, A. Poulain, ed. (London, 1915; New York, 1920); G.R. Hocke, *Das Europäische Tagebuch* (Wiesbaden, 1963), pp. 826–32.

JESSICA POWERS (Sr Miriam of the Holy Spirit)

Jessica Powers combines traditional scriptural images with those drawn from the Wisconsin farming environment of her childhood in order to translate her own spiritual experience into a universally applicable statement of divine love.

To Live with the Spirit

To live with the Spirit of God is to be a listener.
It is to keep the vigil of mystery,
earthless and still.
One leans to catch the stirring of the Spirit,
strange as the wind's will.

The soul that walks where the wind of the Spirit blows
turns like a wandering weather-vane toward love.
It may lament like Job or Jeremiah,
echo the wounded hart, the mateless dove.
It may rejoice in spaciousness of meadow
that emulates the freedom of the sky.
Always it walks in waylessness, unknowing;
it has cast down forever from its hand
the compass of the whither and the why.

To live with the Spirit of God is to be a lover.
It is becoming love, and like to Him
toward Whom we strain with metaphors of creatures:
fire-sweep and water-rush and the wind's whim.
The soul is all activity, all silence;
and though it surges Godward to its goal,
it holds, as moving earth holds sleeping noonday,
the peace that is the listening of the soul.

From the web-site of the Carmel of the Mother of God, Pewaukee, Wisconsin, USA and the Selected Poetry of Jessica Powers, p. 38. See Biography, pp. 234–5.

SR WENDY BECKETT

Sister Wendy has a ready ability, nurtured by profound and immensely wide-ranging acquaintance with works of art, to elicit from them something which, she reminds us, the American critic Harold Rosenberg called '"the formal sign language of an inner kingdom—equivalents in paint of a flash, no matter how transitory, of what has been known throughout the centuries as spiritual enlightenment." We are shy, today, of this kind of language, yet this spiritual dimension is the reason for art's importance, and for our need for it, whether acknowledged or ignored.' Her remarks on Magdalena Abakanowicz's eighty pieces in three sizes constructed between 1972 and 1982, entitled Backs, *and on Rebecca Purdum's 1985 painting* In Three's, *are good examples of this faculty.*

Our need to love and to hope

When the Nazis invaded Poland, Magdalena Abakanowicz saw drunken troopers fire at her mother, leaving her mutilated. It was then that the realization came to her that 'the body was like a piece of fabric – that it could be torn apart with ease' . . . Human cruelty and indifference, human fear of being victimized ourselves: all the evil each knows within his or her own heart, this is what strikes us with fear and compassion as we meet this density of *Backs*. In its helpless misery, the sight may fill us with despair, yet a closer look reveals a strange, silent dignity. Whatever the unintelligible onslaughts of life may do to man, the human spirit can survive intact. Abakanowicz believes that 'Everything that surrounds us makes us and in making us, makes the work. So I believe that, if we were terribly honest with ourselves, what we say or write or do will touch everyone. It will touch others if it comes from deep inside, because there begins the contact between all people'. Paradoxically, the hollowness of the *Backs* speaks only of our need to be centred and to love.

* * *

{ 35 }

In Three's has a mysterious inner unity: paint, form and structure, all three have 'become' the artist, flow in and out of one another, all intimately connected 'off scene', as it were. We see on the canvas a shadowy semi-human form, floating beside a darkness that gleams up from the picture's depth. Around them drift, in and out of focus, faint and gentle luminosities, with a solitary and defined streak of intense blue overhead. Do we distinguish these as the *'Three's'*, to which the title refers? 'Three' has Trinitarian reverberances for the western ear, and it is indicative of Purdum's effect on us that it is to so profound a context that we instinctively turn. In the past, she has worked with the mentally retarded, finding in their brave attempts to communicate a sign of deep hope. At humanity's most feeble, it still seeks and believes in the possibility to reach another, and in the other's willingness to listen. In an age of spiritual retardation, Purdum's mystical certainties, prayer made visible, may also be taken as a sign of hope. She 'sees', and believes that we, too, can 'see'.

Sister Wendy Beckett, *Contemporary Women Artists* (Oxford, 1988), pp. 16, 88

2

Founders, Directors & Advisers

꙰

ST RADEGUND

Queen Radegund founded a monastery of nuns near Poitiers, France, in times of constant violence, and managed to persuade King Clothaire I, her former or estranged husband (who had forced her into marrying him), to endow it. Here she writes to various bishops to describe the aims of her nunnery. She begs them to protect her foundation after her death, and, if need be, to help her successors to continue life there in her spirit and to deal effectively with difficulties without and opposition within. Her letter was preserved by St Gregory of Tours.

Willingly Chosen

I have been liberated from the claims of a secular existence by God's assistance and by his divine grace. I have freely chosen a religious life under Christ's direction. Now my mind and abilities are in the service of others, for the Lord helps me to make sure that my good intentions for them will actually benefit them. The noble Lord and King Clothaire gave me certain assets that allowed me to establish a monastery for young women. After founding it, I transferred to its ownership everything which his Royal Highness so bountifully granted me. What is more, I have given the group of nuns I brought together there with Christ's help the Rule by which the holy Caesaria lived, and which the holy President Caesarius of Arles so wisely drew from the teachings of the holy Fathers of the Church. With the approval of the noble bishop of the area, and at the express wish of our congregation, I have appointed my friend Dame Agnes abbess. From the days of my youth onwards I have loved and educated her as a daughter, and, after the will of God, I have accepted her authority. My Sisters and I have followed the apostolic example and have disposed of all our worldly possessions, warily recalling Ananias and Sapphira, and have kept nothing of our own. Since the risks attached to the events and length of human life cannot be accurately foretold, I now submit this letter containing my request to you. I beg you to grant my petition for the protection and support of my endeavours in the name of Christ.

Gregorius Tur. (Gregory of Tours), *Historia Francorum*, W. Levinson & B. Krusch, eds (rev. & repr., 1916) in *Scriptores Rerum Merovingicarum*, 9, ch. 42.

In a lyrical petition to her sympathetic cousin Hermalafred (modelled on the verse letters attributed to his lovelorn heroines by the classical Roman poet Ovid, and possibly written with some contribution from her poet friend St Venantius Fortunatus), Queen Radegund offers a vivid description of the chaos that threatened the civilized Christian courts and the relatively few oases of cultured convent life in sixth-century Europe. Hermalafred had fled from Thuringia when Radegund was captured, and had joined the army of the Emperor Justinian. After reminding him of their childhood friendship, and of the events leading up to her captivity, Radegund wonders where he is and assures him that but for her foundation she would risk tempest, wind and shipwreck to find him. She tells him that her murdered brother had died lest she be incriminated. She requests news of Hermalafred and his sisters. Apparently Hermalafred, lost in Byzantium, never answered her message. Eventually, a letter from his nephew reported his uncle's death.

Tearful Times

War is a sad and terrifying experience, and it seems that fate cannot tolerate human peace and happiness. Sudden descents into chaos have brought down proud kingdoms, and towering fortresses that had survived for years have crashed to the ground destroyed by fire and siege. I know only too well how curling tongues of flame have swallowed the once magnificent residence of monarchs. Now burnt ash covers the polished metal of a roof that formerly glistened in the sunlight. The enemy has captured those who once held sway in that court, and its nobles have descended to the lower depths. All those ranks of finely-clad servants have been brought to the dust in a single day. Haughty courtiers and powerful favourites have not even been laid to rest, and have been denied all funeral rites.

My father's sister with the golden locks brighter than fire lies milk-wan in death, slain by the invaders. The battle-field is strewn with our unburied warriors, and with the flower of the nation in a single open grave. Like ancient Troy, the Thuringian land has suffered untold slaughter. Chained noblewomen are dragged off by their hair and are denied even a sad farewell to their household gods. Prisoners cannot kiss their thresholds for the last time, or turn to see familiar sights fade for ever. Barefoot wives trample in their husbands' blood and fond sisters tread on their brothers' corpses. The imprint of children is still on the lips of the mothers from whom they are torn. There is no mourning for the slain. The fate of a child that loses its life is less painful than that which awaits the living, for whom these breathless mothers cannot even weep.

If my tears were to flow for ever I could not cry enough to equal all this tragedy. My private sorrow was the sorrow of the nation. The terror was so great that fate smiled on those whom the enemy slaughtered. I alone survive to weep over the many who are lost, and my tears flow not only for my dead but for my living relatives. I am so sad that my eyes can never convey all I feel. Though I utter no cry, I grieve deeply. I look to the winds for some message of hope, but they say nothing.

Harsh destiny has torn away the kinsman whose affection was once my constant strength. You are far from me but my concern is so resolute that you must surely sense it. I cannot think that bitter fate has changed your affectionate nature. You must remember how much I meant to you from your infancy onwards, and how fond of me you were when I was so very young. For you are my father's brother's son, and the most cherished of my kinsfolk. You took the place of my dead father, of my dearest mother, of a sister and of a brother. You held me by your gentle hand. I prized your sweet kisses, and your tender words soothed me as a child. Scarcely a moment passed when I did not see you, but now a long time has gone by since I heard the least word from you. I have to hide my deep distress, my dear wish that I had the power to summon you here, my friend, whenever or wherever it might be possible. Possibly father, mother, or royal duties have kept you from me. It has been so long that even if you hurried to see me now, I would feel your absence sorely.

Perhaps I already sense the judgement of fate, for affection so long unreturned must certainly die. In the past I felt anxious if you were merely in another house, and I thought your least absence meant you had gone for ever. Now you seem as restricted to the east as I am to the west. The ocean is my boundary and the sun-kissed waves are yours. Two creatures dear to one another are separated by vast tracts of land, and a world has come between them, although at one time scarcely any space divided one from the other.

Lord Jesus, hear my prayer. Make sure that my letter reaches my dear cousin, so that his welcome message speeds here in return, and the pain of unanswered hope is banished by good news of him borne on swift wings.

Radegundis 'Carmina', *Venanti Fortunati Opera poetica*, F. Leo, ed., *Monumenta Germaniae Historica, Auct. Ant.* (cf., e.g., repr. 1961), Appendix, No. 3; see also: Lina Eckenstein, *Woman under Monasticism: Chapters on Saint-lore and Convent Life between* AD 500 *and* AD 1500 (New York, 1963).

ST CLARE OF ASSISI

Clare writes her first letter to Agnes of Prague, Princess of Bohemia, in which she praises an example of surrendering worldly goods to the destitute and following the poor Christ in the spirit of St Francis. She probably composed this letter after Pentecost 1234, when Agnes, then 23, decided not to marry the Emperor Frederick II and instead was received into the Franciscan monastery in Prague. Agnes had been the prospective pawn in the political strategies of her father, Otakar I, of Frederick (who had planned to marry her since 1228) and of Pope Gregory IX. In a very material, indeed geo-political sense, Agnes did reject the honours of this world and affected its tripartite power politics most effectively. Instead of marriage, she founded a monastery and hospital in Prague and followed the way of life recommended by Clare's monastery of San Damiano near Assisi. Clare's letter is a scarcely veiled though suitably formal confirmation of the thwarting of particular makers' and movers' plans, yet also a heartfelt lyrical celebration of the appropriateness of Agnes' choice.

A letter to Lady Agnes

I, Clare, the unworthy servant of Jesus Christ and useless handmaid of the enclosed ladies of the Monastery of San Damiano, am your subject and servant on all occasions, and herewith commend myself entirely to you, Lady Agnes, the worthy and most holy virgin and daughter of the highly renowned and illustrious King of Bohemia, praying, with particular reverence, that you will be rewarded with the glory of eternal happiness.

Having heard a most praiseworthy account of your holy conversion and unsullied way of life, which has been related not only to me but almost throughout the world, I rejoice and greatly exult in the Lord. Not only I but all those who serve and seek him are full of joy at this news.

I rejoice because you, more than others, could have tasted public magnificence and honours, and worldly grandeur. After all, you could have been duly married to the illustrious Emperor, for that would accord with your station and with his. But with your whole heart and mind you have rejected all this, chosen instead most holy poverty and physical want, and received a more noble spouse: the Lord Jesus Christ, who will keep your virginity always immaculate and irreproachable.

When you have loved Jesus, you will be chaste. When you have touched him, you will be even more pure. When you have accepted him, you will be a virgin. His power is greater, his nobility more considerable, his appearance more beautiful, his love more tender, and his kindness more just.

You are now held tight in the embraces of the Lord who has adorned your breast with jewels and has decorated your ears with priceless pearls.

He has wrapped you round with shining, sparkling gems, and has placed on your head a golden crown to show how very holy you are.

Therefore, dearest sister – or, should I say, lady most worthy of honour, because you are the spouse and but also the mother and sister of my Lord Jesus Christ, and you have been most wonderfully decorated with the insignia of inviolable virginity and holiest poverty – be strengthened in the holy service which you have chosen because of your ardent longing for Jesus, poor and crucified. For all of us, he accepted the suffering of the cross, and freed us from the power of the Prince of Darkness by whom we were enslaved because of our first parents' disobedience – and thus reconciled us to God the Father.

This poverty is indeed everlastingly generous to those who love and embrace it! This poverty is indeed holy for those who possess and desire it. To them God has promised the kingdom of heaven and most certainly offers them eternal glory and happiness! This poverty is indeed blessed which the Lord Jesus Christ, who ruled and now still holds sway over heaven and earth, and who spoke so that everything that was made was made, condescended to embrace before anything else!

Foxes have dens, he says, and the birds of the air have nests, but the Son of Man, Christ himself, has nowhere to lay his head; instead, he bowed his head and gave up his spirit.

If so great a Lord entered the Virgin's womb and chose to appear contemptible, needy, and poor in this world, so that humans who were utterly poor and destitute, and in absolute need of divine nourishment, might become rich in him by acquiring the kingdom of heaven, you must exult, rejoice, and be full of incredible joy and spiritual happiness!

Contempt of the world has delighted you more than its honours, poverty more than earthly riches, and treasures in heaven rather than those on earth, for in heaven rust does not consume them, moth cannot destroy them, and thieves do not find and steal them. In heaven you will have the greatest reward, for you have truly deserved to be called sister, spouse, and mother of the Son of the most high Father and of the glorious Virgin.

You are aware, I am sure, that the Lord promises and gives the kingdom of heaven only to the poor, because those who love earthly things lose the fruit of love. You know, too, that you cannot serve God and worldly riches, since either the one is loved and the other hated, or the one is served and the other despised. You also know that if you wear clothes you cannot fight with someone who is naked, because the one who wears something to hold onto is more quickly thrown to the ground. You know, too, that you cannot remain glorious in the world and reign with Christ in heaven, and that it is easier for a camel to pass through the eye of a needle than for someone rich to enter the kingdom of heaven. And so you have thrown away your clothes, that is, your worldly riches, so that you will not be vanquished by your opponent, and you can enter the kingdom of heaven by the strait gate and narrow path.

It is indeed a great and praiseworthy exchange to surrender the temporal to gain the eternal, to choose the heavenly rather than the earthly, to receive a hundred-fold instead of one, and to enjoy a life of blessed happiness for ever.

Because of this, I decided that I should do all in my power to help your Excellency and Holiness with humble prayers in

Christ's unlimited mercy, to remain ever stronger in his holy service, and to advance from good to better, and from virtue to virtue, so that the Lord whom you serve with all your heart and soul may freely give you the reward which you desire.

Also, with the utmost fervour, I beg you in the Lord generously to include me your unworthy servant in your holy prayers, together with the other sisters in the monastery, who are all devoted to you. With the help of your prayers, may we deserve the mercy of Jesus Christ and, together with you, enjoy the vision that will never fade.

Farewell in the Lord! Pray for me, Clare of Assisi, I beseech you.

Translated from: *S. Clara Assisiensis Epistolae* ('Prima epistola Agneti'); cf., e.g.: *S Assisiensis Opera* (*Escritos*) (Latin & Spanish), Ignatius Omaechevarria, ed. & tr. (Madrid, 1970); cf. also: *S. Claire d'Assise: Documents*, H. Roggen, ed. (Paris, 1983).

ST GERTRUDE THE GREAT OF HELFTA

Gertrude composed seven exercises for the use of the sisters of her monastery; they describe the process of sanctification of the soul in the religious life: Renewal of Baptismal Innocence; Spiritual Conversion; Espousals and Consecration; Renewal of Religious Profession; Acts of Love of God; Praise and Thanksgiving; Reparation, and Preparation for Death. The exercises take the practitioners back to relive baptism and forward to prepare for death, and constitute something like a psychoanalytical recovery of an individual's growth in religion. The intermediate exercises rehearse the vocation to a religious life, acts of love towards God, and the sacrifice of praise and thanksgiving due to him. Gertrude never lectures or preaches. Instead the individual soul judges, condemns and renews herself. St Gertrude detaches us gently from ourselves and brings us to Jesus by preceding us as an exemplar. Each exercise includes instructions followed by

*a prayer. This summary version of the first exercise demonstrates
her method.*

The Memory of Baptism

If, at the close of your life, you wish to present the Lord with the
robe of baptismal innocence without reproach and the seal of the
Christian faith whole and unbroken, set apart some time in each
year to recall the memory of your baptism, if possible around
Easter or Pentecost. To perform this exercise proficiently, you
should encourage a sincere desire to be born again to God by the
holiness of a renewed life, and to enter once more into a restored
infancy. Say: 'God be merciful to me and bless me; look kindly
and have mercy on me. May my heart praise the Lord in sincerity
and truth; let the whole earth of my heart tremble and be moved
before the presence of the Lord; may my spirit be recreated and
renewed by the Spirit of his mouth; and may that good Spirit
bring me to the land where justice reigns.'

Then recite the Creed and remember the sign of faith which
was first impressed on you at baptism. Make the sign of the cross
on different parts of your body, as you do on your forehead and
on your chest, saying: 'In the Name of the Father, and of the Son
and of the Holy Spirit. Dearest Jesus, my crucified Love, impress
the sign of your cross on my forehead and on my heart, so that
I may live under your protection from now on and for ever.
Give me a living faith, so that I can fulfil your heavenly precepts;
enlarge my heart, so that I may follow your commandments; and
make me fit to become the temple of God and the home of the
Holy Spirit. Amen'.

Ask our Lord to bless and protect you, and to send your angel
to be your guide throughout the voyage of life, saying: 'Jesus
Prince of Peace, Angel of the great counsel, be ever at my right
hand as my leader and my guardian throughout my pilgrimage. Let me never be confused or deflected from my course, or
wander far from you. Send your holy angel from heaven to take
charge of me as the minister of your loving care for me, to lead

me onwards as you wish, to help me to walk in your ways, and to bring me at length to you, perfect and complete. Amen'.

Welcome and greet this holy angel, saying: 'Hail, holy Angel of God, guardian of my soul and of my body. By the sweetest heart of Jesus Christ, the Son of God, shelter me in your faithful and fatherly care, for the love of God whose creation you are, and as I am, and for the love of the Lord who put me into your charge on the day of my baptism. Help me to cross, unharmed and unsullied, the fierce-flowing and hazardous torrents of this life, until I am admitted to behold, like you and with you, the incomparable beauty of the supreme King, the sight of which infinitely transcends the highest joy our hearts can conceive. Amen'.

Turn to Mary the Mother of God, and ask her to obtain a complete renewal of your life for you. Recall the moment when you were plunged into the water in the sacred font in the name of the Father, of the Son, and of the Holy Spirit: 'O Jesus, Fountain of Life, allow me to drink the living water that pours from you, so that I shall thirst after you alone for ever. Plunge me into the depths of your loving mercy. Baptize me in the holiness of your liberating death. Renew me in the blood with which you saved me. Use the water flowing from your pierced side to eradicate all the sins I have committed since baptism. Fill me with your Spirit, and take possession of me completely in purity of soul and body. Amen'.

Recall the holy chrism with which you were anointed on emerging from the water of baptism, and ask our Lord to teach you everything you should know through the blessing of his Spirit: 'Holy Father, through your Son our Lord Jesus Christ, you have remade me with water and the Holy Spirit. Grant me perfect and entire forgiveness of all my sins, and of your loving kindness take me into everlasting life by the anointing of your Spirit. Amen. May your peace be with me now and for ever. Amen.'

Say the following prayer in memory of the white robe with which you were clothed: 'Jesus, Sun of Justice, clothe me with yourself, so that I can live as you wish. Enable me from now on to keep the robe of my baptismal innocence white and unsullied in holiness, so that I can show it in all perfection at the seat of judgement and wear it then throughout eternity. Amen.'

Think of the taper which was put into your hand, and pray for inward light: 'Jesus, unfailing Light, kindle the glowing lamp of your love in me. Keep it always alight within me, and teach me how to make sure that my baptism remains pure and without reproach, so that I can appear in all humility and confidence when I am summoned to be found worthy to enter into the joys of everlasting life, and see you, the true Light, and the beauty of your divine countenance. Amen.'

Adapted from: *The Exercises of St Gertrude Virgin and Abbess, of the Order of St Benedict* (London, 1863), pp. 5–14.

ST TERESA OF AVILA

In her autobiography, letters and 'relations', exhortations to nuns and profound analyses of devotion and of the stages of contemplation such as The Interior Castle, *which are steeped in the language of the Bible, Teresa of Avila returned constantly to the subject of prayer, whether narrating its ascents and descents in her own experience, advising nuns on dryness and plenitude of spirit, or providing simple or sophisticated accounts of approaches to and encounters with the divine for advisers such as Father Geronimo Gracian or her former confessor Alonso Velazquez, later Bishop of Osma. 'No one,' wrote the great Benedictine historian Dom David Knowles, 'can read her books without becoming aware that for her prayer – individual, silent, loving attention to God – is the centre of the soul's life, and the* sine qua non *of growth in the Christian virtues' (*The Life of St Teresa by Herself *[London, 1962], Introduction, xii). Even in translation, 'in the very folds of the language used by Teresa, in the tastes and rhythms of the rough or flowing Castilian ... I feel in all the fibres of my body, in all the light and dark of my spirit ... that power of language, which she manipulates*

*with such genius . . . that loving solitude which in Teresa's pages
becomes subjective lucidity imprisoned by the Other but assured
of its ability to seize and hold the Other captive'* (Julia Kristeva,
Thérèse mon Amour *[Paris, 2008], pp. 120–1).*

How to pray

The first prayer of which I was conscious was, I think, supernatural (which is what I call something that no skill or effort of ours, however hard we try, can reach, though we should prepare ourselves for it, and this preparation will always help us immensely). It consists of a kind of inward recollection of which the soul is aware. Then the soul seems to have other senses within itself, which in some way echo its outward senses. It withdraws into itself, tries to get away from the tumult of its outer senses, and dissociates them from their normal functions by, for instance, closing the eyes so that nothing can be seen, heard, or understood but the soul's present main purpose, which is to be able to converse with God alone. This kind of prayer does not suspend the faculties and powers of the soul; it retains the full use of them, but so that they are taken up with God. This will be easily understood by those whom our Lord has already raised to this state; but those for whom it is a novel experience will not find it easy, or they will need many words and illustrations to have some idea of what is happening. At any rate, this recollection leads to a most reassuring and comforting quietude and inward peace, and then the soul is in a condition in which it seems to want nothing; for even speaking wearies it. And by 'speaking' I mean vocal prayer and meditation alike. All it wants to do is to love. This lasts some time, even a long time. This type of prayer usually leads to what is called a sleep of the faculties; yet they are not so absorbed or suspended that it can be called a trance, and it is not altogether a state of union.

* * *

The prayer of quiet is a little spark of the true love of our Lord, which he starts to arouse in the soul. He wants the soul to understand what this love is by experiencing the joy which it brings. This quiet recollection and little spark will produce great results if they are the work of God's Spirit, and not a subtle temptation, or self-deception. An experienced person cannot possibly fail to understand at once that this is not something you can just manufacture for yourself, though of course human nature is always looking for pleasant moods and events. But this particular spark very soon goes cold since, however we blow on it to make it burn fiercely, just for the fire's sake, we might as well be pouring water on it to put it out completely. But if this spark comes from God, however slight it may be, it causes a great crackling; and if people do not quench it by their faults, it is the beginning of the great fire emitting the flames of that most vehement love of God which our Lord wants perfect souls to possess.

This little spark is a sign or pledge which God gives to a soul, to show that he has chosen it for great things, if it will only get ready to receive them. It is a great gift, and much too great for me to describe aptly. It can be an immense sorrow for me, since I know that many souls come this far, and that those who go farther, as they ought to go, seem to be so few, although there must really be very many who stay the course, because God is so patient with us. I speak only of what I myself have seen.

* * *

This is the order to follow in prayer. First, make the sign of the cross; remember all the faults you have committed since your last confession; strip yourself of all things, as if you were about to die; be truly sorry for your sins, and recite the psalm 'Miserere', as a penance for them: 'God, be gracious to me in your faithful love; in the fullness of your mercy blot out my misdeeds. Wash away all my iniquity and cleanse me from my sin. For well I know my misdeeds, and my sins confront me all the time.' Then say: 'I come to you, Lord, to learn in your school, and not to teach. I want to talk to you, Lord, though I am dust and ashes, and not much more than an ordinary earth worm.' Offer yourself to God as someone always ready to do what he wishes, and think of your suffering Lord peacefully and quietly.

Try to think of the divine nature of God as the everlasting Word, and see the Father united with a human nature that did not exist in itself until he produced it. Consider the extraordinary love and humility with which God changed places, so that the human became God, and God became human. Think of his generosity in using his power to reveal himself to human beings and allow them to share his glory, power, and greatness . . .

Look at Jesus crowned with thorns and try to realize how banal and even blind our understanding of this image is. Ask our Lord to open the eyes of your soul, and shine the light of faith into the dark resistance of your mind, so that you can learn something of who God is, and what we are; and use this humble knowledge to observe his commandments, follow his advice, and always do his will. As you look at his hands and feet nailed, consider his loving kindness and the poverty of what we are prepared to give on his behalf, as well as the enthusiasm with which he seeks us, and our sheer laziness in seeking him. Look at his side opened with a lance to show us his heart, and the intense love with which he has loved us, becoming our harbour and refuge, and the door by which we can enter the ark of salvation, when the deluge of our temptations and trials threatens to overcome us. Ask him to help us to open our own sides and reveal all our worries and needs, to him and to ourselves, so that we can try to face them and put them right.

Approach prayer gently and with humility. Be ready to follow the path God decides to show you, and be absolutely secure in the knowledge that you can rely on him. Listen attentively to his advice. Sometimes he will seem to turn away from you, and at other times to come up to you. Perhaps he will shut the door and leave you outside. Perhaps he will take you by the hand, and lead you into his house. Accept whatever happens with equanimity. If he reproves you, acknowledge his right to do so and the justice of what he says.

When he comforts you even if you have not deserved consolation, think of his kindness in enabling you to experience his goodness ... In prayer, your soul must rest in self-awareness; and when the comforting breath of the Holy Spirit raises it, places it in the heart of God, and sustains it there, revealing God's own goodness, and manifesting his power, your soul will learn to enjoy the favour of admittance to the very presence of God, where he holds you as his favoured bride, in whom he delights ...

Remaining at prayer without obtaining any advantage is not lost time, but a time of great gain, because then we work hard without interest, only for the glory of God. Although we seem at first to labour in vain, that is not the case; it is like sons who work on their father's estate, and receive no wages for the day's work when night comes, yet receive everything at the end of the year.

This is very like the prayer in the Garden of Gethsemane, when Jesus asked for the bitterness and difficulty he experienced in overcoming his human nature to be taken away. He did not ask for his pains to be removed, but only his dislike of them when he had to suffer them. That was when he asked for his weak human body to be infused with the strength of the Spirit. He was told that it was not expedient, and that he must drink his chalice: that is, overcome the cowardice and weakness of the flesh. And just as he was truly God, so he was truly human, for even he felt the same pains as other human beings ...

When we get ready to pray, we should as it were put on a wedding garment – that is, our mood should suit the occasion. No one can be a great scholar or a courtier without great expense and effort. To possess spiritual knowledge and to become a courtier of heaven requires time and devotion.

The Life of St Teresa by Herself, David Lewis, ed. & tr. (London, 1962), pp. 100–1, 402; cf. *The Letters of St Teresa of Avila*, John Dalton, ed. & tr. (London, 1902), adapted; cf. Santa Teresa de Jesus, *Obras Completas*, vol. I (Madrid, 1954), pp. 678–9; *ibid.*, vol. II, pp. 530–33, *et passim*.

BD ANNE OF ST BARTHOLOMEW (Ana Garcia)

In terms that demonstrate her Teresian heritage, Anne recalls her state of mind before she entered the novitiate, as well as later experiences in the Carmelite Order.

Before I entered

He seemed to hide himself from me and leave me in darkness. I was immensely depressed and lonely. I had been a few days in the Monastery of St Joseph when I said to my loving Lord: 'Why are you doing this? Why have you abandoned me? If I did not know you, I would think you had deceived me, and if I had known that you would leave me like this I would never have come to the monastery.'

This abandonment lasted throughout the entire year of noviti-ate. One day at the end of the year I entered the hermitage of Christ at the Pillar to pray. I was scarcely on my knees before my mind changed to a supernatural way of seeing, and our Lord appeared to me on the cross. His first words were in answer to my question whether the thirst he experienced on the cross was a natural thirst. He said: 'I was thirsty only for souls. From now on you must consider this truth, and follow a different path from the one you have taken until now.' It was as if he had said: 'My child, don't seek me any longer.' Then he showed me all the vir-tues in their ultimate forms, which I found exquisitely beautiful. I was even more impressed when I realized how distant I was from their beauty and perfection. After favouring me with this insight, our divine Master disappeared. He left my heart deeply affected by his love, and moved by seeing him on the cross so transfixed by the love of souls. This grace was impressed on my soul. It stayed with me day and night, and my heart was con-stantly with my loving Master. He was always in my heart. This became my everyday state of being. Wherever I happened to be, I experienced an insistent longing to help save souls and to practise the virtues which Jesus had shown me in all their perfection. He assured me that I would acquire them by following the way of the cross . . .

Our Lord granted me so many favours not because I was good, but in order to express his goodness. Although I was unworthy of grace, he sought me out even when I was least occupied with any thought of him, to make sure that I would stay on the right path, and his loving-kindness could take effect. I carried out my various tasks more than willingly when obedience called for them to be done. I deserved no praise for this. I found joy in my work quite plainly and simply, that is, without considering my undoubted inadequacies and the many faults I had done nothing to eradicate. I seemed to do everything entirely out of love of God. Our Lord could see this, and eventually I realized that it was because he loved me that he sent me certain trials to reveal the traces of self-love that were still in me . . .

On one occasion I was seated near the door, because I was acting as portress. I sat there feeling rather hurt, for it seemed to me that the older Sisters were displeased with me and were annoyed that the Prioress had placed me there, because they thought I was still too young for any such responsibility, and eventually I understood why they would resent it . . . It was then that I was granted a spiritual vision of our Lord showing me a withered rosebush in the courtyard; it was covered with red and white roses. The bush was dried up, and anyway it wasn't the season for roses. Jesus said: 'These roses can't be gathered without having to deal with the thorns too.' He wanted me to understand that virtue is acquired only by suffering and contradictions.

I always received some form of consolation from our Lord if I did good to my neighbours when any opportunity to do so presented itself, and if I helped them in their need. Although I inconvenienced myself on such occasions, the difficulty and annoyance disappeared and became true consolations. I owe that transformation to our good Lord, and the same faculty has remained with me until now . . .

My prayer

The kind of prayer I practised on certain days was a profoundly reverent awareness of a light shining in my soul. All my faculties were so penetrated by it that they seemed to have no existence apart from the life which they received from this light. It was neither a vision of Jesus Christ as I saw him usually, nor any other kind of perceived presence. Instead the Holy Trinity seemed to dwell in me somehow. Although my soul saw nothing at all, I felt the same reverence for the Trinity as if I could actually see it present there before me.

My soul as a silkworm

On other days my soul was like a silkworm. This creature is treated with the greatest care by those who raise it. They feed it on tender leaves. When it reaches maturity it starts spinning a thread of very delicate silk with its mouth, and uses it to make a cocoon. It is totally taken up with the pleasure and comfort of this process, and does not think that it might ever cease to exist. Nevertheless, finally its strength is exhausted. It stays fastened up in its cocoon and dies there. I saw (or, rather, I was shown) something like that in my soul. Experiencing a similar sweetness and with the same silent concentration, the soul goes on spinning silk and giving to God what she has received from him. As if she were following the example of the little silkworm, she shuts herself inside her very own self as if in a tomb separating her from all other creatures. With a tender love which she draws unceasingly from the depths of her heart, she actually expresses her deep desire to leave this life. Death is the true life of such a soul, and she longs to have a thousand lives to devote to God and sacrifice for him . . .

Zeal for souls

I was praying on the eve of the Feast of St Denis, the Areopagite, for whom I had a great devotion, when our Lord visited my soul and transformed it into his own soul by a wonderful union.

Although he stayed only a short time, the effects were immense. I became so spiritual in soul and body that I no longer seemed to perform any natural action, or make even the least natural movement. The following day, on the Feast of St Denis, Jesus granted me the same favour after Communion. Although this visit was quite short, the fruits which I experienced, and the state in which it placed my soul, lasted more than fifteen days. Although I saw nothing, I could feel God's sovereign Majesty in the depths of my soul, and felt as I might if I actually saw the Holy Trinity with my own eyes. I saw nothing, but the realization I had of God's presence within me was more striking than if I had actually seen him. During those two weeks I had, indeed, reason enough to be troubled and distraught, but my mind did not allow a single distracting thought to enter it and lost none of its simplicity (I use this expression, because the vision I had of God was simple, quiet and undisturbed).

At the end of the fifteen days, things changed. Admittedly, this grace was not entirely taken from me, but it was not granted me in the perfection which I have just described. The fruits it continued to produce in me were greater courage of soul, more intense fervour, and a more ardent desire to see God and to spend my time serving him as he might decide. This particular state calls for greater activity and less simple looking towards God. Because you are always more energetically employed then, you have to be much more careful not to commit faults, whereas you are preserved from them when you are enclosed in the power of the prayer I have described: that is to say, when you are simply looking towards God. The difference between these two states is not difficult to understand. The soul enjoying this plain sight of God resembles a person who is satiated and has an abundance of all the dishes she might possibly desire, without the trouble of looking for them, or even sitting down to the table. The soul that no longer enjoys this plain sight of God is like a hungry person who wants dishes according to her taste, but has to work hard to obtain them, and has to labour as much to keep them as she did to get them. The soul must act in the same way with regard to the virtues, the knowledge of God and self-knowledge.

Adapted from: Blessed Mother Anne of Saint Bartholomew, *Autobiography*, Marcel Bouis, SJ, ed.; a Religious of the Carmel of St Louis, tr. (St Louis, Mo., 1916), pp. 20, 32–3, 66, 71 *et passim*.

ST JEANNE-FRANCOISE DE CHANTAL

Jeanne de Chantal's spiritual advice often shows the influence of St François de Sales' guidance (and sometimes betrays her rehandling of her notes on the advice she received from him after 1605), yet she is no mere imitator but specializes in the encouragement of anxious souls experiencing the kind of problems she had lived through ('Fear is even more distressing than evil itself'). The text often benefited from the editing of Bossuet, who did not destroy the traditional imagery proper to a bride of Christ which reappears in the writings of so many nuns in the ages of faith.

A little St John

Think of yourself as a minor St John permitted to recline on our Lord's bosom and rest between the arms of his divine providence. Our sole purpose and interest must be the glory of God, and if we had any other concern than that we should get rid of it straightaway. So, as if you were another St John, remain trusting and relaxed in our Lord's arms and surrender your whole being to his will and holy providence. It is happiness indeed to rely on his caring embrace, knowing that a draught of his goodness is better than any wine.

So stay there, dearest sister, like the little St John you are, and while others are receiving all kinds of good things at the Lord's table, rest and support yourself, your head, your love and your spirit on our dear Lord's loving self, for how much better it is to sleep on this sacred pillow than to remain anxiously awake in some other posture.

Live your life in wholehearted reliance on God, and make sure that everything about you is completely free of all covering of artifice, and that this applies to you yourself especially. May our Lord keep you there as a fervent suppliant clinging to his holy cross, liberated from anything that does not belong to him and is not him alone. If he offers you the conviction and consolation of his presence, he does so that your heart may progress from enjoyment of his just being there to direct knowledge of Jesus himself and his will for you.

Worship God as often as possible with short yet ardent movements of the spirit darting out from your very heart. As I have so often advised you, you should admire his goodness, bow to him, throw yourself at the foot of his holy cross, and invoke his help. Give him your soul again and again and again, a thousand times over and again. At times you need never utter a single word but merely contemplate his loving-kindness.

This is one of the main ways to benefit the spirit, for if your soul constantly engages with God, and does so ardently, it will be impressed with all the perfection of God.

My dear daughter, you must know that we are too intelligent to think ourselves poor if we enjoy a state in which we are neither hungry, nor cold, nor treated with disdain, but only find that some of our plans are thwarted in minor ways.

Be daring, be courageous, but never over-particular, for the courage you need means that you must always declare resolutely: 'Rejoice in the Lord!' without reserve, and never worry whether the times are sweet or bitter, or you are passing through light or darkness.

So let us go forward fearlessly, dear daughter, rejoicing in the truly profound, firm and unyielding love of our God, and banish all those spurious temptations to the winds, however often they seek to arrest us on our way.

[Jeanne de Chantal], *Sainte J.F. Frémyot de Chantal: Sa vie et ses oeuvres*, F.M. de Chaugy, ed., 8 vols (Paris, 1874–9), vols 2, 3, *passim*; cf., Jeanne de Chantal, *Correspondance*, Sr Marie-Patricia Burns VSM, ed., 6 vols (Paris, 1986–96).

MARY WARD

Some of Mary's resolutions made around 1616:

1. I will endeavour that no sensible motions, nor occurrent accidents, change easily my inward composure nor external carriage, because freedom of mind and calmness of passions are so necessary both for my own profit in spirit and proceedings with others . . .
2. Seeing my loathness to suffer hath been the cause of so many excuses, I purpose henceforward to embrace all contrary things as due for my sins, and the part and portion which for myself I have chosen, repeating in such occasion that voice of the Prophet, 'I know, O Lord, that thy judgements are right and that thou . . . hast caused me to be troubled.'
3. I will ever fly all manner of esteem, and yet carry myself, so as I may be grateful to all.
4. I will never endeavour that any love me for myself, and yet will I labour to love all for God and in him.
5. I will never contradict in desire, word, nor action the will of my Superior . . .
6. I will every day labour to become perfect in obedience, kissing the five wounds of our Saviour crucified, that I may be such in this virtue as he would have me.
7. When any lights or other motions occur unto me about the Institute, I will commend the same unto the sacred wounds of Christ, and make acts of resignation.
8. I will intend no other thing hereafter in all I do, think, or speak, than the greater glory of God.
9. I will daily endeavour to become more perfect, that my works may be the more agreeable to so excellent an end.
10. Whatsoever I find I want I will make haste to ask it of God.
11. What I would confer with my director absent, I will at my first opportunity confer with God, who is always present.

12. I will labour always to overcome my passions in the beginning.

13. I will never, for any human respects whatsoever, do against or hinder the greater glory of God.

14. I will be always ruled and conform myself wholly to the will and judgement of my director in all things.

15. Always when the clock strikes I will lift up my mind to God, and reflecting briefly that every reasonable soul is made to his image, I will beg grace for myself and all others, especially our company and the Society of Jesus.

16. I will endeavour always to have ready mind and courageous heart to undergo and exercise all means which may help me to perfection.

17. Feel and taste how sweet the Lord is! I will frequent the Holy Sacraments so often as I may be permitted.

18. I will labour to my uttermost to prepare myself well, remembering the greatness and excellency of the thing.

19. After confession I will endeavour to cut off all affection to my former faults.

20. After Communion I will give myself much to God, with an ardent desire to perform his holy will.

21. I will read every day something of some devout book.

22. I will use often with humility to speak unto our Lord, of whose mercy, grace, and especial assistance I have always so much need.

23. I will follow the counsel which Blessed Father Ignatius so much recommended and practised, which is always to walk in the presence of my God.

Mother M. Salome, *Mary Ward: A Foundress of the Seventeenth Century* (London, 1901), pp. 101–4.

She re-stated the unavoidable general principle of her system of perfection.

Knowledge of truth

Now you are to understand how you are to attain this perfection. By learning? No, though learning be a good means, because it giveth knowledge. Yet you see many learned men who are not perfect because they practise not what they know, nor perform what they preach. But to attain perfection, knowledge of verity is necessary, to love it and to effect it. That you may not err, I beseech you all to understand and note well wherefore you are to seek this knowledge. Not for the content and satisfaction it bringeth, though it be exceedingly great, but for the end it bringeth you to, which is God. Seek it for him, who is Verity. Then you will be happy and able to profit yourselves and others.

Till God Will: Mary Ward through Her Writings, M. Emmanuel Orchard, ed. (London, 1985), p. 59.

ST LOUISE DE MARILLAC

Nearly 800 of Louise de Marillac's letters have survived and many of these are addressed to the Sisters of her community. A constant topic is the importance for the Daughters of accepting spiritually what at that time were often very difficult physical changes of place, persons and duties because of the 'respect which they owe to the example of the Son of God who acted in this way . . . such changes can and must occur. If they are not accepted, we shall never enjoy the peace of soul that is essential if we are to please God and to accomplish his holy will . . . Another evil is the disedifying example that we would give our neighbour. We would also find it impossible to practise our Rule faithfully and would be in danger of losing our vocation'. The following subtly

encouraging letter to Margaret, Magdalen and Frances, Sisters of
Charity in Warsaw, is a variation on this theme.

Servants of the sick poor

19 August 1655

Dear Sisters,

Well, the time providentially decided by Almighty God for the departure of the Sisters who will join you there is here at last. We grieve to see them leave us but we rejoice because we never doubt that that they will carry out God's will as they join their efforts to yours, so that his sacred plans can be realized in the Kingdom of Poland. I assure you that those plans are immensely important, for much depends on them, my dear Sisters. I pray fervently that you will experience God's goodness, for I am convinced that this knowledge will inspire deep humility and embarrassment in you at seeing yourselves chosen for this work, and will ensure that you resolve never to fall short of your vocation. But how are you – and I too of course – to do that? In this way: we must totally suppress our contrary passions and desires by repressing our senses. Our hearts must thirst too if, by God's grace, they are to be filled with love. Then God in his goodness will look favourably on the sacrifice of self that you so often offer to him, and on all the things that you do for the poor.

Dear Sisters, you have always told me that the three of you have a single heart. In the name of the Blessed Trinity whom you have honoured and should always honour, I beg you to open your ranks and admit these three new Sisters to this union of hearts so thoroughly that the three last are indistinguishable from the three first. I assure you they are intent on carrying out the plan in a frame of mind that aims only at pleasing God. None of them is out for herself, or is looking for personal satisfaction, any more than I am. Of course, that does not mean that on occasions human nature won't come up with reasons for struggle. That can happen even to the truly perfect, but even then, as you know, this can be a valuable test of the loyalty of people who want to belong entirely to God. So don't be taken by surprise. The self may choose all kinds of ways to rebel, but it is precisely then that our souls must rise to increasingly generous heights in practising heroic virtue. We have to humble ourselves as soon as a contrary inclination is felt. We must calm our feelings, and prove that we intend to be real Christians. Then we shall pay homage to Jesus Christ by exercising the virtues he himself has shown us in his sacred humanity.

I think that one practical thing is necessary. Let me ask you to make sure of this, dear Sisters. It is this: never speak Polish among your three selves without explaining what you say to the others. Then they will learn the language more rapidly, and you will avoid the pitfalls that might cause problems if you did not explain what you are saying. Just think of these Sisters' attitude to God as they set out. They are going to do his holy will by serving the poor in a spirit of love. Think of their attitude to you as well. They appreciate the choice God has decided to make of you as the foundation stones of this new establishment. They think that you should be given all the credit for it, and that God in his providence has sheltered you under his wings to guide you as you go on your way without companionship and in blind trust, with no clear knowledge of the road before you. These thoughts never make them jealous in any way. On the contrary, these Sisters are comforted by following in your footsteps, for they look forward to seeing you practise the customs and duties that God wants from you and from them. They also hope that you, dear Sister Margaret, will always be ready to give them a timely word of advice when they need it, and that the other Sisters will do the same, for they are quite unaware, you must know, how the sick are nursed in Poland.

I am sure, dear Sisters, that I shall never be sufficiently pleased to know how all of you will be united in word and action, as I am certain you will be, both at home (where that will be generally evident to everyone's edification) and outside. In other words, with regard to your own six selves, you must have no secrets whatsoever. With regard to the world outside, you must keep everything secret that happens within your family circle of six Sisters. If you do that, you will accomplish great things.

I pray to our Lord in all his goodness to give you all the blessings needed to carry out the task he has chosen for you. Dear
Sisters, in his holy love I am your humble and very affectionate
servant,

Louise de Marillac

P. S. I assume that I do not have to ask you to pray God for the
well-being of our revered Father Vincent de Paul.

Cf., e.g.: *Sainte Louise de Marillac: Ses Ecrits* (Paris, 1961), pp. 559–60
(Letter 447).

MOTHER CECILE BRUYERE

*The redoubtable founder of the French Benedictine women's
congregation of the modern era offers the Abbess of Stanbrook
and her own nuns advice on silence, meditation and an approach
to dying.*

The spiritual life and meditation

Many people ask me which topics are most suitable for meditation. This is not a trivial matter, especially for those who are
beginning to live an authentic spiritual life, because if you haven't
chosen a specific subject to think about, you merely skip from
one thought to another, times flies away, and arbitrary speculation, which is the fatal enemy of self-control, starts to influence
and eventually takes over your meditation. The great masters
of the spiritual life often tell us to make sure that we choose the
theme for meditation the night before. This is very good advice,
especially for people with little experience of the practice of the
presence of God.

Apart from this general rule, I think it is almost impossible
to establish a precise system for making the right choice of subject. Everyone has her own capabilities and needs and no one has

the same ones. You pray differently depending on whether you are happy or sad, comforted or under trial. Every individual has her own way of recollection and concentration on the essential mysteries. Some people find a few lines of text sufficient to start an effective meditation session, whereas others need more. Some people find a particular mystery most interesting – and sometimes spend too long on it. Others have to follow the sequence of the liturgical seasons and focus on its themes one by one as they come up, even in private prayer. There is no absolute rule or general system that you have to follow in all this, except that it is a good idea to consult known experts and authorities in the field . . .

The sole point of the rule of silence customary in religious Orders is to persuade the soul to a certain degree of introspection and to retreat gradually from the life of the senses; but of course this recommendation of outward silence would be useless if the soul did not manage to check an unruly imagination and keep it on the main theme . . .

True wisdom in this world amounts to putting ourselves in God's hands, and not trying to look too far ahead. God doesn't tell us his secrets beforehand but unfolds them little by little when we are secure in the knowledge that we can trust him entirely . . .

We are told that there are no waves deep down in the lakes to be found in the flatland before the highest mountains. Waves are confined to the surface and the depths of even the oceans of this world are quite untroubled. As the soul approaches God's own depths it is bathed in peace, that unfathomable peace that nothing can disperse or banish: neither the memories of our wrongdoing, nor our pains and suffering, nor those of others, nor anything in this world, because that peace is the onset of everlasting life. Even before we enter that sure and certain ultimate peace on our way to its very source, we already experience something of the peace of God which transcends human understanding and keeps constant guard over our hearts and minds as they rest in Christ Jesus.

Mère Cécile Bruyère, *In Spiritu et veritate* (letters of 1890 and 1897) (Solesmes, n.d.); *La vie spirituelle et l'oraison, d'après la Sainte Ecriture et la tradition monastique* (Solesmes, 1899), pp. 89–90, 148–9.

ST THÉRÈSE COUDERC

Thérèse Couderc knew that the God to whom she said 'Yes' was good, and one day, when she was saying a prayer of thanksgiving after Mass, she had a mystical vision of the goodness of all things: 'I saw the word "goodness" written in what looked like golden letters. I repeated it for a long time with unutterable joy. I saw it inscribed on all creatures, animate and inanimate, rational or not, and even on the prie-dieu at which I was kneeling. I realized that all these creatures and things share in goodness, and that all the services and assistance which we receive from each of them are a blessing that we owe to the goodness of our God, who has given them some part of his own infinite goodness, so that we can find it in everything and everywhere.' In spite of much hardship, injustice and ill-health, she never abandoned her faith in the goodness of God and creation, and the security of surrendering herself to God. Her writings are often sequences of aphorisms that emphasize the same message in a variety of ways: 'My heart embraces the whole world', 'Let me live by love, let me die of love and let my last heart-beat be an act of perfect love,' 'All places are alike to me, because I expect to find God everywhere, since he is the only object of all my desires,' 'My heart doesn't age as far as loving other people is concerned . . .We all know that our heart is exactly the same one we had years ago. It always knows how to love God first and then others in him.' She wrote the following spiritual exercise on self-abandonment and giving everything to God in Montpellier, France, in June 1864.

Surrender yourself

Over the years our Lord had shown me more than once how helpful it was for a soul seeking perfection to entrust herself entirely to the guidance of the Holy Spirit. This morning, however, Jesus had decided to bring this home to me from a quite different perspective. I was getting ready to begin my meditation when I heard the bells of different churches roundabout summoning the faithful to attend Mass. At that very moment, I wanted to join in all the Masses that were being said, and I pointed my meditation in that direction so that I could share in them.

Then I found myself looking at the whole Catholic universe from a wide-angle perspective, and focussed on a vast number of altars where our Lord was offering himself up for us simultaneously. The blood of Jesus the innocent Lamb was shed on each of these altars, which appeared to be wrapped in very delicate clouds of smoke swirling up to heaven. Love and gratitude for the sight of our Lord's total selflessness took hold of me and entered my soul. But I was astonished to think that it had not changed the whole world. I asked Jesus how, if the sacrifice of the Cross offered only once had been enough to save all the souls in the world, it was not enough now to sanctify them all, even though it was celebrated so often. The answer I seemed to hear was that Jesus Christ's sacrifice was certainly sufficient in itself, and his blood was more than enough to make a million worlds holy, but human souls failed to do what they should in response to this. They were not generous enough. The main way to follow the path of perfection and holiness was to surrender yourself to our good God.

But what does 'surrender yourself' mean? Although I understand the implications of the two words, I cannot explain them. I only know that they are very accommodating, and cover both present and future.

To surrender yourself is more than devoting yourself or giving yourself. It is even more than abandoning yourself to God. Surrendering yourself means dying to everything and to the self. It means no longer being concerned with the self except to make sure that it is always turned towards God. To surrender yourself means no longer looking for your own advantage in anything, either spiritual or temporal. It means not seeking your own satisfaction but only what God wants. Of course surrendering yourself also means cultivating the spirit of detachment which clings to nothing, neither to people nor things, and neither to time nor place, but adheres to everything, accepts everything, and submits to everything.

Perhaps you think that all this is very difficult. If so, you are wrong. There is nothing so easy and nothing so pleasant. It all amounts to doing something generous for once and all, and saying with total sincerity: 'My God, I want to be everything for you, please accept my offering'. Then you have said everything that needs to be said. But from then on you must take care to keep your soul in this state. You must not shy away from any little sacrifices that might help you advance in virtue. You should always remember that you have surrendered yourself. I pray to our Lord to help all the souls wishing to please him to understand these words, and to inspire them to take advantage of this straightforward means of holiness. If only people could just understand in advance the sweetness and peace that they will enjoy if they hold nothing back from God who loves them. He communicates himself to a soul that genuinely looks for him and knows how to surrender herself. Once you experience this you will know how to find the true happiness that you search for in vain elsewhere.

The soul that surrenders herself finds heaven on earth, since she enjoys the sweet peace that is part of the happiness of the Lord's own people.

Adapted & translated from the original. Cf. Ghislaine Côté, *Le Cénacle: Fondements Christologiques et Spiritualité* (Paris, 1991); Hélène Caumeil & Chantal de la Forge, *Prier 15 jours avec Thérèse Couderc* (Paris, 2005).

BD MARIE-LOUISE TRICHET

Marie-Louise's sisters had to endure harsh living conditions in the building where she established her congregation: '. . . an old house tacked together from several garrets and shacks, which formerly housed several families of poor weavers who had taken refuge there. It had also been an inn of sorts. The inside left as much to be desired as the outside. There was no furniture, linen or provisions, and not even things the most impoverished think

*necessary. The beds were in the same state as everything else.
They were more like camp beds than domestic beds, for they had
neither bedposts, boards, feet, canopies nor curtains, but were
slats held together with webbing, and an old mattress thrown
down, with sheets and a cover made of numerous off-cuts or
fragments of cloth. Some had been given only a plain straw
mattress. The seats were mean benches made from poor pieces
of planking or a bundle of split wood. The cooking equipment
consisted of a few bowls and plates moulded from heavy clay,
and poorly-fashioned wooden forks and spoons. There were no
chandeliers or candles but only small tinplate lamps, such as the
very poor use, with minute candle stumps in a little foul-smelling
oil. The food had nothing to commend it. Supper was a large
chunk of black bread, as difficult to chew and swallow as it was
to digest. Its cereal content depended on how much the nuns
could afford: rye, barley and pearl barley, occasionally mixed
with a little wheat germ ... Sister Mary of Jesus was used to a
life of frugality and mortification, but from that first evening,
she tells us, she could not stop herself finding these surroundings rather revolting, not on her own account, but on behalf of
her sisters who would shortly join her there'* (Charles Besnard,
La Vie de la Sœur Marie-Louise de Jésus *(Paris, 1985 [original
c.1768]), p. 117. Given such conditions, she knew the work of a
novice mistress was of prime importance and, indeed, the 'most
difficult job of them all, which calls for understanding yet unre-
lentingly firm direction', as shown in this extract from a letter to
a young sister in an outlying community whose development she
controlled most assiduously by correspondence.*

Challenge yourself

You have written to me only once while you have been in the
house, and then without telling me what you are doing. Remember, dear daughter, that you are obliged to write about your
state and to assure me that you are really humble and obedient. I
deeply fear that lack of discipline has made you forget the good

resolutions you made in the mother-house at Saint-Laurent, and that you only want to follow your own inclinations. I advise you to be careful of your temperament, which has a great need of restraint, and I strongly recommend you to do nothing without your Superior's permission. What do you imagine, dear child, will become of you, young as you are, if you do just what you feel like doing? You must realize that all you have to fear is your very own self, and it is a great misfortune if you do not challenge yourself. To attract the blessings of the Lord on all your little tasks, you must practise the great virtues of humility, obedience and kindness towards everyone. I urge you to do just that, and to write about all your little annoyances and troubles to a mother who in all she does wishes only to bring you the happiness of making yourself holy.

Quoted in: René Laurentin, *Petite vie de Marie-Louise Trichet* (Paris, 1993), pp. 125–6.

Yet Marie-Louise was well aware of the importance of treating aspiring nuns with sympathy while inculcating the rules of conduct that would make the religious life possible in the conditions of the time, as is evident from this meticulously defined letter (the pace of which imitates the recommended course of action) to a superior who wished to instruct the novices far too rapidly.

With divine patience

As for Sister X, my dear daughter, you must treat her case with patience. I have very often found myself having to deal with problems as distressing as those which you must now face, and I too have sometimes asked for the same dispensation, that you now ask me to grant, from their having to ask permission to take Communion. I was invariably advised to be patient and not to leave poor sinners to their own devices, and I came to see eventually that I always won more through patience and gentleness than I would have done in another way. These sisters benefited from this approach, and afterwards I was immensely pleased that I had done so rather than show my displeasure. I advise you to use the same technique with regard to Sister X, and I trust that your patience and your kindness towards her will enable her to come to herself, and will finally win her over for God. Do not tell me that you have indeed had to practise patience for a very long time, for I am sure that that is true, but, my dear daughter, if God were to lose heart in the face of our daily acts of disloyalty and upsets, where would you and I be? So let us treat our neighbour with the same patience that God shows to us as he waits for us to be truly sorrowful.

Quoted in: René Laurentin, *Petite vie de Marie-Louise Trichet* (Paris, 1993), p. 126.

BD MARIA ELIZABETTA (Mary Elizabeth) HESSELBLAD

Throughout her life, Blessed Maria Hesselblad, the Swedish convert who, with special papal permission, fulfilled her long dream of reviving the Order founded by St Bridget, and became a great ecumenist, had immense faith in God's providence. She was continually rewarded by extraordinary evidence of the divine in the midst of adversity, all the way from the time when she was locked overnight in the mortuary of the hospital where she worked as a nurse, and in the dark knocked against the body of a supposedly dead man on a slab, found he was still just breathing and was able to save his life; through the difficult years of her young Order's survival during World War I; to the preservation from terrible persecution and murder of all the political and racial refugees she crammed into the Order's small house in Rome during World War II, the most barbaric phase of Italian Fascism, and the Nazi mass-murder of Jews.

With its emphasis on faith, hope and charity, and her undying confidence that 'where two or three are gathered together in my name, there am I in their midst', this composite prayer and exhortation of Blessed Maria, drawn from her memoirs, prayers, and addresses to her nuns, might be a programme for all religious at any time and in any place.

Ut omnes sint . . . May they all be one . . .

In my childhood I saw you in the deep forests of my country and heard your voice echoing in the mountains . . . You were my life on the great ocean . . . I saw you in my new country and you were close to me in my loneliness and in the solitude of my heart. You were my greatest good, for you confirmed my will to do good and the desire to alleviate suffering, pain and misery . . . You walked with me in the dark and narrow streets where the youngest and most obscure of your children live . . . I dreamed of returning to my sweet home country, and to a 'house of peace' there, but your voice constantly summoned me to Rome, the home of St Bridget . . . The fight was long and difficult, but your voice urged me to follow the path of the Cross until the end of my life. *Ecce ancilla Domini!* Behold the handmaiden of the Lord!

When I was a schoolchild, I realized that my companions belonged to many different churches. I started to wonder which was the true Church, because I had read in the New Testament that there would be one sheepfold and one Shepherd. I often prayed to be led to that sheepfold, especially when, walking under the tall pines of my native Sweden, I looked up to the sky and said: 'Dear Father in heaven, where is the sheepfold where you want us all to be together?' A great peace seemed to enter my soul when a voice replied: 'One day I shall show you, my daughter'.

The most perfect act of which we are capable, containing all the other virtues, is our complete surrender to God by renouncing ourselves entirely. I thank you, Lord, for my whole life and for all that you have given me. May I continue to find you in all that happens in my life and in all humanity. I thank you for all that you grant me, for all that you deny me and for all that you take from me. A soul that truly loves God does not want to pass through roses, but through thorns. Let us thank the good Lord for having called us to serve him so intimately. Let us strive to be ever faithful to his inspiration, persevering even if our path is sometimes sown with thorns. Where God has called us, we shall find everything that we need to attain perfection.

I commend recollection and silence to you as the only way of achieving union with Jesus and becoming his worthy spouses. Engaging the soul in constant union with God is the true and effective art of prayer. Our good God desires great things from this Order in the future, for his glory and for the salvation of souls. May we always work harder to maintain a spirit of simplicity and love, with righteousness first among ourselves and then among all those whom we meet outside.

Lord, remember your promise and grant peace to all those of good-will. You are the source of all good desires, counsels and works. Grant peace to the people of the world for the good of all mankind and for your greater glory. Grant peace in families, schools and universities, between those who work and those who give work, and between all kingdoms and governments of the world. Lord, grant peace and brotherly love among all your creation, and the peace and the light of the Holy Spirit between statesmen.

I shall never stop praying for Christians to unite in God's love. Lord, bring us closer to the point where all Christians are united. Hear the prayers of your humble Bridgettine daughters who consecrate themselves to you in love and sacrifice for this intention.

Cf. *Beati e Santi* and Bridgettine sites; the film *Mother Maria Hesselblad: The Extraordinary Woman in Rome* (Turin, 2000).

3

Mothering, Healing & Family Relations

❧

JULIAN OF NORWICH

The following passage from The Revelations of Divine Love *is one of the most profound yet simple and influential presentations of the loving-kindness and motherliness of God in world spirituality. Julian explains her understanding of the great truth that God loves us and by divine grace and goodness our souls will live in heaven for all eternity. The noblest thing God has made is humankind and its highest expression is the blessed soul of Jesus Christ. Jesus is our true Mother in grace, whose motherhood stretches out infinitely. It is all one love: 'The motherhood of mercy and grace restores us to our natural place, where we were created by the motherliness of love, the mother's love that never deserts us.' Julian has found an unfailingly universal image for the truth she knows by intuition, from experience and through contemplation.*

God's indwelling in our souls

Enclosed in us

God's love for humankind is vast and unending. He makes no distinction in love between the blessed soul of Christ and the least soul that will be saved. It is very easy to believe and trust that the blessed soul of Christ is at the highest point in the glorious Godhead; and truly, if my understanding of what our Lord says is correct, where Christ's blessed soul is, there too is the substance of all the souls that will be saved by Christ.

We ought to be overjoyed that God lives in our souls, and even more so that our souls live in God, for our souls are made to be God's own residence, and the residence of the soul is God, who is uncreated. It is a most profound and wonderful thing to see and to realize within ourselves that God, who made us, is living in our souls. It is something even more profound and marvellous to know within ourselves that our souls, which are created, live in the substance of God. We are what we are through this substance, that is, through God.

I could see no difference between God and our substance, for it was as if it were all God, and yet I understood in my mind that our substance was in God: that is, that God is God, and that he created our substance. For the almighty truth of the Trinity is our Father, since he made us and preserves us in himself. And the profound wisdom of the Trinity is our Mother in whom we are all enclosed. The great goodness of the Trinity is our Lord, and we are enclosed in him, and he in us. We are enclosed in the Father, and we are enclosed in the Son, and we are enclosed in the Holy Spirit; and the Father is enclosed in us, and the Son is enclosed in us, and the Holy Spirit is enclosed in us: all power, all wisdom and all goodness: and one God, one Lord.

Our faith is a virtue that originates in the basic goodness of what we are and is felt in our soul by the work of the Holy Spirit, through whom all our virtues come to us, for no one can be virtuous without the Spirit. Our faith is nothing other than a right understanding and true belief, and secure trust, that as far as our innermost being is concerned we are in God, and God in us, even though we do not see him. And this particular virtue, together with all the others that God has decided we should have in our charge, enables us to do great things. For Christ in his mercy is working in us, and we graciously cooperate with him through the gifts and abilities of the Holy Spirit. This process makes us Christ's children and Christian in our behaviour.

Christ is our way

Therefore Christ is our way, leading us securely according to his laws, and through his great power Christ in his body bears us up to heaven. For I saw that Christ, who contains all who are to be saved within himself, presents his Father in heaven with us in worship. His Father receives this gift with great thanks and courteously gives it back to his Son Jesus Christ. The Father rejoices at this gift and action, which are happiness for the Son and delight for the Holy Spirit. Of all the things that we do, the one that most pleases our Lord is that we ourselves rejoice in this joy of the Holy Trinity about our salvation . . .

Notwithstanding all our feelings of sadness or pleasure, God wants us to understand by faith that we are truly more in heaven than on earth . . .

Almighty God is our kindly Mother

When almighty God made us he was our kindly Father, and God the all wise was our kindly Mother, and the Holy Spirit their love and goodness, but all one God and one Lord. In this unity and joining together he is our very loyal husband, and we are his cherished wife and loved one with whom he is never displeased. For he has said: 'I love you and you love me, and our love will never be shattered.'

I saw how the Blessed Trinity worked, and understood that it had three properties: fatherhood, motherhood, and lordship in one and the same God. In our almighty Father we have been happily maintained with regard to our created being from eternity. In the second Person, we have been maintained, restored and redeemed by skill and wisdom with regard to our sensual nature, for he is our Mother, Brother, and Saviour. And in our good Lord the Holy Spirit we have our reward and our peace when our life and suffering are at an end, and they will infinitely exceed anything we might desire, because of his great courtesy and infinite grace.

Our entire life is threefold. Initially, we have our being, then our growth, and thereafter our fulfilment. The first is nature, the second is mercy, and the third is grace. For the first, I saw and understood that the vast power of the Trinity is our Father, the profound wisdom of the Trinity is our Mother, and the great love of the Trinity is our Lord; and we have all this by our nature and in our created being.

I also realized that the second Person, who is our Mother in respect of our nature, yes, that same dear and worthy person, has become our Mother in respect of our sensual nature. For we are God's creation in two respects: our nature as our very being and our sensual nature. Our very nature is the higher part, which we have in our Father, Almighty God, and the second Person of the Trinity is our Mother of our fundamental created nature, in whom we are grounded and rooted, and he is our Mother in mercy in respect of our sensual nature, which he has taken himself. Therefore he is our Mother in various ways and functions, which are united in him but separate in us. In our Mother Christ we benefit and develop, and in his mercy he reforms us and restores us; and by means of his passion, death and resurrection he has united us with our very nature and being. This is how our Mother works in his mercy for the advantage of all his children who are responsive to him and obedient . . .

Jesus Christ is our very Mother

We have all these blessings by mercy and grace, and would never have enjoyed such welcome joy if there had been no opposition to the express goodness which is God. It is because of this that we enjoy those benefits. Wickedness was permitted to rise up against that goodness, and the goodness of mercy and grace opposed wickedness, and turned all of it into goodness and honour, for all those who will be saved. After all, it is the nature of God to oppose good to evil. Therefore Jesus Christ, who sets good against evil, is our true Mother. We owe him our being (which is the very basis of motherhood), as well as all the joyful love and care that never cease thereafter.

God is truly our Father, as truly as he is our Mother. He has shown this at all times, and especially in those loving words in which he says: 'It is I', meaning: 'It is I who am the power and goodness of Fatherhood. It is I who am the wisdom of Motherhood. It is I who am light and grace and blessed love entirely. It is I who am the Trinity. It is I who am Unity. It is I who am the sovereign Goodness of all things whatsoever. I make it possible for you to love. I make it possible for you to long for things. And I am the everlasting fulfilment of all true desires' . . .

Loving-kindness, mercy and grace are our life whole and entire, and give us meekness, mildness, patience and compassion, as well as hatred of sin and wickedness, for the nature of virtues is to hate sin and wickedness. In this way Jesus is our true Mother with respect to our basic nature, as we were created; and he is our true Mother in grace, because she took our human nature upon himself . . .

The noble and beautiful word 'Mother' is so delightful, and is indeed unique, that it cannot really be used except in relation to him and to her who is his own true Mother, and ours. Motherhood essentially stands for love and kindness, wisdom, knowledge and goodness . . . A loving, kind mother who understands and realizes her child's needs will care for him or her tenderly because it is in a mother's nature to do just that. As children develop she changes the methods by which she cares for them, but not her love.

Translated from the Middle English of Julian of Norwich, *Revelations of Divine Love*, chapters 54–60; cf. *The Shewings of Julian of Norwich*, G.R. Crampton, ed. (Kalamazoo, Mich., 1994); *A Book of Showings to the Anchoress Julian of Norwich*, E. Colledge & J. Walsh, eds (Toronto, 1978); *Revelations of Divine Love*, G. Warrack, tr. (London, 1907).

ST HILDEGARD OF BINGEN

Hildegard tells us that compassion is at the very heart of all heal-
ing. For her, the voice of mercy is never strained. It is always there
to comfort us. Hildegard's understanding of health was holis-
tic: soma and psyche, body and mind, action and thought, were
aspects of a whole.

How to cure hardness of heart

Plants exchange the sweet scents of their fragrance and precious
stones present each other with their gleaming brilliance. Every
living thing longs for some other thing to hold it in a loving
embrace. All nature is at the service of humankind. It offers and
provides its treasures for human use out of love and joy. Yet
there are those who persist in offering in return no more than
a harsh and unfeeling gaze and the smoke of discontent in the
harshness of their hearts.

But I am the inexhaustibly sweet herb of mercy and compassion. You can find me in the air, in the dew, and in the fresh
greenness of all that lives. My heart bursts with willingness to
help all those in need. I was already there when God uttered the
words 'Let there be . . .!' and the world that now serves human
beings emerged from nothing. You, Hardness of Heart, have no
love at the centre of your being, whereas I, Mercy, look on all
life's needs with a kindly eye. I feel close to everything that is. I
help the weak and fragile, and show them the way to health and
wholeness. I am a precious balm for all sorrows, and my words
console the sad and suffering and restore them in body and in
soul . . .

Mind and body

There is a connection between physical movement and mental
discomfort or distress. When a human body becomes hyper-

active and cannot keep still, but is always nervously seeking to do something or other, the essential nature of the human mind asserts itself. In reaction to all this nervous hub-bub, it ceases to operate and behaves as if it were asleep. It is like a watermill that sometimes stops working if a heavy onrush of water overwhelms it. Similarly the mind no longer functions but remains still and peaceful until the overactive body is chastened in some way or assailed by fears that make it slow down. Then the mind recovers its strength, shows that it is alert, and starts thinking again. So much so, that the person whose mind and body are in question seems reborn as a totally new being . . .

The virtues of agate

If an insect or some other little creature sprays someone with its venom, but not so as to penetrate the body, then you must heat the agate thoroughly in sunlight or on a preheated brick and when it is hot place it on the painful area, when the stone will remove the poison. Then heat it once again in the same way and hold it over steaming water so that the evaporated water drops into the hot water and let it lie there for an hour. Finally, dip a linen cloth in the agate water and lay it, still wet, on the spot where the insect attacked the victim or on the area where it sprayed its poison, and he or she will be cured.

Hildegard von Bingen, *Causae et curae* [Causes and Treatment], P. Kaiser, ed. (Leipzig, 1903), pp. 41–5 *et passim*; id., *Heilwissen: Von den Ursachen und der Behandlung von Krankheiten* [Medicine: On the causes and treatment of Diseases] M. Pawlik, ed. & tr. (Freiburg im Breisgau, 1994), pp. 192–3; Gottfried Hertzka, *Kleine Hildegard-Hausapotheke* (Stein am Rhein, 1993), p. 23.

ST CATHERINE DEI RICCI

Although St Catherine was an extraordinarily ecstatic mystic who received the stigmata, was recorded even by St Philip Neri as capable of bilocation, and lived to the full the spirituality of an emotionally overcharged age, her correspondence was often practical and compassionate. In a letter of 15 November 1543 to her father, Pierfrancesco dei Ricci, she asks for more understanding of her brother's character and behaviour. Another, of 16 January 1561, to Filippo Salviati, a layman, is a very good example of her ability to convey her sympathy and practical advice not only directly but by using a telling metaphor.

My dear Father

May the Divine Majesty grant you patience and give peace to your troubled soul! May you be enlightened to see what is best to be done, and have the grace to do it. I have received a letter from Ridolfo, begging me to plead his cause with you, and to forward to you the letter he has written to you. I understand only too well why you are displeased with him and the serious faults of which he is guilty. But, Father, I beg you to be patient and prudent. He has acted very wrongly and disobeyed both God and you, his loving father, who have spent so much care on him. In spite of all that, I beseech you for the love of God to forgive him. If you have cursed him – and he deserved it – now restore him to your blessing. Since the harm is done, there is nothing to be obtained by making bad worse and driving him to despair. Justice may be on your side, and the world may tell you to be firm in asserting your rights, but I believe that it is by showing mercy you will please our Lord. When Mother thinks the moment has come, Ridolfo will, I know, ask your pardon. I implore you to grant it when he asks. Tell him the truth gently, promise to help him if he behaves himself, and threaten to withdraw your help should he misbehave. As long as he is afraid to approach you or speak to you, medicine will be precious little use to him. He fully acknowledges that you are in the right and is very humble and most anxious to atone by his future conduct for the offence he has given you. The sooner you forgive him, the more quickly he will recover from his illness. You are the person to restore him to health of soul and body. Speak to your son again. Do not refuse me, Father! If I am truly your daughter and you love me as much as you profess, you will grant me what I ask. I thank you with all my heart for your affection: may our Lord reward you!

* * *

Meeting in Paradise

Dear Salviati, I hear that you are sick. I can believe you though I cannot think of a solution. Religious separated from the world and with no business or family ties necessarily lead a more harsh and rigorous life than others. But you are the head of a great house and have all the cares of a family to bear; you must be very careful about your life and health, not in order to enjoy the pleasures of this world, but to support your family as you should, and to give your children a good Christian education. Never forget that we shall have to give an account at the judgement of our indiscretions as well as of our self-indulgence. Now that you are both at Florence, I am sure no one will offer you soup and biscuits at supper, so I am sending you a basket of chestnuts, and order you to eat at least four each night. We must look to life not death as our goal, and seek to do good in order to honour and glorify God in ourselves.

I so wish you would not do things that are really beyond you. You will do yourself irreparable harm. For example, you ought not to have left here. You were told this often enough, but all you said was: 'I shall go whether it snows or hails'. You cannot argue with someone who has made up his mind, and you were determined to do so whatever the result, although I was sorry to hear of it, and if it had been possible I should have stopped a single drop falling on your dear head. But you wouldn't do what I advised . . .

It is now nine o'clock on Tuesday evening. I assume that your day is at an end and that you have gone to bed. I am sure that this weather is really bad for your health, so I beg you to take care of yourself in all simplicity, at least until mid-April. Do it out of love of our Lord, and to gain time to work for God: that should be our real aim.

The wine got here and I was given some of it at collation last night after reading your letter, for my throat had swollen considerably on hearing of your problems. But your news was so harsh that I ignored the wine's sweetness. Yet this morning it tasted sweet. Thank you. I remembered you last night and this morning and offered our Lord your body, soul, heart, memory, intellect and will. They are the six water-pots whose contents I asked him to change into wine. I prayed that as wine purifies and preserves, so your mind may be liberated from everything untoward, and your good will may be preserved by good actions. Please do the same for me. I look forward to the day when we see one another neither at St Peter's nor at Florence nor at the Prato, but in Paradise when Jesus, his blessed Mother and the whole company of heaven come to fruition.

Yours, Catherine

F.M. Capes, *St Catherine dei Ricci: Her Life, her Letters, her Community* (London, 1905), pp. 94–5, 184–7, adapted; cf. J. Cumming, *Letters from Saints to Sinners* (London & New York, 1996), pp. 101–2.

SR MARIA CELESTE

Sister Maria Celeste, Galileo's daughter, was assigned various tasks in the convent, including the care of the sick and work in the pharmacy. In a letter of 19 December 1625, she sends her father a winter rose which she had found in the convent garden. In accordance with the language of flowers, which often served

for moral instruction as well as messages between close members
of a family, she typically elevates the rose to the level of meta-
phor. It becomes something like an affectionate admonition to
her father not to involve himself entirely in worldly things.

The hope we cling to

You ordered some preserved lemons but I have not managed to
prepare more than a few. I did worry about the lemons being
too shrivelled to preserve them acceptably, and that has indeed
turned out to be the case. I am sending you two baked pears for
this penitential season. But, as the greatest treat of all, I send you
a rose. This ought to please you immensely, since it is a great
rarity at this time of year. Remember that, when you accept a
rose, you have to take its thorns too, which stand for our Lord's
bitter Passion. Of course the green leaves represent the hope we
may cling to that, through the same holy Passion, once we have
passed through the darkness of this short winter of mortal life,
we may reach the brightness and happiness of eternal spring in
heaven. May God of his great mercy grant us that.

I must stop here. Sister Arcangela [her sister Victoria] wants to
share my affectionate wishes for you. We should both be glad to
know how you are at present.

I return the table-cloth in which the lamb was wrapped: you
have a pillow-case of ours in which we sent your shirts, as well
as a basket and a coverlet.

Adapted from *The Private Life of Galileo Galilei compiled principally*
from his correspondence and that of his eldest daughter (Boston, 1870),
pp. 137–8.

On 22 March she writes to her father after her first meeting with
Sestilia Bocchineri, her brother's future wife.

My sister and I were very pleased with the bride's kindly manner, and her good looks. But what gave me the greatest joy was to see that she was fond of you, since that persuades us that she will give you the loving attention and do things for you that we would be delighted to carry out, if we were allowed to. But we will never surrender our own special task, which is to pray to God for you continually. Of course that is our duty, not only as daughters, but as the desolate orphans we would become if you were taken from us.

If only I could explain what I really feel! Then I should be certain that you would never doubt that I love you more affectionately than any daughter ever loved a father. But I do not know how to express myself. After God, I belong to you, and your kindnesses are so numerous that I feel I could risk my own life if only I could save you from any distress, as long as I did not offend almighty God in any way by doing so.

Please, please forgive me if I am tedious. Sometimes my love for you makes me exceed the normal limits of expression. Of course I did not sit down to write about my own feelings, but to tell you that if you could manage to send back the clock on Saturday evening, the Sister sacristan, whose duty is to summon us to matins, would be most grateful. But if you have not been able to set it to rights yet, never mind. It will be better for us to wait a little longer than to have it back before it has been repaired properly.

Please let me know if you would mind making an exchange with us. We want you to take back a lute which you gave us many years ago, and to exchange it for a couple of breviaries, one for each of us. The prayer books we had when we became nuns are quite worn to shreds. They are the instruments we use every day, yet the lute is still hanging there, covered in dust. I am afraid that it could be damaged, as I am forced sometimes to lend it to people outside the house, in order not to be thought discourteous.

If you are prepared to do this for us, please send me a message asking me to return the lute. As for the breviaries, we do not mind if they are not gilt-edged. It will be quite satisfactory if they contain all the saints lately added to the calendar, and if the print is legible, for then they will be of service to us even if we live to be old women.

Adapted from: *The Private Life of Galileo Galilei compiled principally from his correspondence and that of his eldest daughter* (Boston, 1870), pp. 158–9.

On 8 July 1629, Celeste wrote to her father begging him to send her money to obtain the peace, quiet and comfort of private rooms in her convent, for she had been deprived of them by the selfish behaviour of her hypochondriac sister (Sister Arcangela in religion). Eventually he sent her the 20 scudi she had asked for.

I know that you realize, at least to some extent, how uncomfortable I have always been here without a room of my own ... A few years ago I had to surrender the single small cell we had, for which we paid the novice mistress 35 scudi, and allow Sister Arcangela [her actual sister] to occupy it all on her own, so that she could escape as far as possible from the same mistress, who, sad to say, just could not put up with Arcangela's strange behaviour and was therefore a constant threat to her. Arcangela often finds it very difficult to get along with other people, for her character is very different from mine, and quite weird at times. Accordingly, it is better if I let her have her way on many occasions, so that we can live in the peace and harmony appropriate to our resolute love for one another. But this means that I have to spend every night in the remarkably awful company of the novice mistress (even though God does manage to let me survive these nights, for my own good I am sure). And so this means that day after day I am living as a kind of pilgrim without anywhere to get away to for even an hour on my own. I do not want a big attractive space, but a small room like the one now available from a nun desperately in need of cash and willing to sell her room for 35 scudi. Unfortunately I have no more than ten from

Sister Luisa, and five that I look forward to receiving from my regular income. So I need 20 from you, or I will lose the room ... For the love of God, help me, for I am now one of the most distressed paupers ever immured in prison ... I know that you will wish to help and that you can do so ... May the Lord bless you and keep you now and for ever. Your loving daughter.

Adapted from: *The Private Life of Galileo Galilei compiled principally from his correspondence and that of his eldest daughter* (Boston, 1870), pp. 170–2.

On 4 December, Sister Celeste writes to advise her father that he would be receiving from the new Archbishop a request (though in reality something more like an order) to help redress the poverty and inadequate finances of the nuns. The Archbishop had asked the Abbess of St Matthew's convent to send him a list of names of the closest relations of each nun in the house, so that they could be called on to contribute to the relief of the sisterhood during the winter.

I should be very distressed if you were put to any inconvenience, yet, all the same, in all conscience I cannot stand in the way of any help and relief the Archbishop contemplates asking for this poor and truly desolate house. I would, however, suggest that you include a well-known fact in your reply to my lord Archbishop. You would be quite justified to suggest that it would be only right and proper if the relations of many of the nuns here were forced to pay out the sum of two hundred crowns which they have kept back from their dowries, and, over and above those two hundred crowns, the associated interest, which has been owing for many years. Those responsible include Signor Benedetto Landucci, who is a debtor in respect of his daughter, Sister Clara. If something is not done, I fear that you, as Signor Benedetto's surety, will have to pay that sum, or else it will fall upon our poor Vincenzio's shoulders.

If those who owe money could be made to pay, the convent would be relieved in a much better way than by the donations of most relatives, for few of them are rich enough to subscribe. The intention of the superiors is good; they help us as best they can, but the wants of the convent are too great. I, for my part, envy no-one in this world but the Capuchin fathers, who are placed beyond all the cares and anxieties which come upon us nuns. For we have not only to supply the convent charges, and give grain and money every year, but also to provide for our own private necessities by the work of our hands; and our gains are so small that the relief they afford is really scanty. And if I were to tell the truth, I should say that these gains were rather loss than profit in the end, for we hurt our health by sitting up working till seven o'clock (1 am), and consuming oil, which is so expensive. Since I heard from Madonna Piera today that you said we were to ask for anything we wanted, I will make so bold as to ask for a little money to pay a few small debts which make me uneasy. As for the rest, we have enough to eat and to spare, for which God be praised.

Adapted from: *The Private Life of Galileo Galilei compiled principally from his correspondence and that of his eldest daughter* (Boston, 1870), pp. 187–8.

Towards the end of her short life, in a letter of 3 October 1633, and within permissibly prudent limits, Celeste comments on her father's sentence for holding new scientific views that aroused the opposition of obdurate and mistaken church authorities with excessive power over human speculation and creativity.

I will tell you that as a great favour I managed to get someone to show me a copy of your sentence, and though on the one hand it grieved me to read it, yet on the other hand I was glad to have done so, because by doing so I found a way of being of some slight use to you; that is, by taking upon myself that part of the sentence which orders you to recite the seven Penitential Psalms once a week. I began to do this a while ago, and it gives me much pleasure; first because I am persuaded that prayer in obedience to Holy Church must be efficacious; secondly, in order to save you the trouble of remembering it. If I had been able to do more, I would have been most willing to enter a more poverty-stricken prison than the one I live in now, if by so doing I could have set you free.

Adapted from: *The Private Life of Galileo Galilei compiled principally from his correspondence and that of his eldest daughter* (Boston, 1870), p. 265.

SR MARIE DE L'INCARNATION (Marie Guyard)

Marie saw God as a God of love above all else, who had 'never led me by feelings of fear, but always by a spirit of love and trust.' She rejected her son's doubts about the religious life by asking: 'Why do you not want to know ever more closely a God who is so good and loving?' If only he were to rejoice in 'this sweet familiarity with God' in prayer, she asserted, he would be able to demonstrate that love ever more effectively in his own practical works. She never doubted the justification for her own choice of the religious life, for 'the Spirit who has guided me so lovingly has always had the same objective in mind and has inspired my soul to practise the virtues consonant with the spirit of the Gospel . . . and perfect possession of the spirit of Jesus Christ.' (Le Témoignage de Marie de l'Incarnation [Paris, 1932], p. 274). In the following letter, when she is 70 and he is in his fifties, she finally writes to her Benedictine son in France to explain why she left him when he was only eleven, to enter the enclosed religious life in a convent.

Delay no longer!

Quebec, 30 July 1669

My very dear Son,

A ship from France entered our port towards the end of June, but none has arrived since then. It brought news of you which has given me good grounds to praise God for his goodness to you and to me. Indeed, my greatest joy in life is to consider that truth, and I see that your thoughts about your experience affect you deeply and are of great benefit to you. You must be very pleased, my dear son, that I abandoned you to God's sacred guidance by leaving you for the sake of his love. Surely you have found a pearl of inestimable price in that good counsel. I assure you once again that actually separating myself from you was a living death and the Spirit of God, who was unrelenting with regard to the motherly love which I felt for you, gave me no peace until I had done what had to be done. All that had to be suffered, and I was compelled to obey him directly (without reasoning), because he would brook no delay in doing his will, which is absolute. Human nature, which is not inclined to give in easily when its interests are called in question, and especially when a mother's duty towards her son is in question, could not decide. It seemed to me that if I left you when you were so young, you would not be brought up in the fear of God, and that you might fall victim to some evil influence, or adopt some form of behaviour that could endanger your salvation, and therefore I would be deprived of a son whom I wanted to raise only to serve God. I had planned to remain with you in the world until you were old enough to enter a religious order, which was the vocation I had intended you to follow.

But the Holy Spirit was watching me as I struggled to decide one way or the other, and had no pity on my feelings, for he told me in the depths of my heart: 'Come on now, hurry up, you have to make a decision now, you can't delay any longer. The world is no good to you from now on'. Thus he opened the door to the religious life for me. His voice kept pressing me with all his divine insistence; it gave me no rest by day or by night. He managed everything for me and arranged it all with the convent so helpfully that everyone opened their arms to welcome me as if I were the most important lady in the land, who was bring them a vast dowry. I could never have met with greater good will anywhere. Dom Raymond did all that was necessary to arrange matters with my sister, and he himself led me to the place where God wanted me to be. You came with me, and when I said goodbye to you the pain was so extreme that it was as if my soul had been torn from my body. But you must understand that I had a very strong vocation to the religious life from the age of fourteen. I did not act on it because no one would allow me to do what I really wanted. Nevertheless, from the age of nineteen or twenty my mind was made up and I lived with only my body still in the world, so that I could bring you up until the hour of God's will sounded for you and for me.

After I had entered the convent, and when I saw you come crying to the parlour and the choir grille; when you tried to push through the aperture used to give Communion; and when you suddenly saw the main convent door open for the workmen, and you came into our courtyard and, on being told that this was forbidden, you backed out, and you tried to see if you could catch sight of me by some means or other, some of the novices wept and said I was cruel not to cry too, and not even to look at you. Unfortunately, these good sisters did not see the anguish in my heart on your behalf, or my absolute loyalty to God's holy will.

Then the struggle began again when you came crying to the grille asking to have your mother back, or to let you enter and become a religious as well. But the greatest blow of all was when a troop of little children of your age came with you to our refectory windows, crying out weirdly and demanding that they should give me back to you, and your voice stood out above the others calling for me to be given back to you, and insisting that you wanted your mother back. Listening to all that, the nuns were deeply touched with sorrow and compassion, and, although none of them showed any sign of annoyance, I believed they would not put up with it for long, and that they would make me return to the secular world to take care of you. When I came out from prayers and was making my way upstairs to the novitiate, I heard the Spirit of God in my heart saying: 'Do not grieve. I shall look after him'. These divine promises calmed me entirely and made me realize that our Lord's words are spirit and life, and that he is faithful to his promises, so that heaven and earth would perish before one thing that he said would fail to come to pass. If the whole world had contradicted this inward message, I would not have believed the objection.

Since then, I have not worried about any of this. My mind and heart have been quite at peace in the certainty that God's promises would come to pass in you and I saw all things done for your benefit and all the measures taken as I had wished to make sure that you received the education I had wanted you to have. Soon after this, you were sent to Rennes to study and later to Orleans, for God's own goodness had put me in contact with the Jesuit Fathers who were to take care of you. You know how God helped us in this respect. So there we are, my very dear son: you and I have experienced the infinite mercy of such a good Father. Let us leave it in his hands. We will see many more things happen thus if we are faithful to him.

Carry on praying for me as you have done until now.

Lettres de la Révérende Mère Marie de l'Incarnation, L'Abbé Richaud-eau, ed., vol. 2 (Paris, 1876), pp. 407–11 (lettre cxcviii).

ST BERNADETTE OF LOURDES (Marie Bernadette Soubirous, Sr Marie-Bernard)

Bernadette was a straightforward, self-effacing, modest, generous and surprisingly witty young woman. At her convent, she disliked being quizzed by priests and socially advantageous visitors about unimportant details of Mary's appearance, such as her hair style and colour, or how exactly she made the sign of the cross. If pressed by obviously pretentious time-wasters and arrogant or sardonic clerics and others, she was slow to reply.

Once she had been taught French and how to read and write, though she never did so with subtlety or grace, she wrote at least four typically unembellished and even curt accounts of what she saw in the cave at Massabielle in 1858 when she was about 14 and the Virgin Mary appeared to her as a young girl of about 12 speaking not formal French (a language known to relatively few people among the masses at the time) but Bernadette's own patois, or local language of the Lourdes area. In spite of the many emphatic attempts to make her descriptions accord more with standard, 'approved' representations of our Lady, Bernadette's descriptions varied minimally from her oral reports when still illiterate, the most important difference being that between her insistence that Mary was a girl and her use of the more 'polite' term 'young lady'. Of course, clergy, religious, reporters, artists and others wanted her to remember seeing a much taller, older, stately and suitably clothed personage. The following passages reproduce two versions of her vision.

What I saw in the cave

I had scarcely got past the foot of the hill when the wind started to blow as if a storm was coming up. It seemed to be blowing from all the nearby slopes and to move in all directions. I turned to the side where there was a field. The trees there weren't moving at all. I saw some branches and brambles shifting on the side of the cave, but I didn't stare fixedly at them.

I removed my stockings entirely, dipped my foot in the water, and heard the same sound ahead of me. I looked up and saw a cluster of branches and brambles stirring to and fro under the highest part of the opening to the cave, although nothing else was moving there.

Then I saw a young girl dressed in white in the opening. She was no taller than me. She nodded slightly in greeting and at the same time she extended her arms a short distance from her body and opened her hands as you see them in statues of the holy Virgin. A rosary was hanging from her right arm.

I was afraid and drew back. I wanted to call the two children who were with me, but I was too frightened. I rubbed my eyes again and again because I thought I was imagining it all.

When I looked up again, the girl was smiling very kindly and seemed to be asking me to approach her. But I was still afraid. It wasn't the same kind of fear I've felt on other occasions, because I would always stay there to see her, whereas you scamper off if you're really afraid.

Then I thought I ought to pray, so I felt in my pocket and took out the rosary I usually have with me. I kneeled and tried to make the sign of the cross, but I couldn't raise my hand to my forehead. It just dropped down again when I tried to do so.

Meanwhile the girl stood to one side and turned towards me. Now she was holding her big rosary in one hand. She crossed herself, as if she was about to pray. My hand was shaking and I tried to bless myself again. This time it worked. I wasn't frightened any longer after that.

I said the rosary. The girl moved her rosary beads between her fingers but never moved her lips. I looked at her as closely as possible while I was saying my beads.

She had a white dress on. It came right down to her feet, and I could only see their tips. High up around her neck the dress was fixed with a hem with a white cord sticking out from it. She had a white veil on her head. It fell down over her shoulders and arms and covered her almost to the bottom of her dress. I could see a yellow rose on each of her feet. Her sash was blue and hung down below her knees. The rosary beads were strung on a yellow chain. They were big, white and set at some distance from each other.

The girl was very young, lively and wrapped in light.

When I had finished saying my beads she smiled at me, went back into the niche, and disappeared.

* * *

One day, with two other girls I went down to the bank of the river Gave. Suddenly I heard something like leaves rustling. I looked towards the field beside the river but the trees seemed quite still. Obviously the noise came from somewhere else. I looked up and saw the cave where there was a young lady wearing a beautiful white dress with a shining belt. She had a pale yellow rose, the same colour as her rosary beads, on the top of each foot. I immediately started to rub my eyes, thinking I had imagined what I saw, and I put my hands into the fold of my dress where I kept my rosary. I wanted to cross myself but I just couldn't manage it and my hand dropped down. Then the young lady made the sign of the cross herself, and when I tried the second time I succeeded, although my hands were trembling. I started to say the rosary and the young lady's beads slipped through her fingers, although she didn't move her lips. When I had finished saying the Hail Mary, she vanished immediately. I asked the two children with me if they had noticed anything, but they said No. Of course they wanted to know what was happening, and I told them that I had seen a young lady wearing a lovely white dress, but I didn't know who she was. I told them not to say anything about it, and they said I should just forget about it. But I said that was wrong and I went back on the next Sunday, because I seemed to be drawn there . . . On my third visit, the young lady spoke to me and asked me to make sure I came there every day for fifteen days. I said I would do that, and she said she wanted me to tell the priests to build a chapel there. She also told me to drink from the stream. I went over to the river Gave, which was the only stream I could see. Then she made me understand that she did not mean the Gave and pointed to a very small trickle of water nearby. When I was close to it, I could find only a few drops there, and they were mostly mud. I cupped my hands, and tried to get hold of some liquid, but without success, so I began to scrape the ground. I did manage to find a few drops of water but I had to try four times before I had anywhere near enough for any kind of drink. Then the young lady vanished and I went home. I returned every day for fifteen days. Each time, except for one Monday and one Friday, the young lady appeared and told me to look for a stream, wash in it, and make sure that the priests built a chapel there. She said that I also had to pray for the conversion of sinners. I asked her several times what she meant by that, but she just smiled. Finally, she stretched out her arms, looked up to heaven and told me that she was the Immaculate Conception. During the fifteen days she told me three secrets, but said I mustn't tell anyone what they were, and so far I haven't told what she said.

Compiled from letters from, and accounts by, Bernadette: 28 May 1861 to Fr Gondrand of the Oblates of Mary the Immaculate; 22 August 1864 to Fr Charles Bonin of Niort; undated to an unknown lady; cf. F. Trochu, *Sainte Bernadette* (Paris, 1954), pp. 81–3; A. Ravier, *Les écrits de sainte Bernadette* (Paris, 1961), pp. 53–59.

ST THERESE OF LISIEUX

With an extended metaphor drawn from her own practice, Thérèse uses self-analysis as a subtle framework for a description of the conscientious concern for others for which she was known in her convent. In spite of what now seems over-scrupulous exactitude in fulfilling the emotionally harsh and even psychically destructive conventual norms of the period, which called for unremitting self-denial, the carefully considered whole shows considerable literary skill and self-knowledge based on studied introspection.

The two brushes

If an artist's canvas could think and speak, I am sure that it would never complain of being touched and re-touched by the brush; knowing that all its beauty was due to the artist, it would not even feel envious of the brush. Nor could the brush boast of the masterpiece it had helped to produce, for it would understand that true artists are never at a loss, but play with difficulties and, to amuse themselves, often make use of the most unlikely and the most defective instruments.

I am the brush our Lord has chosen to paint his likeness in the souls you have entrusted to my care. But an artist must have at least two brushes: the first, which is more useful, gives the ground tints and rapidly covers the whole canvas; the other, a smaller one, is employed for the details of the picture. You, my dear Mother, represent the valuable brush our Lord holds lovingly in his hand when he wishes to do some great work in the souls of his children; and I am the little one he decides to use afterwards to fill in the minor details.

It was about 8 December, 1892, when the divine Artist first took up his little brush, and I shall always remember those days as a time of special grace.

When I entered Carmel, I found in the novitiate a companion who was about eight years older than me. In spite of this difference in age, we became the closest friends, and to encourage an affection which gave promise of fostering virtue, we were allowed to talk about spiritual subjects. My fellow-novice charmed me by her innocence, as well as by her frank and open disposition; on the other hand I was surprised to find how her love for you differed from mine, and in various ways her behaviour was regrettable. But God had already made me understand that there are souls for whom in his mercy he waits without tiring, enlightening them little by little, and I was determined not to forestall him.

One day, while thinking over the permission we had received to talk so that we might – as our holy Rule tells us – 'incite one another to a more ardent love of our divine Spouse', I realized sadly that our conversations were not producing the desired outcome. I saw clearly that I must either speak out fearlessly, or put an end altogether to what was coming to resemble mere banal chatter. I begged our Lord to inspire me with words that were both kind and convincing, or, better still, to speak himself instead of me. He heard my prayer, for 'those who look upon him shall be enlightened,' and 'to the upright a light is risen in the darkness'. The first of the texts I apply to myself, and other to my companion, who was truly upright of heart.

At our next meeting the poor little Sister quite obviously saw very well from the outset that my manner had changed, and, blushing deeply, she sat down beside me. I told her tenderly what was in my mind; then, pointing out what true love really is, I proved to her that in loving Mother Prioress with such a natural affection, she was in truth simply loving herself. I confided to her the sacrifices of this kind I had been obliged to make at the beginning of my religious life, and before long her tears were mingled with my own. She humbly acknowledged herself in the wrong and admitted that what I had said was quite true; then, begging as a favour that I would always point out her faults, she promised to begin a new life. From that day our love for one another became wholly spiritual, and the words of the Holy Spirit were fulfilled in us: 'A brother who is helped by his brother is like a mighty fortress'.

You know well, Mother, that I had no intention of turning my companion away from you. My aim was to explain to her that true love feeds on sacrifice, and that in proportion as our souls renounce natural satisfaction our affections become stronger and more unselfish.

I remember when I was a postulant there were times when I was so strongly tempted to seek my own satisfaction, and to find some crumbs of pleasure by having a word with you, that I was obliged to hurry past your cell and cling to the banisters to keep myself from turning back. I wanted to ask your permission for many things, and hundreds of pretexts for yielding to my natural affection occurred to me. I am so glad that I learned to practise self-denial from the beginning! I already enjoyed the reward promised to those who fight bravely, and I no longer feel the need of refusing all consolation to my heart, for my heart is set on God. Because it has loved him alone, it has grown, little by little, until it can give to those who are dear to him a far deeper love than if it were centred in a barren and selfish affection.

I have told you of the first piece of work which our Lord was good enough to carry out, together with you, by means of his little brush, but that was merely a prelude to the masterpiece you entrusted to it later.

From the moment I entered the sanctuary of souls, I saw at a glance that the task was beyond my strength, and quickly taking refuge in our Lord's arms, I imitated those little children who when frightened hide their faces on their father's shoulder: 'You can see, Lord,' I cried, 'that I am too small to feed your little ones, but if through me you will give to each what is suitable, then fill my hands, and without quitting the shelter of your arms, or even turning my head, I will distribute your treasures to the souls who come to me asking for food. When they find it to their liking I shall know that it is not to me they owe it, but to you; while if on the contrary they complain, finding fault with its bitterness, I shall not be at all disturbed, but shall try to persuade them it comes from you, and will take care to give them nothing else'.

The knowledge that it was impossible to do anything of myself greatly simplified my task, and confident that the rest would be given me over and above, the one aim of my inward life was to unite myself more and more closely with God. Nor has my hope been ever deceived: each time I have needed sustenance for the souls under my charge I have always found my hands filled. Had I acted otherwise, and relied upon my own strength, I should very soon have been forced to surrender.

In the abstract it seems easy to do good to souls, to make them love God more, and to mould them to one's own ideas. But, when we put our hands to that work, we quickly learn that without God's help it is as impossible to do good to them, as to bring back the sun once it has set. Our own tastes, our own ideas must be put aside, and in absolute forgetfulness of self we must guide souls, not by our way, but along that particular path which our Lord himself points out for us. The chief difficulty, however, does not lie even here. What costs more than all else is to be compelled to note their faults, their slightest imperfections, and to wage a deadly war against them.

Adapted from: Thérèse of Lisieux, *Story of a Soul*, T.N. Taylor, ed. & tr. (London, 1912), pp. 173–6; cf. Thérèse de l'Enfant Jésus, *Oeuvres Complètes* (Paris, 2001), p. 261.

ST MARY OF THE CROSS (Mary MacKillop)

On a number of occasions Mary MacKillop, a resolute and effective founder and superior-general, suffered totally unjustifiable and humiliating accusations of incompetence. She was dismissed from her office and even excommunicated as a result of the machinations of ecclesiastics and members of rival male orders jockeying for positions of power in the world of Australian Catholic education. They were not only envious of her often superior education, and of the work and influence of her Order, but insulted by her sisters' justifiable delation of an abusing priest. Her surviving correspondence reveals Mary's trust in God and her unshaken conviction that this must be conveyed to her correspondents and, above all, to the nuns to whom she remained responsible under God, to whom she prayed: '. . . we wish to serve thee faithfully. But in order to do this, we desire to know ourselves, our complete nothingness, our entire dependence on thee as our first beginning and our last end . . .'. It also shows her firm spirit: 'O, let us, if we cannot agree to what our poor dear old Bishop requires, at least be humble in the way we refuse' (from a letter of 21 September 1871 to Sister Francis Xavier Amsinck).

Letters to friends

To Father Woods, 14 Oct 1871, after her excommunication: The pain I have felt about it all has been something terrible, and but that I dared not, I would have fled where you or anyone else would never find me. I had to write to a good Father who at a great risk took pity on me and kindly gave me comfort, assuring me that good would come of it all. I have been much easier since. My only trouble was for the Bishop, and all the scandal.

To Monsignor Kirby, 22 May 1873: His presence is before me almost in everything, and I love to come to Him in prayer as to my dearest and only Friend. I do not care for using books at prayers – unless it be at meditation or other prayers in community – at other times these would seem obstacles, something stepping in between the freedom and ease with which, like a child to a fond parent whom she knows is ready to listen to her, I love to go to Him. But for all that, I serve Him with so little love, so little perfection, or attempt at them, in my ordinary actions . . .

I cannot tell you what a beautiful thing the will of God seems to me. For some years past, my Communions, my prayers, my intentions have all been for God's will to be done. I can never pray for a particular intention, a particular person, or anything particular about our own Institute, but in God's loved will, that is – whilst I desire with all my heart to pray for these, I cannot help at the same time desiring that He only use my prayers for the intention that His own will most desires at this time. Thus I feel a joy when things go well, for I see His will in this, and an equal joy when they seem to go wrong or against our natural desire, for there again I see His will, and am satisfied that He has accepted my prayers and those of many more for some other object at the time nearer to His adorable will . . .

The end of my prayer was that I would not cease to implore His mercy for grace to do entirely His Will only, no matter at what cost, when He would require it of me, but I felt that I could not from my heart *then* say that I did not feel it hard. This was a terrible task to me and caused me much suffering which nothing but the thought that God required it of me could have supported me under.

To Monsignor Kirby, 18 July 1874: Your letter, too, in which you spoke of God's goodness, encouraged me very much. He is good to me, good in all He sends, and if I only loved Him more, I should not mind when now and then He permits me to feel my way difficult. I live, for all that, in hopes that some day His love will really reign supreme, and that He will never permit me to lose heart in His sacred cause . . .

To Sister Bonaventure April 11, 1876: If I dared I would complain, for my heart is literally crushed with sorrow. The stand-off coldness of Father Director, the inconsistencies of his letters at one time telling me that he cheerfully accepts the decision of Rome, and at another writing in the reverse strain, misunderstanding me so grossly, and avoiding me as he does. I tell you Sister these things have crushed me to the heart, and I have even dared to envy the dead.

To the Sisters, 14 April, 1882: My dearest Sisters, I owe many of you letters and have been waiting for a time to write separately to each. As this seems as far off as ever, I must, at any rate, send a circular which I beg of each of you to accept as if from my own hand. I know that many of you have had a good many troubles and difficulties, but I am sure that you know very well that such will always be the position of a true Sister of St Joseph. We may feel our crosses hard at times, but our courage should rise with them . . .

Remember, that we must always expect, from time to time, to receive crosses and know that we also give them. What poor, faulty nature finds hard to bear, the love of God and zeal in His service will make easy and sweet. Try always to be generous with God.

To her Sisters, 4 March, 1891: My own dear Sisters . . . God has done wonders for us. He has tried us sorely – and comforted us wonderfully. He has protected St Joseph's work, and brought good out of many evils . . . pray to have the true spirit of St Joseph – that prosperity may not elate, nor adversity ever shake your courage and generosity in the service of God. We must all have our moments of trial and weariness . . .

A Sister of St Joseph [Sr Chanel O'Loughlin], *Life and Letters of Mother Mary, Foundress of the Sisterhood of St Joseph of the Sacred Heart* (Sydney, 1916), *passim*; cf. canonization resources, and the Josephite Sisters' archives, Mary MacKillop Place, North Sydney.

BD MARIE DE LA PASSION (Hélène Marie Philippine Chappotin de Neuville)

Marie established and supervised the work of her Franciscan missionary Order in spite of ill-health, several attempts to remove her permanently from her position as Director of the Institute, and severe setbacks in the field, such as the martyrdom of a number of her Sisters at Chan-Si during the Boxer rebellion in China. Her 19,000 letters, largely to her nuns but also to the Pope and other prominent church people, as well as her allocutions, collected meditations and other writings on the missionary task, emphasize a code of behaviour and attitude typical of those which encouraged and sustained missionary Sisters of so many Orders to work in the most taxing physical conditions and among people suffering from incurable diseases, such as leprosy. Marie's call to nuns to work among lepers received answers from more than a thousand volunteers, from whom she chose the first six who disembarked at Mandalay in January 1898. By 1903 they were caring for more than 300 lepers.

We can never do enough!

10 September 1897

My dear Daughters,

I am writing to you today about something that concerns us all. We intend to found two leper hospitals, and the first in December, in Burma. You know, dear Children, how very dear lepers were to our Lord, to all the saints, and especially to our Father Francis and his first disciples.

Since its foundation, our Institute has always been concerned for lepers, with caring for them, helping them . . . but until now we have never actually had charge of one of those refuges where these despised and wretched of the earth receive heroic and loving care. God calls us this year to two such endeavours. I would not be sincere if I did not admit that my natural reactions and my heart are very troubled when I have to call on my daughters to carry out work of this kind. But even if I am humanly faint-hearted about this, my soul rejoices to think that God is summoning us to follow Jesus, St Francis and our first Fathers in this new way.

Of course, my dear Children, I shall never force anyone to dedicate herself to the care of lepers, who are so dear to Jesus' heart because the world and every worldly impulse rejects them with horror. You have to be called, to have a special vocation, to devote yourself to a cause like this. I ask those of you who want to do this, and really have the will to do it, to send me their names, and with the grace of God, the help of the Holy Spirit, the assistance of our Lady and of our Father St Francis, I trust I shall be able to make a worthy choice of Sisters to carry out this work of heroic love.

This choice should be seen by you all as a heavenly as well as an earthly reward, since I am sure that the martyrs of our Order already in heaven will eventually be joined by some of those who decide to nurse the lepers. Those of you who wish to help them must also seek support from unflinching obedience to the Rule of the Order and the grace of the religious life.

Never forget that the age we live in, as the nineteenth century comes to a close, is a sad time when truth is captive and charity has been swept away. We have to follow our vocation in all its requirements, and realize that we may be called on to be victims for the Church and for the souls we serve.

May God do with us whatever he wishes and enable us to fulfil our special calling from beginning to end. I send you my blessings.

The nursing Sisters sent regular reports to Mother Marie, and she included excerpts in the Annals of the Institute that showed how her nuns responded to her injunction that they should: 'See

Jesus in your poor lepers and try to follow St Francis by serving them lovingly.'

Today, 21 January, we bandaged our patients for the first time. Mother Superior showed me the women. We are surrounded by all those who want help. We uncover the diseased part, wash it carefully, and then cover it as the leper wishes. But the sickness is incurable and whatever we put on them scarcely brings them any relief.

The other day a poor man was unwilling to be looked after, but today he agreed. Sister Marie Redempta started to remove the bandage but had not finished before she realized that there was only one finger left on his hand and the wound was so terrible and gave off so vile a stench that the unfortunate patient could not stand it. Luckily our missionary hearts are tough enough not to give way in the face of something as minor as that.

Georges Goyau, *Mère Marie de la Passion et les Franciscaines Missionaires de Marie* (Paris, 1935), pp. 248–53.

MOTHER GENEVIEVE GALLOIS
(Marcelle Gallois)

When Marcelle announced that she was going to be a nun, her father was unbelievably angry. He accepted her becoming a Catholic but he could not come to terms with her forsaking 'her real vocation' as an artist for that of a religious. He ceased all communication with her and her friends, and refused to answer any of her letters. When he retired, he put the family furniture in store and, quite unnecessarily, took his wife to live in a bleak hotel. This situation was a constant distress for Marcelle, who had entered the Order hoping that with God's grace and her prayers he would have a change of heart. This letter to her parents was illustrated with sepia ink drawings of a man dressed like a weeping hermit weighed down by sin, pain and death. Another image shows God blowing a trumpet and indicating another way. Yet another is of the hermit in the stable at Bethlehem holding the child Jesus and letting him take possession of his soul. Another drawing shows the child carrying his own cross, with a monk following him and bearing a cross with the help of three women (who are Faith, Hope and Charity). Her letter is an attempt to explain the ultimately inexplicable changes that can occur in the 'haunted labyrinths of the heart' (Edwin Muir).

Old and new worlds

31 December 1928

My dear Parents,

Don't be alarmed by this drawing. It is the old world which, since Adam, has been weeping and carrying its burden, which for the most part means all of us, including you and me (pain, original sin, death, pride of life, lust of the eyes and lust of the flesh). But the consolation comes later. At one time, the old world heard the voice of the prophet Isaiah heralding the Redemption. Isaiah talks about this at great length and I cannot repeat it all here: 'Comfort yourselves . . . I will save you. I am your Lord, your God and your Redeemer – Unto us a child is born, unto us a Son is given and his name shall be called Wonderful, Counsellor, the Mighty God, Everlasting Father, the Prince of Peace'. A voice like that announcing such momentous things brought the old world to a stop, and made it listen. From time to time, the old world not only stops to hear what is said but actually responds. This kind of dialogue is known as Advent. When we get to the final week, the old world of what has already happened finally understands and cries out with great intensity: 'Wisdom uttered by the Most High, teach us the way of Prudence. Splendour of eternal light, illumine those who are still sitting in the shadow of death!' Every day he lets out his cry and goes before his Saviour, hobbling there, never free of his baggage. Eventually he gets there, sees his Redeemer and actually receives Him . . . one moment he

is smiling politely, a long way off, and then he is taking possession of his Creator, his Saviour, his God, his Life which is life
indeed. He receives the free gift of absolute Goodness, without
which he cannot live. His own pain and suffering are forgotten
because he now has absolute, everlasting happiness. Remember,
this is not fiction, it actually happens to you and me. We know
and receive ultimate Goodness in communion and can take it
like that, for ourselves. Perhaps you think that means it is all
over, and that the old world has nothing to do now but cross its
arms? No. When the Child God has made sure of our love, he
says 'Take up your cross and follow me'. And the old order of
things, now in its robe of innocence and eternal life, takes up its
cross. The cross replaces that hideous burden from the past, and
those three indomitable women, Faith, Hope and Charity help
him to carry it. It can be a very heavy and dark cross, and one
you cannot always change shoulders for, even though it always
hurts you in the same place. The three women will not take it
away from you, but teach you through suffering such ineffable
things, that no one could know them if they had not suffered
themselves. They make sure that the old world that is passing
away does not lay down his cross, his heavy black cross, for
anything in the world. This, in a nutshell, my dear parents, is the
mystery of Christmas; this is what has happened to the old world
– and that old world is you and me. You see, my dear Mama,
that in spite of your suffering and the sadness of being bed-ridden and in pain, you have not missed the grace of Christmas.
On the contrary, none of the divine mysteries is intended for the
people in this world who are happy and contented. Even when
the Child Jesus has only just been born, and there is no sugges-
tion of his Passion about him, we cannot approach him without
renouncing everything. And that is what I wish for you, and for
me too. If George suggests helping you to find a place to live, I
trust that you will let this happen. Dear Papa, please accept the
offer, as you just can't carry on where you are, you and Mama.
Goodbye, dear Mama and Papa, I send you my best wishes for
the New Year, with all my love and kisses,
Sister Genevieve

P.S.: Forgive me for the late arrival of my letter. It is the fault of the old world. It seems to have taken rather a long time to extract itself from the old order of things and to commit itself entirely to the new one!

Noël Alexandre, *Mère Geneviève Gallois* (Brussels, 1999), p. 138.

MOTHER MARIBEL OF WANTAGE

Mother Maribel's advice for novices and her recommendations for superiors are equally straightforward and reveal her ability to share widely different yet exacting experiences, whether of beginners or of seasoned directors. When Bishop Trevor Huddleston asked: 'What is it, in the life of Mother Maribel, that shines out most clearly and distinctly and speaks to us still?' he answered: 'I would use a word which is fundamental to any real understanding of monastic or community life; the word St Benedict made central to his Rule – "stabilitas" or "steadfastness". I believe that for most people the quality they long to discover in others, the quality which draws them and holds them faithful, is precisely this quality of steadfastness.'

Advice for novices

What a tremendous step you are taking and yet what a glorious one! It is just flinging yourself wholeheartedly over the precipice of God's love, and the rest of your life is proving that 'underneath are the everlasting arms'. However tardy I know my response to have been, I would not change places with anyone for a million pounds. Have done with all questionings on your Profession day. There will be lots of suffering, heaps of things of which you don't approve or like, any amount of temptations and difficulties, but 'be alone with God in your inmost heart', trust him and nothing else will matter. That is strong enough to carry you through everything. Don't try to *do* things. All you have to do is to provide a channel sufficiently clear of rubbish for God to work through. It is his love coming through you, his light shining through you that matters. Our poor little efforts are nothing. It is all so simple, and like all simple things so hard to do.

* * *

Advice for Superiors

The spirit of love is the chief thing. Be a mother, as Rule tells us, 'Seek rather to be loved than feared'. In love maintain Rule as exactly as possible, first in your own life, then in your house. Always lead, don't ever drive. If you lead, the sheep will follow. You can't expect anything of your Sisters which you do not do yourself.

The Superior is the servant of all. St Francis de Sales substituted 'Sister Servant' for Superior everywhere. I wish we could. You serve them, you wait on them, not they on you. To be a Superior is an increased opportunity of service. Resist (what they will always try to do!) having anything extra, anything different, from your sisters. If anything has to be different, let it be less, not more. Choose the poorest thing, resist lunch trays, mend your own clothes, do your own cell, fetch your own water, carry your own bag (unless you can do these things for them!) In short, be first in humility. Your only position is 'beneath the feet of all' – a door mat, in fact! They have a right to deposit on you their moods and tensions, troubles and tribulations and to wipe their feet upon you. But train them not to do it in silence times.

Dog-tiredness is such a lovely prayer, really, if only we would recognize it as such. Sometimes I hear, 'I'm so dog-tired when I get to Chapel, I can't pray'. But what does it matter? We don't matter. Our Lord can pray just as well through a dog-tired body and mind as through a well-rested one, better perhaps. It is the same with pain and suffering of all kinds. Our advance guard on the Infirmary Wing would tell us that. So just when our backs and heads are aching and it is a battle to keep awake, then is the time when to say our Office becomes a worthwhile offering . . .

'He emptied himself', means literally, 'He poured himself out'. We are not only to receive Christ, we are to be identified with him. We, too, are to say, 'This is my body – this is my blood', poured out for the glory of God and the good of our fellow men. Should we complain of being 'spent' when that is exactly what we ought to be?

Sister Janet CSMV, *Mother Maribel of Wantage* (London, 1972), pp. 34, 64–5.

4

Prayer, Preaching & Mission

꙰

EGERIA OF SPAIN

Some of the earliest known superiors of communities of women religious earned the title 'Mother' (amma, or 'spiritual mother') because they were sources of wisdom and saving counsel for the sisters, and therefore 'elders of exceptional merit'. Here Mother Egeria offers an exemplary account of her pilgrimage in 381–4 AD to the Holy Land, Egypt, Edessa, Asia Minor and Constantinople in which she confirms the faith of her readers by describing the evidence of God's enduring purpose among the signs of ineluctable transience. Her own journey becomes one of the models followed by the sisters of her community on their own pilgrimage towards salvation.

My visit to the Jordan Valley

I decided to follow God's will and go as far as Arabia, to Mount Nebo, where God commanded Moses to go up, saying to him: 'Go up to the mountain of Abarim, to Mount Nebo, which is in the land of Moab, over against Jericho, and behold the land of Canaan, which I give to the children of Israel for a possession, and die on the Mount which you ascend'. So Jesus our God, who will not forsake those who hope in him, thought me worthy enough for my wish to be granted.

Therefore we set out from Jerusalem and travelled with holy men, with a priest and deacons from Jerusalem and with certain brothers, that is monks, until we came to that spot on the Jordan where the children of Israel had crossed when holy Joshua, the son of Nun, had led them over Jordan, as it is written in the book of Joshua, the son of Nun. The place where the children of Reuben and of Gad and the half tribe of Manasseh had made an altar was shown us a little higher up on the west side, on that side of the river-bank where Jericho is. Crossing the river we came to a city called Livias, which is in the plain where the children of Israel encamped at that time, for the foundations of the camp of the children of Israel and of their dwellings where they abode appear there to this day. The plain is a very great one, lying under the mountains of Arabia above the Jordan; it is the place of which it is written: 'And the children of Israel wept for Moses in the Arabot Moab, the plains of Moab, on the Jordan over against Jericho, forty days'. This is the place where, after Moses' death, Joshua the son of Nun was straightway 'filled with the spirit of wisdom, for Moses had laid his hands upon him', as it is written. This is the place where Moses wrote the book of Deuteronomy, and where he 'repeated to all the congregation of Israel the words of this song until it was ended'; it is written in the book of Deuteronomy. Here holy Moses, the man of God, blessed the tribes of Israel one by one, in order, before his death. So, when we had arrived at this plain, we went to that very spot, and prayers were said; there, too, a certain part of Deuteronomy was read, as well as the song of Moses, with the blessings which he pronounced over the children of Israel; after the reading, prayer was made a second time, and giving thanks to God, we moved on from there. For it was always customary with us that, whenever we succeeded in reaching the places we wanted to visit, we should pray before doing anything else, then the set passage should be read from the book, an appropriate psalm should be said, and then another prayer. At God's bidding we always kept to this custom, whenever we were able to get to our desired destinations. After this, in order to ensure that the work we had begun would be completed, we began to hasten on our way to Mount Nebo. As we went, the priest of the place, that is, Livias, whom we had asked to accompany us, because he knew those places well, advised us: 'If you wish to see the water which flows from the rock, the same water that Moses gave to the children of Israel when they were thirsty, you can see it if you are willing to take the trouble of going about six miles out of your way.' When he had said this, we were very eager to go, and turned out of our way immediately, following the priest who led us.

In that place there is a little church under a mountain, not Nebo, but another height behind, yet not far from Nebo. Many truly holy monks dwell there, whom they call here ascetics. These holy monks were willing to receive us very kindly, and permitted us to enter and greet them. When we had entered and had prayed with them, they were good enough to give us small loaves, called 'blessings', which they usually give to other ecclesiastics and to those whom they receive kindly.

There, in the midst, between the church and the cells, a great stream of water flows out of the rock; it is very beautiful and limpid, and excellent to the taste. Then we asked those holy monks who dwelled there what was this water with so good a flavour, and they said: 'This is the water which holy Moses gave to the children of Israel in this desert'. So we prayed there as the set passage was read from the books of Moses and a psalm was said, then – with the holy clergy and monks who had come with us – we went out to the mountain. Many of the holy monks who lived by that water, and who could manage the effort required, also decided to ascend Mount Nebo with us. And so we arrived at the foot of Mount Nebo. It was very high but the greater part could be ascended sitting on asses, though a little bit was steeper and had to be climbed laboriously on foot, which we did.

Mount Nebo

We arrived at the summit of the mountain, where there is now a church of no great size, on the very top of Mount Nebo. Inside the church, near the pulpit, I saw a raised place about the size of a tomb. I asked the holy men what this was, and they answered: 'Here the angels laid holy Moses, for, as it is written: "No man knows how and when he will be buried", since it is certain that he was buried by the angels. His tomb, indeed, where he was laid, is shown to this day; for we show it to you, just as our ancestors who dwelled here where he was laid showed it to us, and our ancestors said that this tradition was handed down to them by their own ancestors.' So we prayed again, and everything that we usually did in every place was done in due order; then we began to leave the church. The priests and holy monks who knew the place said to us: 'If you wish to see the places that are mentioned in the books of Moses, come out of the door of the church, and from the very summit, from the side on which they are visible from here, look out, and we shall identify each place that can be seen from here.' We rejoiced at this and immediately went outside. From the door of the church we saw the place where the Jordan runs into the Dead Sea, for it appeared below the spot where we stood. On the opposite side we saw not only Livias, which was on the near side of Jordan, but also Jericho, which was beyond Jordan; for the lofty place where we stood, before the door of the church, rose to so great a height. The greatest part of Palestine, the land of promise, was in sight, together with the whole land of Jordan, as far as it could be seen with our eyes. On the left side we saw all the lands of the Sodomites and Segor, which is the only one of the five cities that exists to-day. There is a trace of it, but nothing appears of those other cities but a heap of ruins, just as they were turned into ashes. They showed us the place where the inscription concerning Lot's wife was once to be seen, which we read of in the Scriptures. But believe me, reverend ladies, the pillar itself cannot be seen, and only the place is shown, for the pillar is said to have been covered by the Dead Sea. Certainly when we saw the place we saw no pillar, and I cannot pretend that it was visible there. The bishop of the place, that is of Segor, told us that it is now some years since the pillar could be seen. The spot where the pillar stood is about six miles from Segor, and the water now covers the whole of this space. Then we went to the right side of the church, out of doors. Opposite us they pointed out two cities, one Esebon, now called Exebon, which belonged to Seon, king of the Amorites, and Sasdra, the city of Og the king of Basan. Fogor, which was a city of the kingdom of Edom, opposite us, was also pointed out. All these cities which we saw were situated on mountains, but the ground seemed to be flatter a little below them. Then we were told that in the days when holy Moses and the children of Israel had fought against those cities, they had encamped there, and indeed the signs of a camp were visible there. [From] the side of the mountain which I have called the left, which was above the Dead Sea, a very sharp-cut mountain was shown to us, which was formerly called *Agri specula*. This is the mountain on which Balak the son of Beor placed Balaam the soothsayer to curse the children of Israel, and God refused to permit it, as it is written.

Then, having seen everything that we desired, we returned in the name of God through Jericho back to Jerusalem along the whole of the route by which we had come.

Adapted from: *The Pilgrimage of Etheria*, M. I. McClure & C. L. Feltoe, eds (London, 1919), *passim*.

ST CATHERINE OF SIENA

Catherine became a Dominican tertiary when very young and did not take up a full religious life, for, as she said: 'My cell is not to be made of stone or wood. Instead it will be the cell of self-knowledge.' She stressed a religious life outside the strict Rule of a community, and did not talk or write as a theologian but as one whose profound spiritual experiences empowered her to speak by the voice of the Master within to whom she surrendered herself entirely. As in the following passages, she concentrated on self-knowledge, on that fruitful awareness of her own nothing-ness which took her ever closer to essential things: love of God, of others, and thereby of oneself in a truly commendable way.

The way of love

God has shown me that as long as we think of him, he will think of us, for a soul that is truly united to God is not conscious of itself. It neither sees nor loves itself, nor anyone else, but keeps its thoughts on God alone, not on any creature.

A soul in this state sees that in itself it is nothing, that all its virtue and all its strength belong to God, its Maker, alone. So it abandons itself and all other creatures completely, and takes refuge in its Creator, our Lord Jesus Christ, to such an extent that it casts all its spiritual and physical actions wholly on to him, in whom it sees that it will find every blessing and total goodness. This means that it has no desire to look for anything outside this intimate knowledge of him, for any reason whatsoever.

Being united in love in this way – a love which increases day by day – the soul becomes as it were changed into our Lord, so that it can neither think, nor understand, nor love, nor be conscious of anything but God or what belongs to God. It sees itself and all other creatures only in God; it is conscious of itself and of all other creatures only in God, and is aware only of the presence of its Creator, and that nothing should concern us other than to think how to please him to whom we have entrusted everything that we do, both in body and in soul.

Our Lord taught me that to acquire virtue and strength of mind we must follow him . . . It would have been possible for him, because of the divine virtue in him, to have vanquished evil in any number of ways, but he chose to do so only by accepting death on a cross, so that he could give an example in terms of his humanity. If you want to overcome your spiritual enemies, you must learn from this example and take up your cross. If you keep the Lord's suffering in mind you will find that awareness a great comfort in times of temptation. The suffering of the cross might well be called comfort in temptation, for the more suffering you bear for love of Christ, the more like him you become. And if you can share in his suffering, then you can share in his joy.

So, for the sake of God's love, learn to suffer the harsh things in life with patience, and not only to enjoy its delights. Do not be

afraid. You will find enough strength to bear everything patiently
. . .

Anyone who uses God's grace in this way will soon be victorious in everything he or she does. Whenever anything new happens to you (whether it brings you good fortune or bad), you must tell yourself: 'I can learn something from this experience.' If you do this consistently, you will soon be rich in virtue . . .

If you want to be truly pure in soul, you must avoid passing any sort of judgment on your neighbours as well as idle gossip about what they might have done. You should see nothing but God's will in everyone. You should not judge people in any way, and you should not be ready to condemn them, even if they are open sinners. Instead, you should feel compassion for them and pray for them, and not feel superior to them or blame them. Put all your hope and trust in divine Providence, for I know from experience that Providence will never disappoint those who trust in it . . .

All virtues and defects come through our neighbour

You should know, too, that every virtue is obtained by means of your neighbour, but also every defect. Therefore people who to all intents and purposes hate God, injure their neighbours and themselves . . . and this injury is both general and particular. It is general because you are obliged to love your neighbours as yourself, and if you love them, you ought to help them spiritually with prayer, and by words of advice, and, depending on their needs at the time, you ought to assist them both spiritually and temporally, at the very least with your good will if you have nothing else to offer. If you are not a loving person, you will not help yourself or others but do yourself harm. Without love, you will stop grace reaching you, and you will hurt your neighbours by depriving them of the benefit of the prayers and of the good intentions that you are bound to offer to God on their behalf. In fact, every act of assistance that you perform should proceed from the charity which you are able to practise because of your love for God.

Every evil act is also done by means of your neighbours, for, if you do not love God, you cannot be in charity with your neighbours. All evils derive from a soul's lack of love of God and of love of its neighbours; for, if you do no good, it follows that you must do evil. Against whom is this evil directed? First of all yourself, and then your neighbours. It is not directed against God, for no evil can touch God, except in so far as he counts whatever you do to yourself as done to him. Of course you can injure yourself by sin, which deprives you of grace, and you can do nothing worse than this to your neighbours. You harm them by not paying them the debt of love which you owe them, and which you ought to use to help them by praying to God for them and offering him your good intentions on their behalf. You owe this kind of help in general to every rational creature; but it is more specifically useful when you render it to those who are close at hand and under your eyes.

Of course we are all obliged to help one another by word and instruction, and by giving an example of good works, and in every other way that might help our neighbours when we see that they are in need. We have to advise them exactly as we would ourselves, without any self-love. If you do not love God, and have no love for your neighbours, neglecting your bounden duty to help and advise them, you do them a special injury. You do them evil, not only by not doing them the good that you are capable of, but by injuring them positively and by what amounts to an attitude of constant evil. In fact, sin causes a physical and a mental injury. The mental injury is already done when sinners take pleasure in the idea of sin, and in hatred of virtue; that is, when they enjoy sensual self-love, for that deprives them of the movement of love which ought to flow from them towards God, and towards their neighbours. Without that love, self-love will make them commit one sin after another against their neighbours, in various ways that happen to please them at the time. Sometimes they will even do cruel things, in general and in particular . . .

Physical cruelty has its origin in cupidity, which not only prevents people from helping their neighbours, but makes them take others' goods, and rob the poor creatures roundabout them.

Sometimes they do this by the arbitrary exercise of power, and sometimes by cheating and fraud, so that their neighbours are even forced to pay to recover their own goods, and often indeed themselves . . .

In all places, and in all kinds of people, sin is always committed against your neighbours, and through them. There is no other way in which sin, either secret or open, could ever be committed. A secret sin is when you deprive your neighbours of what you ought to give them. An open sin is when you carry out positive acts of sin . . .

How virtuous acts are done by means of our neighbours

All sins are carried out by means of your neighbours if you are without love, which is the light of every virtue. Similarly, self-love, which destroys charity and affection for your neighbours, is the principle and foundation of all evil. All scandals, hatred, cruelty, and every sort of trouble proceed from this perverse root of self-love, which has poisoned the entire world, and weakened the mystical body of the Church, and the universal body of believers in Christianity . . .

Similarly, the virtues of patience, good will and kindness are shown in a time of anger when sweet patience is evident in God's servants, and envy, vexation, and hatred elicit their love, and their hunger and desire for the salvation of souls. Virtue appears in those who return good for evil, but is often even more evident when good people give back fiery coals of love to dispel the hatred and rancorous hearts of angry men and women. Therefore benevolence often emerges from hatred because of the love and perfect patience of those who suffer the anger of the wicked, and bear and support their inadequacies. The virtues of fortitude and perseverance are demonstrated by long endurance of the injuries and detractions of wicked people, who, by injuries or flattery, constantly try to prevent others from following the way of truth and its teachings.

'Profitable Teachings from the Life of the Bride of Christ, Catherine of Siena', in *The Cell of Self-knowledge*, John Griffiths, ed., John Griffiths

& Charles Crawford, trs (Dublin & New York, 1981), pp. 27–37; *The Dialogue of St Catherine of Siena*, Algar Thorold, tr. (adapted) (London, 1907), *passim*.

ST PHILIPPINE DUCHESNE

From 1805 on, Philippine felt a call to be a missionary. In a letter to Saint Madeleine Sophie she described the grace she received during an all-night vigil before the Blessed Sacrament on Holy Thursday, 1806: 'I was in the New World all night long, and I travelled in good company. First, I reverently gathered up all the Precious Blood from the Garden, the Praetorium, and Calvary. Then I took possession of our Lord in the Blessed Sacrament. I held him close to my heart and went forth to scatter my treasure everywhere, never fearing that it would be exhausted. St Francis Xavier helped me to make this priceless seed bear fruit. From his position before the throne of God, he prayed that the light of truth might shine in new lands. St Francis Regis was our guide, together with many other saints anxious to proclaim the glory of God. All went well, and there was no room for unhappiness, not even for holy sorrow, in my heart, for it seemed that the merits of Jesus were about to be applied in an entirely new way.' It was only in 1818 that Philippine could realize her great dream. The following conflation of letters of 1822 to Sacred Heart nuns in France reveals something of the dedication and lively interest in her new environment of the nun whom Native Americans of the Osage, Sioux and Iroquois nations called 'the woman who prays always.'

Getting used to strange behaviour

My dear Sisters,

I often long to be with you to profit by our holy recreations. I should prefer to be a mere listener, but you would tell me: 'It is for you to do the talking, for you have crossed the sea and must have many a tale to tell us'. But I am thoroughly rusty, and without wanting to displease you I should often fall silent. While awaiting that meeting which I trust will be one day in heaven, I have put together some incidents to buy your prayers in return.

What pleases us most is the deputation sent by the Osage Indians to Bishop Du Bourg. The chief came to St Louis to ask Monseigneur to visit his tribe. His Lordship will go there next month with some traders from Missouri who have promised to help him in every possible way to win respect for his sacred character. The Bishop gave the Indian chief a crucifix which he accepted with respect. Later, when he entered one of the stores in St Louis the shopkeeper, anxious to see if the crucifix was treasured, offered to give in exchange a fine saddle, then liquor, and finally a large sum of money. Each time the chief refused, saying that never would he give away what he had received from the 'one who speaks to the Author of Life'.

Bishop Flaget has lost three of his missionaries who returned to Europe, one was the founder of the Daughters of Penitence and a saint. We have four children from Prairie de Chien, a month's journey from here. That is where the Councils between the Indians and the representatives of the Government are most often held. They carpet the place of assembly with beaver skins. The most skilful Indian is the speaker and always begins: 'the Author of Life has made all things and he has made the earth for all men to enjoy'. He concludes with a request for liquor, gunpowder and bread.

Love of the 'Blackrobes' is general among the Indians everywhere, even among the Sioux, a most savage tribe. A priest who has been among them and who often comes here tells me that they would supply all his needs were he willing to accept their help, but that he does not want to be indebted to them for fear they ask him for fire-water, that is, brandy. One Indian was strikingly converted. As he lay on his death-bed he spoke of a previous illness during which he had thought he was dying, and he said aloud: 'I then saw the Author of Life and he said to me, "Go back, your hour is not yet!" But I know that this time I shall go to the Author of Life'. Francis, a Christian Iroquois present, said to him: 'The Author of Life probably sent you back so that you might have water poured on your head'. The dying Sioux answered: 'Indeed, I think it was precisely for that I was told to return to life'. Francis replied: 'Do you want me to go to find a Blackrobe to pour water upon you?' The Sioux answered: 'Go quickly. There is need to hurry'. The priest who came at once was quite satisfied with the dying man's answers and baptized him; a few moments later he died. He was solemnly buried by the priest, who also baptized the dead Sioux' son who was very ill. The priest was Father Acquaroni, a Lazarist from Rome, and one of our most zealous friends.

I am sending you a writing portfolio and some Indian slippers which will show you the handiwork of the natives. They give the names of animals to those who go among them, calling the pastor of St Genevieve 'the son of a white fish'. A Canadian Iroquois who had been in Florissant returned home and died at a season when journeys are impossible. His father hollowed out a tree trunk with one of his weapons, put the body inside, and tied it to a tree. When Spring came, he was told by other Indians that the dead boy was crying out: 'Let us go to Florissant!' The father then brought his son's body these eighteen hundred miles, and gave the pastor of Florissant two hundred francs to bury him in consecrated ground.

I have been told that there is in this country a soil which has all the properties of soap and is used as such by the savages who wash and massage themselves with it and exchange it for gunpowder, necklaces and blankets. Every householder here makes his own soap from ashes steeped for several days in water and then slowly filtered. They then mix it with oil and boil it for several days, and at the end they have a red and very good soap. As to plants and grains, the most common is Indian corn from which bread is made. We often eat this sort of bread, which many Americans prefer to that made from wheat, which grain also grows abundantly here. There are beans, pumpkins, cantaloupe, and water-melons. Potatoes are much in use; there are white, red, yellow and bluish or purple ones, and sweet ones that taste just like strawberries, which grow wild here, as does a small fruit having rather the shape and taste of a lemon; it is called citron in English. Maize or Indian corn is eaten on the cob while it is tender.

My letter has often been interrupted for the love of God. May we have the happiness of making him loved, and of loving him ourselves with an effective and generous love.

Marjory Erskine, *Mother Philippine Duchesne: 1769–1852* (London, 1926), pp. 239–41, 277–9.

MOTHER MARIE-LOUISE HARTZER & SR MARIE MADELEINE

Mother Marie-Louise's Daughters of Our Lady of the Sacred Heart worked with great courage and endurance in mission stations in many remote corners of the world, which were difficult to reach and to communicate with in the nineteenth century. Mother Marie-Louise thought that Our Lady's presence was especially evident in this dedicated work, for she was: '. . . present in the Church's mission, and present in the Church's work of introducing into the world the Kingdom of her Son.' Her assurance that 'Many girls, attracted by the devotion to Our Lady of the Sacred Heart, will want to come and share the way of life of the Daughters of Our Lady of the Sacred Heart . . . You will have flourishing works and numerous houses' proved to be justified. Long letters from her nuns enabled Mother Marie-Louise to judge and adjust the effects of her world-wide missions. This extract from a letter sent by Sister Marie Madeleine from Yule Island on 2 August 1887 is typical of the detailed accounts on which the Superior relied. Marie Madeleine was one of four nuns on their way to share the way of life of the people of New Guinea whom they were to care for and nurse.

Very Reverend Mother and Dear Sisters,

You ask me what this name means and whether there a Mission in York. Well, we have never heard of one. No, there isn't a Mission, but there is a boat that passes and stops there, today, for a few hours, and four sisters are on that boat on their way to Yule-Island, they are: Mother Liguori, Sister Claire, Sister Marthe and me. Very Reverend Father Navarre arrived from Yule last Saturday, and gave us this good news, and as he wished to see us leave before his departure for France, he wanted to take advantage of the first boat.

It was not without a certain sadness that we left Thursday and our dear Mother Paul, to whom we are and remain very attached, having always lived together. It was very hard to say goodbye, perhaps for ever.

So we left, accompanied by Father Navarre, and Father Bontemps, after bidding farewell to some friends who wanted to accompany us right to the last minute. Arriving at the steamer, we started to feel a sense of panic, because we could only see a rope ladder to climb on board and we had never done anything like that before. Finally, taking our courage into both hands, we went up without too much difficulty. The priests, a brother, Mother Paul, Sister Marguerite, and three young women also ascended the ladder. We visited the boat. The captain gave us his cabin; he will sleep on a bench. Two of us will be in this little room, and two in the dining room on very narrow beds without sides, that are used as seats for the table at meals, and from which we fear that we might roll off at any minute, when the boat is moving. We are happy to learn that we are to be the only passengers; so the whole room is for us. After a very short time, Father Navarre told us that the captain wanted to set sail so that we could sleep as far away as possible, because we should travel for no more than a night as the sea off this coast was very dangerous.

After receiving a blessing from our priests, we embraced Mother Paul and dear little Sister Marguerite-Marie. We were very sad to go but we restrained our tears. For several days now,

I have been trying to put this thought out of my mind; because I felt broken-hearted and even now, while writing these lines, I have had to force myself not to cry. Our last word was our cherished motto: May the Sacred Heart of Jesus be loved everywhere!

Everyone on board and on the quayside waved their handkerchiefs until we gradually disappeared on the horizon. We followed our Fathers and Sisters with our eyes until they reached their house, and they had barely arrived when they waved all the more intensely; then suddenly we saw the Sacred Heart flag hoisted in our honour. They ran it up and down three times, these were three salutes, and all the while we were in view, we saw it; at last we were out of sight; then we went below and said our rosary. Afterwards we went up to the bridge. At six o'clock we had dinner and, after taking the fresh air, we did our best to get to sleep preferring to suffocate and sleep together. We were already feeling sea sick. It eased off a little during the night. The next morning, we tried to get up and go quickly to the bridge. Mother Liguori courageously ate her meal, but Sister Martha, Sister Claire and I were unable to eat anything. Soon we were being sick over-board and it was the fish that benefited. The rolling was extreme, the smell of a rotting rat permeated our cabin and maintained the sea sickness.

Darnley, 30 – That night we were tossed about fiercely, and at one time we felt as if we were going aground. The captain made no attempt to deny that we were in the most dangerous part of the journey, as the sea was full of rocks hidden under three feet of water, which were difficult to see. That night, I can assure you, there was pandemonium on the bridge. Finally, in the morning we were again able to get some rest. Darnley is a magnificent Island full of coconut palms and there are many houses. The king arrived with his royal diadem on his head and his incised ears; he was accompanied by many of his subjects; one of them had a white hat; he came before us and with a great bow he took his hat in both hands. Everyone was decently dressed, but we thought that their clothes were not often worn, because they were worm-eaten. They left and we lifted anchor. The captain and all the crew were immensely kind. All the covers and pillow-cases were put at our disposal.

Yule-Island, 2 August, – We arrived yesterday morning at six fifteen. Towards half past five, I was suddenly seized with a desire to look out of the cabin's porthole and I saw the *Promised Land*. Hurriedly, I called out and awakened everybody: 'New Guinea! New Guinea!' How great was our joy. We were very excited! But before sharing this with you, my good Mother and dearest sisters, allow me to tell you what happened earlier.

We left Darnley towards midday and we were on the open sea; under normal weather conditions, we would have expected to be at sea for a day and a half but the wind was so fierce that the sea became mountainous. We spent all Saturday night in prayer. We offered our lives as sacrifice, hoping for the protection of Our Lady of the Sacred Heart. We had an unfavourable wind.

But our fear didn't take away all our good humour, and after we had prayed, we sang, spoke of France, Sydney, Thursday, then said: 'Dear Father Navarre did not tell us how entertain-ing it would be to travel to Yule! He had told us that we would suffer somewhat, but not like this!' . . .

At last, so be it! Sunday, Mother Liguori and Sister Martha tried to go up to the bridge, but Sister Martha had hardly arrived before she rolled on the floor. Our Mother was even braver and withstood the shock throughout the morning on the bridge. Sister Claire and I stayed in bed, or rather in torment, because it was a real martyrdom to be tossed about in every direction fol-lowing the pitching of the boat . . .

The closer we came to Yule the jolts became less acute. Finally we saw our dear Mission. Quickly, we went onto the bridge, prayed and then we took Yule as a subject for contemplation, as well as the house of our Fathers, ours etc. Then we saw the flag of the Sacred Heart being hoisted. Brother Salvatore had seen us and had given the alert. The captain blew the whistle and little by little we saw, with the help of opera glasses, the coming and going of the Community. Towards six-thirty, a little boat set out from Yule. This was the Reverend Father Couppé and the good Father Verjus, who, with a brother and some natives, came to meet us.

How happy we were! Surprised to see four (nuns) rather than three, the good Fathers quickly took care of our luggage. Meanwhile the young native boys and two girls formed a group around us: *Babinè ròvè*! 'Holy women!' they said. We shook their hands and smiled at them, and then the one who held the rosary said: *Jesu Keriso*! 'Jesus Christ!' and the other who saw our medal said 'Mary'; a third took our arm affectionately. At last the bridge filled up, as little by little the natives rushed out in their pirogues. I had copied, on Thursday (Island), one of their refrains in Kanak. I spoke a few words (in their language) to them and then they all sang: *Houi, Houi, Jesu Keriso, houi, houi, Jesu Keriso!*

The good captain wanted to land us personally in his rowing boat, where we took our places with the Reverend Father Couppé and his little goat, which we called Mignonnette. Father Verjus followed us with the luggage. On land all the natives were waiting for us at the water's edge. Some Fathers were also there. The nice dog of our Fathers, Toto, who had only been a few days on Thursday (Island) recognized us and wagged his tail in delight. The native girls carried our bags, and even the goat, and we arrived, escorted in this way, first at the Fathers' house and then ours. We made a short stop at the Fathers', during which time we worshipped Our Lord in their little chapel. The Reverend Father Couppé immediately led us to our home and blessed it. Then, lunch was brought to our refectory. The Reverend Father wanted to say grace over our first meal and ourselves, and we ate with a hearty appetite the sago and coconut milk as well as the eggs that we were given. The food of Yule appeared preferable to that of all the other islands. We thought everything was delicious. All credit to the cooking of Brother Salvatore! After lunch Mother Liguori came to an agreement with Father Superior over the allocation of the rooms. I have a nice place because, my bed being the last to be put up, I found myself, guess where . . . behind the altar of our little chapel where the very blessed Sacrament is reserved. A simple partition of leaves separates me from it. After having unpacked everything and putting things in order, we hastened to prepare the room of the good Jesus and the next morning, during mass, Our Lord came down upon us to live there day and night, until the brick church was to be built.

All day the natives surrounded us and wanted to work with us, filled with good will. One of the chiefs came up with his family, Raouma. They were so happy to see us! As a sign of respect, one of his daughters shaved her head, because, she said, she had too many insects in her hair to appear in front of us.

Now, my good Mother, I am going to give you a tour of the house. The walls are all made of leaves, held together by creepers; bamboos serve as crossbeams. The floor is wooden, but all the planks are rounded and keep their form of a tree trunk cut in two; numerous large holes allow us to breathe through our feet, because the house is on stilts; the roof is also of leaves; the exterior doors are made of wood, similar to those in France. The windows have only bamboo shutters, through which we can see. For furniture: a table, a little bookshelf and three wooden stools, and a chair for visitors. We brought our beds from Thursday (Island), and while in France it is a penance to sleep on straw, here I take great delight in my straw-filled mattress, on which I sleep like a baby. Our altar is made of a table standing on bamboo poles, a little tabernacle covered with paper to hide its mean appearance, and for decoration, a piece of red curtain that conceals the space in front of the altar, then another piece behind the altar, to shield our wall of leaves from the heat of the candle. Two empty boxes, made of tinplate, act as flower vases; two other smaller ones filled with damp earth act as containers for the candles. A little bouquet of flowers, given to our Mother Liguori for her feast day, is in a glass at the foot of the tabernacle. We have had to write out the Mass texts for the altar in some haste; lastly, our altar cloth is an old piece of hemmed muslin. Three paper images are attached with pins. We have made a holy water stand, and two curtains to hide the entry while we wait for a door. Our stools follow us everywhere, to every room. Our veranda is made of the same wooden planks as in the house. In the midst of all this, we are happy and serene, because we are sure that we are where the Sacred Heart wants us to be. With the help of the Sacred Heart of Jesus, we will do our best.

We see nothing but greenery and the sea around us; the village is half a league away . . .

Sister M. Madeleine, Daughter of Our Lady of the Sacred Heart

Fernand et Léopold Hartzer, *La Révérende Mère Marie-Louise Hartzer: Fondatrice des Filles de Notre-Dame du Sacré-Cœur et les Missions d'Océanie*, (Issoudun, Truin & Paris, 1913), pp. 144–50.

MOTHER CECILE BRUYERE

Mother Bruyère offers classical advice on progress in the spiritual life and in prayer in the great patristic and monastic traditions to which she owed her own inspiration. Her treatise was intended at first for the sisters of the community where she was Superior but soon became a popular work among a public in search of sure spiritual guidance in their prayer-life.

Our sole interest

The sole interest of all human beings is to fulfil the purpose of God in creating them from nothing. The most reasonable, intelligent and necessary activity that our minds and souls can engage in is to know how to get to that desirable goal, to realize what obstacles might stand in the way of our progress, or keep us from our sole end, and to seek enlightenment about the forms of opposition and resistance that we bear within ourselves.

The mysteries of the spiritual life are not, as is generally believed, necessarily reserved for a small company of select souls or specialists in religious affairs. We are all created by God and are all summoned to save ourselves. We are all born anew in exactly the same way and, as St Paul says: 'There is one Lord, one faith, one God, one Father of us all, who is the one over all, the one working through all, and the one living in all.' One and the same intuitive vision will allow us all to enter into possession of eternal life and happiness.

But of course we all need due preparation for this, and God allows us various degrees of grace '. . . until the time comes when, in the unity of common faith and common knowledge of the Son of God, we arrive at real maturity – that measure of development which is meant by "the fullness of Christ".'

Nevertheless, in the midst of this earthly life, and our apprenticeship and preparation for our future eternal life, the law of eternity already applies in every respect. In fact, the only real value of this life, as we seek to pierce the shadows of faith and find its reality, is to help us to reach a trial version, indeed an initiation into, what will eventually prove to be the full flowering of everlasting life. God's intention in this period of trial through which we must pass is always to help us towards our supernaturally perfect condition, and the full development of our faith should take us right up to the borderland of intuitive understanding, enabling us to enter a state of unyielding hope in which we know for certain what we shall eventually possess when the love we already sense here becomes eternal life in all its fullness.

All human beings, whether Christians or not, are looking for happiness, but the idea which various human beings have of what is true happiness differs according to their way of life and the means available to them. It is really astonishing to see how many Christians are profoundly affected by the ways of the world around them, and try to be happy without thinking about God at all or his intentions in any way, even to the extent of absolute exhaustion in searching for something they can never find like that . . .

Pain and suffering may seem authentic means of correcting our nature when it goes astray from its one true end . . . but it is useless and even dangerous to try to suffer just for the sake of suffering. This is an illusory and disastrous tendency among even very well-intentioned people in these uncertain times. They talk easily of suffering and of wanting to suffer, but this is rather a sign of weakness and a means by which Christians often try to hide their own inadequacies. A longing for suffering becomes a means of covering up cowardice or even neurosis. People often forget that suffering is not an end in itself, and far from being a substitute for one's duty and purpose in life. Pain and suffering are far from necessarily holy or edifying experiences . . . too many religious people take pleasure in them and even cultivate them until they exult in their dolorous condition and mistake their own interests for God's intentions . . .

'Now I want to give you some further information in some spiritual matters . . . I want you to understand that people have different gifts, but it is the same Spirit who gives them. There are different ways of serving God, but it is the same Lord who is served. God works through different people in different ways,' St Paul told the Corinthians. The gifts of which he speaks and which God distributes among human beings quite freely are exceptional, for 'each person is given a gift by the Spirit to use it for the common good' . . .

Any Christian cultivating the spirit of prayer and union with God has been accustomed to follow an exceptional spiritual guide. Of course, a few hardy spirits who have reached the status of trustworthy guides are able to advance without any master. Generally, however, it is indispensable to have a guide to lead us along the pathways of God, and this guide must be unusually wise and enlightened, for we must always remember that 'when one blind man leads another blind man they will both end up in the ditch!' These are, of course, Jesus' own words.

Mère Cécile Bruyère, *La Vie Spirituelle et L'Oraison d'après la Sainte Ecriture et la tradition monastique* (Solesmes, 1899), *passim.*

SR ESTHER (Emma Caroline Silcock)

Not long after reaching Australia, Sister (later Mother) Esther and her first helpers visited a somewhat ineptly run 'Gospel Hall', 'the weirdest kind of place, women off the street coming nearly always drunk, or stupid with opium . . . we all sang hymns and someone got up and asked: "Who will sign the pledge?"' As they left Sister Esther said: 'We must think out a better way than that.' She realized that prayers and hymns were not enough and that help in the way of food, education, medicine and ready comfort in all life's tribulations was needed. To provide this and to give an effective example, a religious community had to live among the poor and outcast. This extract from Esther's notes for her Sisters' first Rule stressed 'deeds of Christian charity' almost to the extent of excluding formal prayer. Her notes can scarcely be bettered as a succinct statement of the aims of a religious community.

The future is in the hands of God who loves us

The aim and object of this Community into which these Sisters have been called is two-fold. First, the glory of God and the perfection of those he calls out of the world to serve him in the religious life, under the perpetual vows of poverty, chastity and obedience. Second, the Community has been founded for active mission work in the Church for the honour and glory of our blessed Lord Jesus Christ. Our life will be one of sacrifice and work, always ready to serve the poor and those in need. But all work must be done for the love of Jesus, otherwise it will be barren and of little value. These Sisters must not look back to the world they have left for God or compare it with that of our present state, nor should the Sisters look forward to the future with fear or dread. The future is in the hands of God who loves us.

Cf. John W. Stewart, 'Sister Esther: An Anglican Saint', in *The Melbourne Anglican*, (September, 2001).

ST MARIA SKOBTSOVA

St Maria Skobtsova, the martyr of Ravensbrück, was executed in a gas-chamber because of her compassion for her fellow-humans. Mother Skobtsova provided the perfect summary of her life and thinking when she wrote: 'No amount of thought will ever result in any greater formulation than the three words, "Love one another," so long as it is love to the end and without exception.' Most of her writings are illustrations, in one way or another, of this principle and include this novel exposition of asceticism in the Orthodox tradition.

The second gospel commandment

'The sign of those who have reached perfection is this: if ten times a day they are given over to be burned for the love of their neighbour, they will not be satisfied with that, as Moses, and the ardent Paul, and the other disciples showed. God gave his Son over to death on the Cross out of love for his creature. And if he had had something more precious, he would have given it to us, in order thereby to gain humankind. Imitating this, all the saints, in striving for perfection, long to be like God in perfect love for their neighbour.'

'No man dares to say of his love for his neighbour that he succeeds in it in his soul, if he abandons the part that he fulfils bodily, as well as he can, and in conformity with time and place. For only this fulfilment certifies that a man has perfect love in him. And when we are faithful and true in it as far as possible, then the soul is given power, in simple and incomparable notions, to attain to the great region of lofty and divine contemplation.'

These words from St Isaac the Syrian, both from the *Philokalia*, justify not only active Christianity, but the possibility of attaining to 'lofty and divine contemplation' through the love of one's neighbour – not merely an abstract, but necessarily the most concrete, practical love. Here is the whole key to the mystery of human relations as a religious path.

For me these are truly fiery words. Unfortunately, in the area of applying these principles to life, in the area of practical and ascetic behaviour towards man, we have much less material than in the area of man's attitude toward God and towards himself. Yet the need to find some precise and correct ways, and not to wander, being guided only by one's own sentimental moods, the need to know the limits of this area of human relations – all this is very strongly felt. In the end, since we have certain basic instructions, perhaps it will not be so difficult to apply them to various areas of human relations, at first only as a sort of schema, an approximate listing of what is involved.

Let us try to find the main landmarks for this schema in the triune makeup of the human being – body, soul, and spirit. In the area of our serving each of these main principles, ascetic demands and instructions emerge of themselves, the fulfilment of which, on the one hand, is unavoidable in order to reach the goal, and, on the other hand, is beyond one's strength.

It seems right to me to draw a line here between one's attitude toward oneself and one's attitude toward others. The rule of not doing to others what you do not want done to yourself is hardly applicable in asceticism. Asceticism goes much further and sets much stricter demands on oneself than on one's neighbours. In the area of the relation to one's physical world, asceticism demands two things of us: work and abstinence. Work is not only an unavoidable evil, the curse of Adam; it is also a participation in the work of divine economy; it can be transfigured and sanctified. It is also wrong to understand work only as working with one's hands, a menial task; it calls for responsibility, inspiration, and love. It should always be work in the fields of the Lord.

Work stands at the centre of modern ascetic endeavour in the area of man's relation to his physical existence. Abstinence is as unavoidable as work. But its significance is to some degree secondary, because it is needed mainly in order to free one's attention for more valuable things than those from which one abstains. One can introduce some unsuitable passion into abstinence – and that is wrong. A person should abstain and at the same time not notice his abstinence.

A person should have a more attentive attitude toward his brother's flesh than his own. Christian love teaches us to give our brother not only material but spiritual gifts. We must give him our last shirt and our last crust of bread. Here personal charity is as necessary and justified as the broadest social work. In this sense there is no doubt that the Christian is called to social work. He is called to organize a better life for the workers, to provide for the old, to build hospitals, care for children, fight against exploitation, injustice, want, lawlessness.

In principle the value is completely the same, whether he does it on an individual or a social level; what matters is that his social work be based on love for his neighbour and not have any latent career or material purposes. For the rest it is always justified – from personal aid to working on a national scale, from concrete attention to an individual person to an understanding of abstract systems of the right organization of social life. The love of man demands one thing from us in this area: ascetic ministry to his material needs, attentive and responsible work, a sober and unsentimental awareness of our strength and of its true usefulness.

The ascetic rules here are simple and perhaps do not leave any particular room for mystical inspiration, often being limited merely to everyday work and responsibility. But there is great strength and great truth in them, based on the words of the Gospel about the Last Judgment, when Christ says to those who stand on his right hand that they visited him in prison, and in the hospital, fed him when he was hungry, clothed him when he was naked. He will say this to those who did it either on an individual or on a social level.

Thus, in the dull, laborious, often humdrum ascetic rules concerning our attitude toward the material needs of our neighbour, there already lies the pledge of a possible relation to God, their spirit-bearing nature.

From: 'The Second Gospel Commandment,' in *Mother Maria Skobtsova: Essential Writings*, Helene Klepinin Arjakovsky, ed., Richard Pevear & Larissa Volokhonsky, trs (New York, 2000).

MOTHER TERESA OF CALCUTTA

In her Nobel Peace Prize acceptance speech of 11 December 1979, in Oslo, Norway, Mother Teresa restated the principles of loving care, concern and sacrifice that she had always advocated. This extract from the speech is an impassioned plea for the general acknowledgement of and commitment to those guidelines.

Love as I have loved you

As we have gathered here together to thank God for the Nobel Peace Prize, I think it will be beautiful that we pray the prayer of St. Francis of Assisi which always surprises me very much. We pray this prayer every day after Holy Communion, because it is very fitting for each one of us. And I always wonder that 400–500 years ago when St. Francis of Assisi composed this prayer, they had the same difficulties that we have today as we compose this prayer that fits very nicely for us also. I think some of you already have got it – so we pray together: Let us thank God for the opportunity that we all have together today, for this gift of peace that reminds us that we have been created to live that peace, and that Jesus became man to bring that good news to the poor. He, being God, became man in all things like us except in sin, and he proclaimed very clearly that he had come to give the good news. The news was peace to all of good will and this is something that we all want: the peace of heart. And God loved the world so much that he gave his son – it was a giving: it is as much as if to say it hurt God to give, because he loved the world so much that he gave his son. He gave him to the Virgin Mary, and what did she do with him? As soon as he came in her life, immediately she went in haste to give that good news, and as she came into the house of her cousin, the child – the child in the womb of Elizabeth, leapt with joy. He was, that little unborn child was, the first messenger of peace. He recognized the Prince of Peace, he recognized that Christ had come to bring the good news for you and for me. And as if that was not enough – it was not enough to become a man – he died on the cross to show that greater love, and he died for you and for me and for that leper and for that man dying of hunger and that naked person lying in the street not only of Calcutta, but of Africa, and New York, and London, and Oslo – and insisted that we love one another as he loves each one of us. And we read that in the Gospel very clearly: 'Love as I have loved you; as I love you; as the Father has loved me, I love you.' And the harder the Father loved him, he gave him to us, and how much we love one another, we too must give to each other until it hurts. It is not enough for us to say: 'I love God, but I do not love my neighbour.' St John says that you are a liar if you say you love God and you don't love your neighbour. How can you love God whom you do not see, if you do not love your neighbour whom you see, whom you touch, with whom you live? And so this is very important for us to realize that love, to be true, has to hurt. It hurt Jesus to love us. It hurt him. And to make sure we remember his great love, he made himself the bread of life to satisfy our hunger for his love – our hunger for God – because we have been created for that love. We have been created in his image. We have been created to love and to be loved, and he has become man to make it possible for us to love as he loved us. He makes himself the hungry one, the naked one, the homeless one, and he says: 'You did it to me.' He is hungry for our love, and this is the hunger that you and I must find. It may be in our own home. I never forget an opportunity I had in visiting a home where they had all these old parents of sons and daughters who had just put them in an institution and forgotten [them], maybe. And I went there, and I saw in that home they had everything, beautiful things, but everybody was looking towards the door. And I did not see a single one with a smile on their face. And I turned to the sister and I asked: How is that? How is that these people who have everything here, why are they all looking towards the door? Why are they not smiling? I am so used to seeing the smiles on our people, even the dying ones smile. And she said: 'This is nearly every day. They are expecting, they are hoping that a son or daughter will come to visit them. They are hurt because they are forgotten.' And see: this is where love comes. That poverty comes right there in our own home, even neglect to love. Maybe in our own family we have somebody who is feeling lonely, who is feeling sick, who is feeling worried, and there are difficult days for everybody . . .

I never forget some time ago about fourteen professors came from the United States from different universities. And they came to Calcutta to our house. Then we were talking about the fact that they had been to the home for the dying. (We have a home for the dying in Calcutta, where we have picked up more than 36,000 people only from the streets, of and out of that big number more than 18,000 have died a beautiful death. They have just gone home to God). And they came to our house and we talked of love, of compassion. And then one of them asked me: 'Say, Mother, please tell us something that we will remember'. And I said to them: 'Smile at each other, make time for each other in your family. Smile at each other.' And then another one asked me: 'Are you married?' and I said: 'Yes, and I find it sometimes very difficult to smile at Jesus because he can be very demanding sometimes'.

SR JOAN CHITTISTER

Sister Joan Chittister is a celebrated contemporary leader of a religious community but primarily a worldwide preacher with a mission, especially to women religious and peacemakers. She is concerned to renew and refresh conventional ideas of the religious life. Her talk and writing, though always clear and directed unmistakably to central questions, sometimes approach the time-less quality of parable and wisdom literature, as in her famous recasting of the Sufi account of an old woman on her arduous way to a place of pilgrimage at the top of a mountain in the high monsoon season. When the innkeeper said it was too dark and wet to reach the shrine, the woman said that was no problem, since her heart had always been there and she had only to take her body to join it. Sister Joan draws the lesson that in these times of religious turmoil we must continue our pilgrimage, 'ignore the storms around us' and 'press on, press on, press on to where our hearts await our bodies this very day'. In the following typical passage she reminds us that the human community may provide the model for the religious life, not vice versa.

Another rank of holiness

Modern society has the idea that if you want to live a truly spiritual life, you have to leave life as we know it and go away by yourself and 'contemplate,' and that if you do, you will get holy. It is a fascinating although misleading thought. The Rule of Benedict says that if you want to be holy, stay where you are in the human community and learn from it. Learn patience. Learn wisdom. Learn unselfishness. Learn love. Then, if you want to go away from it all, then and only then will you be ready to do it alone.

There is, of course, an anchorite lurking in each of us who wants to get away from it all, who finds the task of dailiness devastating, who looks for God in clouds and candlelight . . . [Benedict] himself set out to live the spiritual life as a hermit and then discovered, apparently, that living life alone is nowhere near as caring of our souls as living it with others. It is one thing to plan my own day well with all its balance and its quiet and its contemplative exercises. It is entirely another rank of holiness to let my children and my superiors and my elderly parents and the needs of the poor do it for me.

Quoted in: *The Monastic Way: Ancient Wisdom for Contemporary Living*, Hannah Ward & Jennifer Wild, eds (London, 2006), pp. 6–7.

SR EMMANUELLE

Sister Emmanuelle conveys her conviction that 'The authentic human characteristic, in all the grandeur and misery of the human condition, is to keep on searching and never to be satisfied with things as they are or with ready-made beliefs of any kind.'

What's the point of being alive?

My reason for writing this book was to make it possible for my brothers and sisters everywhere to share the benefits of almost a century of experience. The event which started me asking questions about things took place shortly before my sixth birthday. I was at the seaside, watching the coming and going of the waves and the sparkling foam. It was fascinating. And then I saw the foam close over my dear father's face. Had he disappeared beneath the waves for ever? If so, where exactly had he gone? I listened to people talking about eternity for the first time. Inside my little brain, I wondered how he could have passed from the froth on the surface of the sea to eternal life. It all seemed quite crazy, as did the death of my father and the explanations they supplied me with.

Here, I think, the basic experience of my psychological make-up merges with the fundamental question of our time. My fellow humans today are obsessed by a lack of meaning. Life for these often deeply distressed questioners seems to be no more than a chaotic series of moments and events. But events (both those of our individual lives and those of human history) only count insofar as they mean something. Yet an event, something that happens to us, has no intrinsic meaning. Of course an event should enable us to understand its tragic implications and distinguish between them and its possible beauty and fruitful outcomes. We should be able to relate it to something. When an event becomes intelligible for us, we realize that there is something else to be glimpsed through and beyond apparently tragic, exceptional or banal happenings. Historical events are only temporarily obscure. Once we grasp their significance they open up and no longer seem mysterious.

Most men and women nowadays need to give a meaning to their lives. I meet a lot of people today who are burdened with insecurity and even heavy anxiety: 'What's the point of being alive?' I understand exactly what they are getting at with this question. I too have known the anxiety of nights of dead-end situations and no answers, and I shall tell you about them in the rest of this book.

But that isn't where the real problem lies. Our lack of certainty about meaning is actually necessary, indeed beneficial. It has always been a very human experience. Of course the real problem is that something else is missing, for there is no way to resolve the contemporary anxiety I refer to. I have a very poor opinion of those who try to exploit this deficiency, and of well set up people who can offer our puzzled selves no more than clichés, banal and emotional answers or sheer pathos. In the worlds of media, politics and sometimes even religion we are subject to the rule of sensation and of events for events' sake.

Nevertheless I very much prefer this kind of lack to the false contentment that was the rule when I was young. I am talking about the beginning of the last century when the ground seemed solid under our feet and everything seemed destined to go on snoring away peacefully for ever . . . Yes, it was peaceful but horribly superficial. Sacred values (and what were claimed to be sacred values) seemed eternal but were actually monuments with clay feet that owed much more to tradition and custom than to profound inward conviction . . .

Sœur Emmanuelle, *Vivre, à quoi ça sert?* (Paris, 2004), pp. 5–7.

SR PIA BUXTON CJ (Judith Buxton)

Sister Pia, a much respected and inspirational Ignatian retreat director and speaker, and former president of the Conference of Religious of England and Wales, spent two months 'sitting at the feet' of a Buddhist community in the Chilterns, England. Here she hands on the fruits of her 'walk into the unknown' and her respectful inquiry into contemporary practice drawn from another tradition.

Light from the Buddha

It was a typical English February night, after days of dampness with clouds of uncertainty in the winter sky and the occasional appearance of a full moon. In the Buddhist monastery it was the Magga Puga, the full-moon festival. We were celebrating one of the founding stories of Buddhism: the gathering of the first bikkus who had come to hear Gotama's teaching 2,500 years before. We had begun the evening liturgy at 11 pm in the great temple. There had been a quiet waiting in the semi-darkness, then the simple three-note Pali chant started. Later we ambulated slowly, conga style, through the lamp-lit spaces of the temple and eventually out into the big field and three times round the shrine there. The moon, whose cycle controls so much of Buddhist life, took a nonchalant look at us now and then. The huge bonfire had been prepared, the white robes of the novices and the saffron robes glowed in the fire light. The still, reflective faces of my friends were illuminated. There was very quiet conversation, affection, mystery and mirth. Then, contrary to the ancient rule of no food after noon, out came a supply of marshmallows to be toasted on sticks. A strange pre-eucharist, I wondered. An expression of a deep human need to remember, to give thanks, to reach atonement. At 3 am, we dispersed along the little paths through the monastery.

This Magga Puga night had come towards the end of my retreat. By then I had grown accustomed to the pervading influence of the Three Refuges of Buddhism: the Buddha, the Dhamma (his teaching), the Sangha (the community). That morning in the dhamma talk, the Canadian-born abbot had described the work of Buddhism as quietly giving witness to the truth of Buddha by doing mindfully, reflectively, the small and ordinary things of daily life. Without some sort of spiritual living people destroy nature, each other, and themselves, he had said.

I had come to Amaravati nearly two months earlier. The community of about twenty-four monks and twelve nuns, all young, all shaven-headed, mostly from the Western world via Thailand, were making their annual two-month winter retreat. This mixture of monks and nuns is unusual in a Buddhist monastery, but Amaravati is a place of gentle innovation. For example, as a member of an Ignatian apostolic congregation, and a total newcomer to Buddhism, I was invited to live with the sisters and share fully in the retreat. They welcomed me especially because I was older than they: only one of them had yet reached forty.

Having finished a six-year stint in leadership, I was seeking solitude; I wanted to get away from other people's expectations. I wanted to shed my cultural religious certainties and walk into the unknown. I did not want to learn about Buddhism with my head but to experience something of it by immersion. I did not realize, then, that immersion would mean eight hours of meditation daily and only one meal, and getting up at about 4.30 am. But I knew that I needed the discipline of a structured life for my exploring. Through various helpful friends I was led to the Theravadian or Forest Buddhists and to the largest of their four monasteries in Britain, Amaravati in the Chilterns.

Obviously the place looks different from most retreat houses. At the centre of everything a large, beautiful, brick temple points heavenward from a curving roof. It has a spacious gravel forecourt and there are statues of the Buddha and bells about the place. The saffron-clad abbot greeted me, avoiding my extended hand (a monk may not touch a woman and this one was charmingly amused by my confusion), and handed me over to the sisters among whom I would live on the far side of the monastery. Beyond the temple area the architecture deteriorates rapidly into blocks and rows of Nissen huts extending in all directions. Built for the Canadian army during the war and now renovated somewhat, these form the living quarters of the community, the offices and workshops, the retreatants' dormitories, the many shrines and meditation rooms, the well-stocked ecumenical library.

Many Christians and others come to Amaravati for retreats and courses, staying in the simple accommodation provided for them. During the winter retreat, however, most of this activity stops and only a voluntary team of lay people is there to enable the monastery to function. They participate in the practices as time allows. The rule forbids the fully professed monks and nuns from cooking, growing things, killing, or touching money. When they beg they cannot request anything; they just wait with their bowl. This begging bowl and their long strip of saffron material is all they possess, so they are dependent on others.

As a fully committed retreatant I found this fringe community of helpers very supportive. Together we formed hoi polloi at the end of the dinner queue during the long religious process of inspecting, blessing, gracing and reflecting on our daily meal. Some of them, like me, had a chair to sit on at meditation (after four weeks I could manage the semi-lotus position for stretches of half an hour; at the corpse position I excelled).

You cannot be long at Amaravati without appreciating the radical commitment of its members. Everything in the monastery emanates from the Buddha's fundamental teaching on the universal human experience of dissatisfaction (anxiety, fear, unhappy experiences, incapacity and the rest), that this suffering exists, has origin, has ending, and that there is a path to its ending. So much of what we call religion is the interpretation of deep experience and ordering of the resulting codes and practices to express it. Out of his original experience of suffering, Buddha taught how to clear the mind, little by little, through detachment from all forms of grasping, aversion and delusion, in order to achieve a state beyond suffering, called enlightenment. All around me were men and women practising this teaching through mindfulness and meditation, by exercises of physical and mental control and harmony, and through constant self-reflection and analysis.

Buddha did not make statements about God, for he witnessed the violent controversy this could cause. So neither God nor grace are named at Amaravati. The path to enlightenment is the hard work of constant mindfulness, and it is walked alone. A monastic community is not there for companionship or friendship, but to teach. This jarred with my own faith and with my understanding of the Church as a community of sinners who know they are loved by God. At Amaravati I often marvelled at the resilience and humour of those around me on this unyielding path.

Unlike members of most religions or Churches, a Buddhist does not belong to any self-defined institution. Buddhism does not have excluding edges and avoids definitions. Where Christianity so often seeks to answer questions with a tidy definition, a Buddhist teacher will be content with an enigmatic 'Who knows?' The teaching of Buddha, the dhamma, is the authority and every member of the community brought their own experience to that teaching for analysis and measurement. Before the abbot could give a dhamma talk it had to be requested of him, literally, from the floor, where his audience was sitting. I wondered how this practice might affect Sunday sermons in church.

Buddhism and Christianity start in different places. Christian energy began and was nurtured in the cultures that emerged from the Middle East, and onward through Greece and Rome. This was the ferment through which reason was harnessed to facts and religion to action and in which an incarnational spirituality could flourish. Buddhism, on the other hand, emerged and spread and took shape in cultures absorbed by detail and infinite refinement, or engrossed in metaphysics. When Arnold Toynbee reflected that the meeting between Buddhism and Christianity would be one of the most important events of the twentieth century, he was describing a complex event.

Christians will search for revelation and life in everything and will seek to share what they find. Christianity is intrinsically involved and missionary. Like the cultures that have nurtured it and to which it has given spiritual form, it will struggle to spread and ramify. Buddhism leads inexorably inward to a selfless detachment and, until recently anyway, has not been missionary.

At Amaravati there were proto-Buddhists from many of the Christian churches or none. Westerners are attracted to Buddhism's counter-cultural simplicity and peace, to its stringency and challenge. This is very understandable. 'Consumerism is the ultimate superstition, and a consumerist society will destroy itself,' said the abbot one early morning as we sat around him on our safus, sipping runny porridge from our plastic mugs. He added, with a smile: 'Fashion is the lowest form of ideology . . . you can see, we are not very fashionable here.'

In fact, Buddhism is in fashion. It offers an obvious alternative to the hedonism and greed of Western society that has so often forgotten the vocabulary of Christianity, let along its message. Much of the teaching of Buddha resonates with the wisdom of the Christian Scriptures, with the wisdom of the Christian saints and mystics, and with the deeds and words of Jesus. Meeting with Buddhism can point us ordinary Christians to the spirituality, the mysticism, the spiritual freedom, of our own incarnational inheritance; it is there waiting for us.

Love, compassion and forgiveness were taught and practised in abundance at Amaravati. God's love was incarnated as it always is, where human beings live virtuously. We often used one or other of the beautiful Buddhist meditation texts on forgiveness or compassion or loving kindness: 'So with a boundless heart should one cherish all beings, radiating kindness over the entire world . . .' and so on.

I shared my hut with a gentle, young Russian doctor. She lived these meditations for me. An entry in my diary reads: '15 February: This morning my little Russian was sad; she had heard of the death of her uncle, and asked for prayers. However, this evening she wears her woolly hat at a jaunty angle to cheer us both up, and brings me a terrible brew of lotus-root tea to help improve my lotus position without pain.'

At times I felt like an alien in an oriental world, and I was often saddened by the hardness of the life of those around me and at the vacuum into which they looked; but there was much that was familiar and the hard was never harsh. Often I was lonely, lost, hungry, my mind confused and my spirit in darkness, yet my abiding memories are of the stillness of that crowded shrine-room and of returning to my hut in the darkness after the last sitting. The final entry in my diary reads: '1 March: Again I come back from meditating in the shrine-room tonight with a hunger for prayer. Reading from the Word of God in my Daily Missal and finding the presence of Jesus pervading my room. Perhaps a Christian's prayer is always a listening for the incarnation and a recognising of the kingdom . . . but it is all gift.'

A Buddhist retreat may sound esoteric; I began it as a very ordinary person and finished much the same. My first diary entry reads: '2 January: These women are so intelligent, amusing and human.' Indeed they were.

The Tablet (London, 19 June 1999)

SR ELIZABETH A. JOHNSON

In the course of an account of her spiritual influences, Sister Elizabeth Johnson describes the conflicts that beset her when she was deciding to make a commitment to the religious life.

To the whole of humanity

It was the summer of 1965. In preparation for making final vows in my religious order, the Sisters of St Joseph of Brentwood, New York, I and sixty classmates were spending two months of extended reflection at our cloistered, beautifully green and rolling Motherhouse on Long Island. My heart was very conflicted about whether to make this life-committing decision. The reason for my hesitation was the contrast between the spirituality of religious life at that time, which required world-denying detachment, and my own growing inclinations. The trouble was: I was fascinated by this world.

On the one hand, our congregation was living the religious life-style typical of the era: strong top-down authority, strict daily horarium, full habit, restricted human relationships, emphasis on distance from the world, commitment to saving one's soul and the souls of others in a church where conciliar renewal had not yet begun. Indeed, the Council in progress was a distant event with next to no impact on daily life. On the other hand, the sixties were in mid swing: John F. Kennedy newly dead, Joan Baez and Bob Dylan singing protest songs, Martin Luther King dreaming his dream, riots in the cities, LBJ's war on poverty, my own peers in 'the outside world' beginning to rebel against the older generation. My sympathies lay with the latter. In contrast to what our vow preparation was teaching, I kept thinking that if God created and loved this world, then shouldn't those of us radically seeking God in religious life be in the forefront of engagement with this world? Wouldn't final vows box me into a narrow life of perfection when the evolving, struggling world needed to be embraced with the love of God? Wouldn't I be denying the divine call that I felt in my own spirit?

And so I struggled.

One day we were handed, among other materials for personal reading, a poorly printed pamphlet. It was the draft of a con-ciliar document not yet voted on. Out of curiosity, I took it on my daily walk. Coming to a large, favourite pine tree I settled in its shade and began to read. The opening words riveted me: 'The joys and the hopes, the griefs and the anxieties of the people of this age, especially those who are poor or in any way afflicted, these too are the joys and hopes, the griefs and anxieties of the followers of Christ.' Stunned, I read that sentence over and over again. Exactly right! And weren't nuns supposed to be followers of Christ? Here was the highest authority in the Church chal-lenging the spiritual tradition in which I felt encased, endorsing rather than warning against involvement with the world. But more than that. This document painted a theological vision of humanity created in the image of God, defaced by the evil of sin, but redeemed by Christ and now led in history by the Spirit through the witness of the Church. This was a vision I had never before encountered, and it was so beautiful.

All afternoon long I slowly read that draft of *Gaudium et Spes*, drinking it in like water in the desert. The sun began to slide down the sky but in a very real way the light was rising. I loved the way the Council aimed its message to the 'whole of humanity' in a spirit of respect and love. I admired the way it admitted that atheism often arose as a critical reaction to deficiencies in the way believers themselves acted. I thrilled to the idea that the Church and the world should be in mutual relationship, each learning from the specific wisdom of the other – the gospel on the one hand, and science and humanities, on the other hand. I resonated with its analysis of changed conditions in the modern world – new technologies, a new humanistic spirit, the desire for freedom even on the part of women, enormous inequity of material wealth resulting in poverty and hunger, the danger of nuclear weapons – and the impact all of these conditions had on religion. Marriage and family, culture, socio-economic justice, political participation, war and peace, international co-operation: I stirred to the way these issues were addressed in the spirit of the Gospel.

Most of all, I revelled in this work's emphasis on the dignity of the human person. Every human being is created in the image of God. This anthropology grounds the essential equality of all persons, the fierce and repeated call to treat every human person with respect, and the need for an ethic that serves the common good. What ringing words: 'With respect to the fundamental rights of the person, every type of discrimination, whether social or cultural, whether based on sex, race, colour, social condition, language, or religion, is to be overcome and eradicated as contrary to God's intent'.

Excerpted from: Sister Elizabeth's personal website at Fordham University, and from: Elizabeth Johnson, 'Worth A Life,' in *Vatican II: Forty Personal Stories*, William Madges & Michael Daley, eds (Mystic, CT, 2003), 200–4.

5

Autobiographers, Diarists &
Chroniclers

⁂

SR JEANNE DE JUSSIE

---

*Many nuns over the centuries have kept diaries, journals and
chronicles, which are sometimes more than personal documents,
for they illuminate not only the contemporary practice of the
particular Order but the history of the times. Jeanne de Jussie's
unique chronicle of the transition from Catholicism to Calvinism
in sixteenth-century Geneva is one of the most brilliant and reve-
latory of these documents. Here a sequence of entries shows both
how a Poor Clare of the time, writing in French between 1526
and 1536, saw the often savage unfolding of the confrontation
of faiths before, during and after the expulsion and rehousing
of her community elsewhere, and how reports of miraculous
incidents were accepted as equal evidence of events alongside
what we think of as more reliable accounts. Jeanne has a sense
of the dramatic and an unusual ability to perceive and convey
the impact of events by describing the psychological tension they
arouse. She describes her purpose thus: 'Your chronicler saw
those unhappy times with her very own eyes ... You may rest
assured that I know everything I write to be true. Even then, I set
down only an infinitesimal part of the main events so that they
will not be forgotten, and in future people who suffer for God's
sake in this world will learn that our forebears suffered just as
much as us, and as those who come after us will suffer to differ-*

ent degrees, following the example of our Lord and Saviour, who was the first to suffer thus and suffered the most.'

A clash of faiths

1532

On a Sunday morning in June of this year, a certain number of ill-intentioned brutes placed big printed notices on all the church doors of Geneva, which contained all the main articles of faith of the cursed Lutheran sect. Good Christians tore them down. When matins had been said, one of the canons of the cathedral [Father Peter Werly of Fribourg], a good, devout Catholic, confronted these heretics and tore down the notices which they had attached to the church of St Peter. That angered these wrong-doers and one of them drew his sword and struck him on the arm, so that, even though he did not bleed to death, he had to lie up for a long time fearing he would die, and all people of good will wished him well. By the grace of God for whose sake he had risked his life, he was cured through the expert attention of the surgeons. On the feast of St Barnabas a prohibition on posting any such notices was promulgated by the sound of the trumpet on pain of three twists of the rope and banishment from the town for a year.

15 March 1534

Today the Grey Friars executed a young thief who belonged to the Lutheran sect. He was urged to convert so that he could die repenting of his heresy and in the true faith, but he was taken on the way to the gibbet and handed over to the Reformer Faret and his companion, so that they could preach at him and convert him to their heresy. Afterwards a miracle occurred: a woman who had been hanged on the scaffold a year before, and who had died in the faith of our holy Mother the Church, rose miraculously from the dead, stood before this Lutheran robber and bit him on his bare neck, and because this was so remarkable the city published the news of this event, and many people went to see what had happened. In fact, more than 4000 people from all sides came on the same day to see this miracle.

On Misericordia Sunday, in the octave of Easter, a rich Lutheran lady whose sister was a nun at the Convent of St Claire came to speak to the sisters, and since they had no idea that she had been converted to Protestantism, she was taken to the grille, where she greeted the nuns very courteously. Then, after a few words, she could not restrain her venomous spite and spat it out, right into the hearts of the poor nuns, saying that the world had been following the wrong faith until then. The Mother Superior answered her fiercely, saying: 'Madame, we do not want to listen to that kind of talk. If you want to take part in our devotions as you have done in the past, we shall be delighted to pray with you, but otherwise we shall simply ignore you.' But she would not stop her waspish remarks, so the nuns shut her out of the convent, saying that the bishop had forbidden them to listen to that kind of heresy. Nevertheless, she stayed there for a long time, ranting against the door, and since then she has never ceased seeking to arouse the heretics against the nuns and trying to release her sister from the religious life.

On the eve of Pentecost, the heretics knocked the heads off six statues in front of the entry to the Franciscans, then threw them into the well at St Claire's. It was heart-rending for us to see these headless bodies.

Just before the end of July, the citizens of Geneva caught sight of some bands of people near the town, and they quickly took up their arms. This was how they lived in Geneva, constantly subject to fear and unhappiness, especially the poor nuns of St Claire. When they heard the tumult they always thought that the Protestants were coming to do them harm, and were quite afraid.

One night, quite by accident, one of the young nuns was praying in the church and fell asleep there. The Mother Superior forgot she was there and locked her in and all the others retired to the dormitory as usual. Just before eleven at night, the poor sister woke up and caught sight of some dead souls who happened to be haunting the church. She ran to the door to get out. Finding it locked she was too scared to shout but started to hit the door as hard as she could. Hearing the noise, all the nuns suddenly woke up terribly shocked. She knocked again, twice, three times, with all her strength. They rose from their beds, trembling and at their wits' end, thinking that the heretics had arrived at last to do their worst. The poor sisters did not know what to do, for they could not see how anyone could help them. The Abbess tried to calm them: 'My dear sisters and dear children, I beg and require you to be steadfast and to entrust yourselves to God's blessing, which by my authority I now pronounce over you. For my part, I am going to see exactly what is happening. If you wish to accompany me, you can, but before I open the door I want to know if all my sheep are in the sheepfold.' With praiseworthy courage she looked at all their beds and had all the nuns assemble before her. She found one missing. That very nun was now growing even more frightened and at that very moment banged on the door even more vehemently than before. 'Follow me,' said the Abbess, 'Let us leave the convent and go to the church, for we shall be more secure before God than in the dormitory. So she opened the door as best she could and found this poor distraught girl there. When she saw the community so upset, she realized what she had done, and how her own fear had affected them, and fell at the nuns' feet as if in a seizure, and they were extremely sorry for her. Several nuns were very ill as a result of this incident, and very often experienced similar anxieties, and lived in constant fear of what might happen, for the threat was very real.

In the first week of August, St Victor's monastery was completely pillaged and they gave fifty florins to a band of toerags to lay it waste. For some time it was reported by I know not whom that if you happened to go near that church you would hear the poor departed complaining and lamenting hideously day and night, and this was a most distressing experience, with good reason, for many people were buried there since it was the oldest church in Geneva and one of seven parishes, together with the priory of St Benedict.

In the last but one week of September, we received one Triboulet, the civil commander of Berne, whom the citizens of Berne had appointed over the town. After greeting him Mother Abbess and her Superior described their way of life and how they were enclosed out of love of God, and that no one entered their convent. But he grew angry and the poor nuns, fearing some even greater misfortune, opened the door and he came in roaring like a lion. The poor sisters all took refuge in the church, prostrating themselves and praying. There were many tears and they were very afraid. Triboulet came by the front of the church, stopped, did not enter but took pity on the nuns and asked the Abbess to tell them to get up from the ground. She asked him to do his best for this poor desperate community and ordered the sisters to greet him and ask him to be merciful, so that he would let them serve God as enclosed nuns for the rest of their lives. In fact it pleased God to change his heart entirely and he was quite overcome with compassion for the nuns. He could think of nothing but to comfort them and to assure them that they would never be caused any distress by any action of his. In fact, he said he would do everything possible to protect them, and departed with a changed attitude without anyone hurting them on that occasion.

On Christmas Day, to prevent any scandal, the magistrates passed by the churches with a number of armed members of the town watch, who stayed at the church doors until divine worship was at an end. The Lutherans did not celebrate the feast and dressed in their meanest clothes as on ordinary working days. They baked no white loaves, because Christians did so, and mocked them, saying: 'The papists are celebrating their feast-day. They'll eat so much white bread that it will kill them.'

Le Levain du Calvinisme, ou Commencement de l'hérésie de Genève, fait par Révérende Soeur Jeanne de Jussie, Ad.-C. Grivel, ed. (Geneva, 1865), *passim*; Jeanne de Jussie, *Petite Chronique: Einleitung, Edition, Kommentar*, Helmut Feld, ed. (Mainz, 1996), pp. 132–209 *et passim*.

SR MARIA CELESTE

Sister Maria Celeste (Galileo's daughter) describes the insanity of a novice-mistress.

A veritable tempest

Now that the tempest of our many troubles is somewhat abated, I shall not wait any longer before telling you about them, hoping that this will make the burden on my own mind lighter, and also wishing to excuse myself for writing twice in such a hurry, and without the usual respect I owe you. The fact is, I was half out of my senses with fear (and so were the other nuns) at the furious behaviour of our mistress, who has tried to kill herself on two occasions in the last few days. The first time she hit her head on the floor so violently that her features became quite monstrous and deformed. The second time she gave herself thirteen wounds, of which two were in the throat. You may imagine how shocked and worried we were to find her totally covered in blood and wounded like that. But the strangest thing of all was that, when she inflicted these injuries on herself, she made a noise to attract someone to her cell, and then asked for a confessor. During this confession, to avoid anyone else seeing it, she gave the priest the instrument which she had used to cut herself (as far as we can guess, it was a penknife). It seems that, though mad, she is quite wily. I suppose we have to conclude that this is some incomprehensible judgement on her from God, who lets her live when human judgement would say she must die, for all those wounds were mortal in the surgeon's opinion. Consequently, she has had to be watched day and night. At present we are all well, thank God, and she is tied down in her bed, but is liable to be just as frenzied as ever, so that we are in constant terror of something dangerous happening.

Adapted from: *The Private life of Galileo compiled principally from his correspondence and that of his eldest daughter Sister Maria Celeste* (Boston, 1870), p. 165.

As the convent apothecary, Sister Maria Celeste was most concerned that her father should avoid the plague.

I am sending you two pots of a sweetened medicine as a protection against the plague. The one without the label consists of dried figs, walnuts, rue, and salt, mixed with honey. A piece the size of a walnut is to be taken in the morning, fasting, with a little Greek wine (or any other good wine). They say it is most marvellously effective. It is true that what is in the pot is baked rather too much because we didn't take into account the tendency the figs have to lump together. The other pot is to be taken in the same way. Its taste is rather more tart than the first one. If you want to carry on taking one or other of them, we shall try to make that one more proficiently next time.

You said in your letter that you had sent the telescope, but I think you must have forgotten to put it in, and so I am reminding you about it, and also about the basket in which I sent the quinces, because I want to send you some more if I can find them.

Adapted from: *The Private life of Galileo compiled principally from his correspondence and that of his eldest daughter Sister Maria Celeste* (Boston, 1870), p. 184.

She managed to obtain another panacea made by Abbess Ursula, a Pistoian nun who had such a great reputation for sanctity that the precious medicine, once produced, was treated almost as if it were a relic by the nuns, who were forbidden to part with it. Maria Celeste begged her father to swallow it.

I beseech your lordship to have faith in this remedy. After all, if you have so much faith in my poor miserable prayers, you have much more reason to trust the petitions of such a holy person. In fact, her merits are so considerable that you may feel certain of escaping all the dangers of the plague.

Adapted from: *The Private life of Galileo compiled principally from his correspondence and that of his eldest daughter Sister Maria Celeste* (Boston, 1870), p. 185.

Her letter of 26 November describes the death of Sister Violante.

On Sunday morning, at the fourteenth hour, our Sister Violante passed away to a better life. We may hope that she is now in a state of blessedness, having borne a painful and lingering illness with much patience and submission to the Lord's will. Truly for the last month she was reduced to such a distressing state of weakness, being unable even to turn in her bed, and taking nourishment with extreme difficulty, that death appeared to her almost desirable as an end to her many sufferings. I wanted to tell you about all this before now, but I had no time to write. I have only enough time now to add that we are all well by the grace of God, and that I want to know whether it is the same with you and your tiny household, especially in the case of our little Galileino [Galileo's grandchild]. The counterpane you sent is really too good for me. Thank you. I shall pray to the Lord to repay you for your constant kindness by allowing you an even greater share of his grace now, and the glory of Paradise hereafter.

Adapted from: *The Private life of Galileo compiled principally from his correspondence and that of his eldest daughter Sister Maria Celeste* (Boston, 1870), p. 186.

MOTHER ANGELIQUE DE SAINT-JEAN ARNAULD D'ANDILLY

Together with other 'Jansenist' nuns, she was arrested in August 1664 and held at the convent of the Annonciades belonging to the 'Blue Nuns' until 1665 for refusing to sign the papal condemnation of Jansenism. Their supposed heresies included not only such fundamental opinions of Jansen or his followers as that humans cannot obey God's commandments without his special grace, but, say, a belief in the superiority of a Council of the Church over and above the authority of the Pope, and a distinct lack of fervour about the Immaculate Conception. The following is an extract from her reasoned account of her unjust incarceration and the constant pressure put upon her to subscribe. It has been recognized as a major work of women's 'prison literature'. Mother Angélique was a learned and subtle if austere theologian whose scope extended well beyond the neo-Augustinianism for which she is either celebrated or castigated. She said that she had indeed 'seen the gates of darkness and the gates of hell, and was preserved only by the grace of God'. In her prolific writings she expounded the same ethical non-compliance with coercive civil and ecclesiastical authorities, when they commend error or illicitly take over the individual conscience, that she was so often called on to practise. As she wrote in her Thoughts to Prepare Nuns for Persecution: 'Faith raises us up and enables us to master our passions, whereas self-love makes us slaves of an infinite number of masters, whose rule, if we are not vigilant, will deprive us of the true freedom of the Children of God.'

They carried me off and held me prisoner

The Archbishop insisted not only that we should sign his formulary, but set a condition to govern that signing, viz. that it had to be signed with the correct disposition of genuine inward submission . . . therefore the reprehensible disobedience which was at issue was not our refusal to sign but a refusal to believe what we were signing, for it was not the signature alone which the Archbishop demanded, but a firm conviction of the truth of the propositions to which we were required to subscribe . . .

On 26 August 1664, after my Lord Archbishop had addressed us in the Chapter and had read out the list of all the nuns he wanted to arrest and take from the house, our Mother Abbess and all of us protested that this ordinance was illicit, as already stated in the record, but the clerk had forgotten to note that at that point the Archbishop had interjected angrily: 'Oh yes, I am well aware that you have no intention of obeying me.' Thereupon he looked at his ecclesiastical assistants, and said: 'Gentlemen, you know what you have to do!' Then we knew that they were going to bring the archers in, because some of them moved off as if to do just that. As a result, our Mother and some of us told the Archbishop that we would not put up any kind of resistance and that we were prepared to leave, but without prejudice to our protest and to our appeal. I must admit that such an open show of violence almost emptied our heads just then of the other things we had planned to deal with this business. Since we were evidently surrounded by officers of the law, and archers were on their way to take us off by naked force of arms, I concentrated on uniting myself with Jesus so that I could offer in silence, like him and with him, all that God might will. When I entered the choir where the Archbishop had ordered the nuns he had selected to be taken away to assemble . . . I was convinced that I would never again see the house and people I was leaving . . .

When my room in the convent where we were to be held was ready, the Abbess took me there . . . As soon as I was alone, I prostrated myself before the Lord who is present everywhere and who had led me into this solitude to live only for him and with him. I thanked him for his grace and dedicated the successful outcome of my struggle to him. That took up all that was left of the day. But when night had fallen and I had completed my prayers, I thought of lying down to sleep. But I felt as if my spirit had been suspended in mid-air until then and had then suddenly been dropped from a very great height, and my heart had been bruised all over by the fall. All at once I was wrought and torn from every direction by all the separations that I had suffered, and the sufferings of all those whom I had left behind and who were just as afflicted as I was. I wanted to be rid of all these thoughts and did everything possible to efface it all from my mind, but, whatever I did to close my mind to these thoughts proved useless, and I could not staunch my wounds. I just had to weep and, I must admit, I cried many tears that night when I myself was the battlefield where grace and nature were in conflict, and I had no other arms to defend myself than the shield of truth, which fended off all the gentle onslaughts of nature, persuading me that I should seek the happiness which God associated with the suffering imposed on me . . .

I had no form of exercise in that prison house, being always shut up, and I was afraid that this would do me harm in the long run, so every evening I forced myself to walk about my room, which was quite large. I had composed something like a litany of the names of all our Sisters of Paris and Port Royal des Champs, as well as those of the novices and postulants without, and of all our friends, and in general of all those for whom I thought I ought to pray especially, and I offered them all to God one after the other, saying in each case: 'Have mercy!', and adding other prayers such as psalms, which I chose as my devotions required. This took up the whole time I spent walking, three quarters of an hour at least, and throughout that winter I never lighted the lamp at that time, since I could walk just as well without a light, and anyway I also worked on the little cords for vestments which they made me plait, so that the nun deputed to watch me, who quite often arrived around then, couldn't understand what I was doing with the means at my side yet working away in a place where nothing whatsoever was visible, but I told her I had quite enough light to walk up and down, pray and complete my task . . .

I told one of their Mothers that I considered myself to be in purgatory, and that I remembered certain visions in which souls in purgatory were portrayed as being made to pass from one place to another to suffer different kinds of purifying punishments, and I decided they wanted to do just that to us, although the only difference between them and us was that the souls in purgatory would suffer less and less as the time of their liberation approached, whereas our sufferings were bound to increase until the last. She did not contradict me, saying only that she had no idea what was in store for us . . .

Angélique de Saint-Jean Arnauld d'Andilly, *Aux portes des ténèbres: Relation de captivité*, preface by Sébastien Lapaque, notes by Louis Cognet (Paris [1711], 2005); cf. *Les Ecrivains de Port-Royal*, Maurice Catel, ed. (Paris, 1962).

BD MARIE DE L'INCARNATION (Madame Barbe Acarie)

In a letter sent shortly after Easter 1615 to her cousin, Cardinal Pierre de Bérulle, Marie describes an intense mystical experience of meeting the Jesus 'before whom she would bend the knees of her heart' during the week before her actual profession when she was a nun in the Amiens Carmel. It is typical of the intense practice of the presence of God inherited from earlier medieval currents of devotion, and the Teresian spirituality by which this account is coloured, as well as the experience of receiving the stigmata.

Identification with Christ

Reverend and dear Father,

I promised to write to you from time to time to describe the state of my soul and devotions. There have been some changes in this aspect of my life recently, and they are so important that I am very anxious to know what you think of the doubts and fears which I have experienced.

Before I recount my doubts in greater detail, it seems necessary to describe my attitude to prayer, because I think this will help you to reach a more accurate judgement of the other things I want to tell you about.

On Holy Saturday, I became very self-critical because, during the few days beforehand, I was scarcely aware of the pains and torments which our Lord Jesus Christ suffered for my sins and for the sins of all humankind. I was terribly distressed by my ingratitude and lack of sympathy. Some time after that, when I happened to look (with my physical eyes) at a crucifix, my heart was moved so suddenly and intensely that I could no longer see it outwardly but only inwardly. I was amazed to see the second Person of the Holy Trinity placed in this position for my sins and for the sins of humanity as a whole. I could never explain what I felt in the depths of my being, and it would be impossible for me adequately to describe the excellence and dignity of Jesus Christ as I saw him then. The sight I was allowed of his person was so clear and had such an effect on me that I could not admit, and of course I could never understand, how, when he had so many other ways of saving the world available to him, he had been prepared to reduce his infinite nobility to so abject a condition. Eventually, however, the same Jesus decided to relieve my anguish (which, I truly believe, if it had continued, I could never have borne), and taught me so specifically and effectively, and especially with such intense clarity, that I could never doubt that it was indeed Jesus himself who shone his light into my darkness. He taught me just as a good father would teach a child, or a good master his disciple, so that I can never describe in any way whatsoever, and certainly never in human language, what I felt deep down within me. I remember that my soul marvelled at his wisdom, goodness and especially his abundant love for the human race. Joy and suffering combined to produce a whole range of effects and to make me think of an astonishing number of things. I had so much to say to the Lord who was so vividly present with me. Were my needs, my hopes and desires forgotten? I made an infinite number of acts of thanksgiving to the whole of heaven and above all to the Blessed Trinity. I implored God to make sure that what he had done for my salvation and for the salvation of all humanity would be effective.

I still experienced the physical pains in hands and legs which I had suffered for so many years, but somehow they had become quite tolerable. I was able to thank Jesus for this but even more for the way in which he wiped all fear from my mind and removed all darkness from my spirit.

Although I can tell you all this in the words I have used, I could never accurately describe my real feelings or decide what truly happened on this singular occasion. I do know that the whole experience lasted as long as morning prayer, and that must have been at least four or five hours . . .

Since then, I have had greater help and ease in mental prayer than ever before. It brings solid, fruitful and infinitely delightful nourishment, particularly after Communion, when I am so conscious of its effects that I no longer need faith to believe that this authentic reality is in my soul, in the midst of all my senses assembled there, as it were, to worship it. I would deny everything else to uphold this truth, which has such effects in my soul that it feels entirely consumed, and is often unable to stand that presence. My soul is so replete with peace and serenity that I cannot describe what I feel. So many things are at work in me that I cannot write about them proficiently, and need help to deal with them adequately.

If God had enabled you to travel as you had planned, my soul would have been immensely relieved. If your sacred occupations would allow you a few days' absence, I should be most humbly grateful if you would make the journey and submit entirely to what the Lord decides. Since I have been here, I have been enormously afflicted by this inward agony, so much so that I cannot understand how I am still alive. I have been feeling better recently and can sleep at night. Nevertheless, the inward fire which I suffer from and which I thought would be reduced with advancing age, is increasing to such an extent that sometimes it almost takes the life from me. I am in great need of advice about this, and for someone to explain what exactly this is that is increasing in me. I do not think this advice can be sent in a letter. With regard to the pains in my hands and my feet, I am very afraid of what they might mean, for I recall something of what the Capuchin Father Benet told me about them seventeen to eighteen years ago.

I really need help in respect of several aspects of this change in me. If you cannot come yourself, please let me know the name of someone I can talk to about this, though I fear that any such confidence to another would be inappropriate, since he would not be aware of all that you know about my problems.

The unworthy Carmelite Sister Marie de l'Incarnation

Sœur Marie de l'Incarnation, *Lettres* (Paris, 1800 &c); cf. *Les vrays exercices de la bien-heureuse sœur Marie de l'Incarnation. Composez par elle mesme. Très propres à toutes Ames qui désirent ensuyvre sa bonne vie* (Paris, 2nd ed. 1623).

ST THÉRÈSE OF LISIEUX

Thérèse had chosen her name in religion long before she became a nun. Perhaps the image of the Child Jesus reminded her of her dead brother or fulfilled her maternal instincts. Both names were closely linked to her childhood and to her theology.

My beautiful name

In the course of the morning, when I had to go to the parlour, when I was still on my own in bed (where I prayed most deeply and, unlike the spouse in the Song of Songs, was always able to talk to my beloved Lord), I wondered what name I would take later on as a Carmelite; I knew there was already a Sister Teresa of Jesus; but I could not bear to lose my beautiful name of Thérèse. Suddenly I thought of the Holy Child to whom I bore such devotion, and I felt how happy I should be if I could be called Teresa of the Child Jesus. I was careful, however, not to tell you of my wish, so you can imagine how surprised and pleased I was to hear Reverend Mother say: 'When you come to us, little one, you will be known as "Teresa of the Child Jesus".'

Adapted from: *Story of a Soul*, T.N. Taylor, ed. & tr. (London, 1912), p. 69.

At that time it was usual to associate contemplation of the mystery of the Child Jesus with the sorrowful mystery of the Holy Face. Many holy pictures showed the Child Jesus in his cot dreaming of his passion, or with outspread arms on the cross. In

1896 Thérèse painted a coat-of-arms at the end of her first manuscript in which she portrayed herself as Thérèse of the Child Jesus of the Holy Face. One part of the shield depicts the child Jesus in the crib in one triangle. The other shows the Holy Face with a harp, indicating Thérèse's wish to sing everlasting praises to Jesus. A vine separates the two images, for: 'I am the Vine and you are the branches. Those who abide in me and I in them bear much fruit, because apart from me you can do nothing' (Jn 15.5). Thérèse obtained permission to add 'of the Holy Face' to her name from the time she was clothed. The reason was her father's illness, which reminded her of the humiliations of Jesus during his passion. Mother Geneviève of St Teresa, who founded the Lisieux community, placed a reproduction of the Veil of Veronica in the convent chapel. Thérèse welcomed this devotion. Her sister Pauline encouraged her to be the little Veronica whom Jesus could contemplate when she was in her enclosed garden.

Until then I had not appreciated the full beauty of the Holy Face, and it was you, my little Mother, who unveiled it to me. Just as you had been the first to leave our home for Carmel, so too were you the first to penetrate the mysteries of love hidden in the Face of our Divine Spouse. Having discovered them you showed them to me – and I understood . . . More than ever I realized the nature of true glory. He whose 'kingdom is not of this world' taught me that true wisdom consists in wishing to be 'unknown and esteemed as nothing,' and the joy that comes of self-forgetting. I wished that, like the Face of Jesus, mine 'should be, as it were, hidden and despised, so that no one on earth should esteem me'. I thirsted to suffer and to be forgotten . . .

Adapted from: *Story of a Soul*, T.N. Taylor, ed. & tr. (London, 1912), p. 125.

MOTHER GENEVIEVE GALLOIS (Marcelle Gallois)

In the notebooks that constitute the closest she came to writing a diary or journal, Mother Gallois records the times of profound anguish as she teetered on the edge of the abyss and confirmed her choice of the religious life as the essential alternative to a descent into nothingness through anger, dark sighs, regrets and temptations, without the possibility of any return. For her, the religious life was ultimately a foretaste of the praise and contemplation to which, given her nature, she must yield or be lost: for '. . . belief in salvation from God in Jesus Christ is a conviction, freely accepted . . . in the conditions of our transitoriness – of our "exaltation" above this finitude, thanks to the absolute freedom and generosity of the merciful presence of the God who takes our part, which we may experience in faith in our impenetrable finitude, though there what we experience corporeally is more his absence' (Edward Schillebeeckx, Christ: the Christian Experience in the Modern World *[London & New York, 1980], p. 838).*

The centre of life

I abandoned the struggle just to keep myself alive and found another battle that was much more exacting and decisive: my attempt to combat the passionate bitterness of nature and of a disordered and tumultuous life surging up in me against God. Verlaine's poem came to mind: 'Voice of love, voice of pride, voice of hatred . . .' All those wayward instincts inveighing against life. As powerful as the sea. This fight is an opportunity we are granted so that we can say we want to be with God just when the soul believes it has gone under for ever and lost all sense of his presence. Will I revert to that sad time when I wanted to commit suicide and longed for the void? No! Faith is now anchored in me; I believe in doubt, in annoyance and impiety. And this agonized suffering of the soul because it can no longer see God is surely an act of faith and love of greater integrity than one made in joy.

My God, you are completely whole in just one word of the office, as in a tiny particle of the Blessed Sacrament. Each liturgical prayer is a resumé or a paraphrase of another. The mysteries of the year's cycle are you, my God, under each of your miracles. The enchantment of the time after Pentecost is you completely whole in the glory of all your perfections. What shall I do once I have known my God in this way? I shall abandon myself to him. But how can I do that? Surely we are separated by the sinfulness that comes between us – but Jesus has redeemed us. I shall unite myself with him in the holy sacrifice of the mass. That is the centre of life and it is to reach that centre that I am a Christian and that I have become a nun.

Noël Alexandre, *Mère Geneviève Gallois* (Brussels, 1999), p. 115.

SR KATHLEEN BRYANT

Kathleen Bryant records the joys and disappointments of a Sister in religion in the modern era.

How can God call a California beach girl to be a Sister?

It all began when I was a junior at San Clemente High. A gentle tug in my heart to consider religious life was the beginning of an exciting life that I could never have imagined at that time. It is as if God took the simple piece of who I was at that time, full of fears and self-doubts, and has continued to create a living quilt full of diverse ministries, people and countries.

That was forty-six years ago (when I was a junior in High School and ran the LA Marathon nine times). As a Religious Sister of Charity (RSC), God has given me more than I could ever have hoped for. I lived in the bush of Africa for the happiest five years of my life where I was nicknamed 'Sister Namoonga.'

God called me to teach in Ireland and to study spiritual direction in Wales. As a pianist I earned a degree in music, taught elementary and high school in California and worked on retreats and liturgies. Along with fifty other Sisters and priests I ran the LA Marathon for vocations five times. My life has been so full and rich that I couldn't ask for more.

How did God move me from fears about becoming a Sister to such enthusiasm and peace? Through prayer and more prayer. For an hour a day I sat and listened to God. And God's love enabled me to let go of fears and doubts in order to be an active, loving and joyful Sister today. That hour a day still keeps me energized.

Since I am the oldest of eight children, my brothers and sisters were concerned that my life as a Sister would be boring and lonely. I can honestly say that I have never had one boring day. I have had some lonely moments and times, but my life has been blessed with intimate, loving relationships with many people.

Whether I have lived in the United States, Ireland or Africa, I have lived in community with our other Sisters. Because each community shares a common bond and vision, I discovered that I could walk into a convent of ours in other countries and feel right at home even though I knew no one. This experience taught me that each religious community creates an atmosphere that grows out of a shared history and tradition. Even though I didn't know the Sisters, there was a common understanding of who we are and have been for years.

I think that the happiest time in community for me was in 1983 when I was living in a community with four RSCs, each from a different country, yet there was a unity of minds and hearts that bound us together. We lived in Namwala, Zambia, a place so remote that there was no telephone, TV, newspaper, or gas station for miles. Our community life consisted in not only praying together but also sitting around a fire at night telling stories. What happened there around the fire was the same thing as what first drew me to enter the convent. I discovered that Sisters could have a great time and a lot of fun just being with one another. I have enjoyed the times we've spent singing together, storytelling, teasing and joking with one another, as well as moments when we shared our faith.

I remember a time when I was living in Zambia, when the pump at the river broke down, and consequently there was no running water for ten days. We had some water for drinking but none for washing! The river was not safe for swimming as it was infested with crocodiles, snakes, hippos and bilharzia. On the tenth day, two African Sisters and myself went down to see what we could do. We brought buckets and skimmed water off the top, poured it through a net and began washing. Since we were also singing and laughing the hippos resented this noisy intrusion and began to bellow. All of a sudden God's sense of humour was very vivid. Here I was on a riverbank, with the hippos complaining, with my community, in the middle of Africa. I started laughing and rejoicing at the way God could bring me from the beach in California to this particular riverbank.

It's not that there haven't been hard times. Once I remember waking up in the middle of the night in Zambia feeling lonely. I went into the little chapel and prayed: 'God, you got me here so you had better take care of me.' Any letter written to my family would take three weeks to arrive and six for a response. There was no phone to pick up and call a friend. I opened my Bible without direction, and there lay the passage in which Jesus promises that anyone who leaves the country, family, etc. will receive hundreds of mothers, fathers, sisters and brothers. With that I went back to bed.

The next morning at school, a Zambian teacher walked up to me and said: 'Sister Namoonga, I am your uncle and you are my niece.' I wondered what he meant until I discovered that the role of the uncle in the Tonga tribe was to advise the niece, protect and look after her. And so that promise of Jesus came true to me. It has come true many times as I tearfully left different places, where I have lived, to become part of another family.

In my thirties, the issue of family emerged again. I really struggled with the fact that I would never have my own child. The reality was brought home by seeing the Zambian women carrying babies on their backs and their allowing me to carry a little boy, Emmanuel, on my back. I felt the pain of not ever having my own baby. My community helped me deal with this issue. The Sisters that lived with me allowed me to talk about it and work it through. Looking over my entire life, I came to the sense of how I still would choose the celibate lifestyle. I felt a call to give life wherever I lived. The presence of God within became very real for me. We, like Mary, can bear Christ to others.

The other struggle that I have experienced has been that of people needing more than I had to give. Whenever I feel 'on empty' and aware of my own poverty, I experience God providing me with whatever I need to say or do. It may happen by my consoling a second-grader whose mom is dying of cancer. Sometimes when I am asked to speak to a large group, I feel frightened, but after prayer and trying to leave it to God, it always goes well. When I act as a spiritual director, and have heard another person's story, at times I am aware of my own poverty and have nothing to say. Later on, the person comments on something that I said that just 'hit the spot.' These are all invitations for me to let go and let God's grace work in whatever ministry I am called to for the time.

My life as a Sister has consisted of some very unexpected turns. My name has been changed many times, which reflects the different stages of my life. I entered when the community was still wearing the long traditional habit, and I was called 'Sister Mary Joseph.' Later we returned to our baptismal names and I was 'Sister Kathleen.' In inner-city Dublin, the high-school students called me 'Sister Kahy' for Kathy with their distinct brogue. In Zambia the teachers gave me the last name 'Namoonga' as part of the Tonga tribe and the students gave me the name 'Choolwe', meaning lucky or blessed. So for five years I was called Sister Choolwe Namoonga. I travelled to Vietnam twice to visit the underground novitiates and seminaries and was given the name Sister Kim Binh by our Vietnamese in Los Angeles on my return. With each new mission God gave me a new name. Along with each new name came the grace for my current ministry.

As a woman in the Church I have seen opportunities evolve in ministry. At first I believed that the most I could do ministerially would be to teach religion. With changes in the Church I find that I have been asked to bring the Eucharist and preach to communities that have no priest. I studied spirituality for a Master's degree at the University of San Francisco and earned my Doctor of Ministry a few years ago. I would never have imagined myself doing these things when I was a teenager. I was Vocation Director for the Archdiocese of Los Angeles for twenty-one years and interviewed men who wanted to enter the seminary. I also interviewed women and helped them to find which community they might be called to enter. Through organizing programmes at the archdiocesan level, I found that the challenge of being a woman religious in the Church had taken on new directions.

Even though my life has been full of different opportunities, I feel God holding it all together and continuing to call me forward. Trust God to do the same for you.

Based on an article on the vocation.com website, considerably revised for this book by Sister Bryant.

6

Community, Politics & Solidarity

જ⊱

HROSWITHA

In the prefaces to her dramatic reinterpretations of biblical and other sacred narratives, the nun Hroswitha explains her approach and apologizes, somewhat tongue-in-cheek, for her lack of opportunity, as a woman, to rival the knowledge and scholarship of others.

Reading and writing

Although the style of this little book is scarcely mellifluous, it is the fruit of much hard work, so I shall be grateful for comments from learned but well-intentioned readers who offer not scorn but helpful improvements. There are faults of style and composition that certainly deserve tough criticism, but I hope that my admission will meet with a sensible reaction.

Moreover, if some commentators object that I have occasionally used apocryphal sources, this was due to ignorance not presumption. When I planned this work, I did not know that the authenticity of the material I was about to work on was doubtful. When I learned this, I decided to keep to the same subject-matter, arguing that what now seems false to some investigators may eventually be proved to be true by others.

In these circumstances, my need of defenders of the propriety of this little work which I have now completed is exactly proportionate to my initial lack of innate ability to carry out the task.

I was too young, unscholarly and cowardly to reveal my project by consulting any learned individuals, fearing that they would stop me writing because the style seemed crude.

Therefore I worked on my own without recourse to others. Sometimes I wrote with great effort, and then might destroy what I had composed inadequately. I did my best, however, depending on my own admittedly inferior skills, to turn the thoughts in the writings I had read within our monastery at Gandersheim into a finished composition. I had become acquainted with those works first through the incomparable teaching of the learned and kindly Riccardis, and others who replaced her, then thanks to the considerate help of the Emperor's niece Gerberga, under whose rule as abbess I now live. Though she is younger than me, she is more learned, and very generously introduced me to various authors whom she had studied under the guidance of brilliant teachers.

Although the art of prosody may seem difficult and arduous for me as a feeble woman, I relied entirely on God's merciful help and did my best to convey these narratives in dactylic metre. I wanted to make sure that my definite if slight natural talent did not lie idle in the dark corners of my mind until it faded through neglect. I kept it going by constant devotion so that it would make some small contribution of praise to God who gave it to me. I had no opportunity to profit from it in any other way, but I wanted to be sure that it eventually produced something of value.

If you, the reader of this work (whoever you are), are truly wise, you will use your intelligence to correct the inadequacies of these pages which, I readily admit, are not the work of a master hand. But if you find something in them that is worthy of approval, ascribe this success to God and all the blemishes to my lack of care. However you react, do not read in a censorious but in a kindly spirit, and never forget that it is best to let humility and self-deprecation blunt the keen edge of censure . . .

Remember that in composing this work I have been swayed this way and that by different considerations: by joy and apprehension. On the one hand, I am profoundly happy that I am able to praise God through my work, for he has made me the person I am. On the other hand, I do not want to pretend to abilities greater than those I actually possess. It seems quite as wrong-headed to deny the gifts God has given you as to claim that you are better-informed and more intelligent than you are.

I do not want to see my natural abilities wither through neglect, and I am well aware that women's understanding is generally held to be behind that of men, so I have supplied what is missing in the threadbare garments in which I now appear before you by plucking a few threads from the fine robes of others' efforts and working them into my own. That is the best way, I believe, to pay tribute to the divine origin of all good work.

Adapted from: Sr M. Gonsalva Wiegand, OSF, *The Non-dramatic Works of Hroswitha: Text, Translation and Commentary* (St Meinrad, Indiana, 1937), *passim*.

MECHTHILD OF MAGDEBURG

Mechtild's exposition of the convent as the perfect metaphor for the shared life of peace and concord seems startlingly original but is actually a novel presentation of the traditional view of the religious community as a model of the principle that should rule the world as a whole. This is the perennial understanding of God as love. As Jacob Boehme, a spirit of the same cast, still expressed it in the seventeenth century: 'Love, that is, divine love, hates all egotism, hates all that which we call I, or I-hood ... As heaven rules the world, and as eternity rules time, even so ought love to rule the natural temporal life, for no other method is there, neither can there be, of attaining to that life which is supernatural and eternal, and which you so much desire to be led into.'

A spiritual convent

Healing roots

I was worried because I felt just as tiny and unworthy as when I started to write thirty years ago. But our Lord showed me a little sack he was holding in his hand and said: 'These are healing roots.' I answered: 'I've never seen anything like that, Lord!' And he said: 'You will know what they are if you look closely. You can use them to heal the sick, make the strong stronger, bring the dead to life, and make the good better.' Then I saw before me a Spiritual Convent established on all the virtues.

The Abbess

She is true love and is filled with holy intelligence which she uses to rule the community in body and soul to the honour and glory of God. She offers the Sisters a wealth of sacred instruction founded on God's will, and in this way she liberates her own soul.

The Chaplain of love

He is totally infused with love so that pride is completely banished, for there is no room for it.

The Prioress

She is God's holy peace and is granted patience in addition to her good intentions, so that she can instruct the community in holy wisdom.

The Assistant Prioress

She is loving-kindness, and assembles the little ones so that they can learn godliness. All wrongdoing will depart from their minds so that God can increase human goodness through them.

The Chapter

It requires four things: evidence of holiness in worship; gentle care in ruling, which opposes sin, glorifies God and evokes joy; avoidance of pride; and assistance to others in genuine service of their needs. For all this God will reward it.

The Chantress

She is hope, so holy and humble in devotion that even shyness in singing in God's sight sounds so noble that he loves this music of the heart . . .

The Schoolmistress

She is wisdom and diligently teaches the ignorant, thus both sanctifying and honouring the convent.

The Cellarer

She is replete with help for everyone, doing her work most joyfully, and thus earning the fruits of God's holiness, so that his most nutritious gifts flow into her heart and into the hearts of all who assist her.

The Steward

She is gentleness and always does good willingly. She gives more than she has and thus obtains special gifts from God. The recipients of her bounty thank God most devotedly with the fervour that fills their hearts like a fine vintage in a pure goblet.

The Infirmarian

She is compassion and is always intent on caring for the sick without restraint. Her reward from God is that she always serves others willingly, and if she is in need he never denies her his help.

The Portress

She is a ready guardian always wishing to do whatever she is asked. Nothing she does is ever wasted and she seeks God out swiftly when she wishes to pray, knowing he will be there with her in holy peace to soothe her sorrow.

The Disciplinarian

She is holy regularity, always illumined in heavenly freedom like an everlasting candle, reminding us that we should bear all our sorrow and pain gently until we come to a holy end.

The Provost

He is divine obedience to whom all the virtues are subject, ensuring that the convent remains always in God.

All who enter this convent will dwell for ever in holy joy, now and in eternity, and all those who live there are blessed.

God's message to the soul

My nature is to love you constantly, for I myself am love. I wish to love you ardently, since I long to be loved greatly. I love you long from my eternity, for I am everlasting and have no end.

The soul's message to God

My joy is that I must love the One who loves me. I pray that I shall love him immeasurably and continually until the day I die. I am joyful because he died out of love for me, and now I must love him so much that I would be willing to die for love of him. Then I shall be an inextinguishable spark alive in the great fire of God's own living Majesty.

I shall be filled with the very fire of love, so that my life is joy and I need no more instruction, for I can never abandon love. I am imprisoned in love for otherwise I would have no source of life. In death as in life, I shall live in the house of love for ever.

Leben und Offenbarungen der heiligen Schwester Mechthildis (von Magdeburg), Jungfrau aus dem Orden des heiligen Benediktus, Johannes Müller, ed., 2 vols (Regensburg, 1880–1); cf. Wilhelm Schleussner, *Das fliessende Licht der Gottheit nach einer neugefunden (Würzburger) Handschrift* (Frankfurt am Main, 1929).

MOTHER WALBURG SCHEFFLERIN VON EICHSTÄTT

Mother Walburg, Prioress of the Maihingen Bridgittine Convent in Nuremberg, Germany, describes some of the nuns who lived there in the fifteenth and sixteenth centuries before and during the peasant uprising which brought their comfortable way of life to an end.

A dove in flames

Sister Anna Mayerin of Nuremberg was pious and godfearing. She was a most spiritual person outside the convent and inside it too, for she was inspired by our Lord's life and Passion in her work and whatever else she did. She had also been to Rome, and when she was about to depart from Nuremberg and make her way to Rome, she found that the dear companion whom she had to leave behind had fallen ill, and was in fact entering her last sickness. Sister Anna was able to say goodbye to her friend and ask her, if she were to die before she, Anna, returned, to make sure, God willing, to visit her once dead, and let her know whether she was suffering in the fires of hell. Anna would be very grateful, however, if she would take care not to appear before her in any frightening form. So the sick friend promised that, God permitting, she would indeed seek her out with her news, but in the form of a dove. So Anna made her way to Rome and, as she was kneeling there before a priest whom she had chosen as confessor, a dove suddenly flew into the church and settled on her head. Spotting it there, the priest made as if to seize the bird, whereupon it flapped its wings and belched out a mass of exceedingly fierce flames. The priest took fright at this and the dove left immediately. Anna told him about the arrangement and that the bird was actually her friend's soul, which he found rather shocking. Sister Anna told us this story herself and when she came back from Rome she entered our convent as a lay sister, brought all her food with her, and was in the Order for ten years before she died in the fifty-fifth year of her age in 1586 on the feast of the Conversion of St Paul. May God have mercy upon her soul and upon the souls of all the faithful. RIP . . .

A salutary warning

Sister Barbara Nörlingerin of Nuremberg was a pious, reserved and peaceful sister who tried to help and befriend everyone, whatever their station. Her father and mother were dead when she came to us and the worthy old Abbess of Kirchheim spoke on her behalf instead. But Barbara had a brother in Welschland. He arrived at the convent after her induction, accused his sister of giving the convent his inheritance and many other things too. He demanded an immense sum of money from the Order which he said his sister had handed over to us. This was a lie, for she brought scarcely anything with her. So the good Mother rejected his claim and refused to have anything to do with it. The brother departed with threats and foul language, after sticking a letter of resignation on his sister's behalf in the fence enclosing our courtyard, and slandering our gracious Lord Wallerstein behind his back. The Count heard of this and our good Mother sent him the letter of resignation for inspection. He set up a hue and cry for the brother, who was betrayed by his own companions. They arrested him at Nordlingen, the Count threw him into prison, and the poor fellow had no one to vouch for him or speak on his behalf. Then the Count decided to behead him, not just on our behalf, but for his own reasons, because the brother had slandered him so vilely and similarly anyone who wanted to defend and protect us. As a result, he received a sentence of death by beheading. When dear Barbara learned of this, she and the other sisters were very distressed, and the entire convent fervently prayed God to make sure (should that be his will) that the poor man would live. The next day, when his head was to be struck off, the daughter of the King of Poland (who was married to the Margrave), arrived with a vast retinue. When Reverend Mother heard this, she sent Brother Sandicelli (who happened to be there by God's grace) to Nordlingen to beg her Royal Highness to plead for the brother's life. Then not only she but many pious people spoke on his behalf against the Count, so his life was spared and they set him free. In fact, he never turned up here again, and never caused the Convent or anyone else any harm. But dear Sister Barbara found out every detail of what had happened and went into a deep depression. She worried so very much about it all, perhaps more than anyone suspected at the time, and of course she hardly got any sleep while her brother was in his dungeon, and grew ill in the head. She was so very sick that you would have thought she was an infant and not a rational grown-up person. Before all this, she had been a very intelligent, reasonable individual, but anger grubbed away at her mind to such a degree that she could no longer make the same use of it, and, even though she still served the sisters quietly, she just wasn't right in the head in the way other people are. Yet she was in the Order for forty years. All this should be a warning to young people and the inexperienced to be very careful about their reactions to unpleasant events. She became physically sick in her sixtieth year, and died in 1521, two days before the feast of St Mary Magdalen. God grant her eternal joy and happiness. She was an assistant in the tailoring shop for many years. RIP.

Georg Grupp, 'Maihinger Brigitterinnen aus Nürnberg,' *Mitteilungen des Vereins für die Geschichte der Stadt Nürnberg*, 13 (1896), 79–97

ST TERESA OF AVILA

'Teresa's passionate, ideal nature demanded an epic life: what were many-volumed romances of chivalry and the social conquests of a brilliant girl to her? Her flame quickly burned up that light fuel; and, fed from within, soared after some illimitable satisfaction, some object which would never justify weariness, which would reconcile self-despair with the rapturous consciousness of life beyond self. She found this epic life in the reform of

a religious order'. Thus the novelist George Eliot in the 'Prelude' to Middlemarch *(*Middlemarch: A study of provincial life *[London, new ed. 1893, p. vii]). In her just anxiety for the good of her Order, Teresa could be most severe. Yet, like George Eliot's Dorothea, 'However just her indignation might be, her ideal was not to claim justice, but to give tenderness' (ibid., p. 149). From this letter which she wrote in 1582, four months before her death, to Mother Anna of Jesus, Prioress and Religious of the Convent of St Joseph at Granada, to complain about her taking too many nuns with her, and for sending no report, we learn something of the exhausting difficulties of supervising a religious foundation with a strict Rule, at such a distance.*

Restraining an unruly prioress

Dear Mother Prioress and nuns of St Joseph, the grace of the Holy Spirit be with you all.

You have made some very odd complaints against our father-provincial, considering how negligent you have been in writing to him since your first letter, in which you told him about having made the foundation. You have behaved in the same way towards me. His Reverence was here on the Feast of the Finding of the Cross, and said he knew nothing about you except what I had told him: this I merely learnt from a letter which I received from the prioress of Seville, who told me you were thinking of purchasing a house for twelve thousand ducats.

It is not at all surprising that rather severe rules should be made for a convent in which such great prosperity reigns. But I have been hurt very deeply by the deviousness of the ways in which you have tried to conceal your disobedience, both on account of the bad example it may give to the rest of the Order, and because the prioresses will get used to taking liberties, for which they will find plenty of excuses. You say that the lady and gentleman who let you occupy their house next door were stingy, but the truth is that you were very unwise to have taken so many (eight) religious with you, and to have sent so many others back who had only just arrived. I cannot imagine how you had the heart to make them come such a long distance.

You should have sent those who arrived to Veas, and others with them: you did very wrong in having so many in the house, especially as you saw that gentleman and his sister were against it; and yet you thought of sending for more from Veas: how *could* you have done so, when you had no house which you could call your own? I certainly am surprised that Don Luis Mercado and his sister Ana were so patient. The whole affair was badly managed from the very beginning . . .

I could not help laughing at the fright you gave us by saying that the Archbishop would suppress the convent. At present I see no sign of such a thing, nor do I see why I should make so much of it. He could not do anything like that if he lived to be a hundred. If any want of obedience should be introduced into the Order, it would be much better there had never been a convent, because our advantage does not consist in having many houses, but in having nuns who are holy to live in them.

I do not know when your letters can be sent to our father-provincial. I fear it will be nearly six weeks before he can have them, and even then, I do not know *how* I shall send them by a safe courier, because he has left here for Soria, and from there he goes to so many places on his visitation, that we cannot possibly tell in what town or city he may be found: neither can we know for certain when we shall hear from him, or of him. As far as I can learn, he was at Villanueva when the poor sisters arrived. I was very upset when I thought of the trouble and shame he would have on seeing them for, as the town is so small, it is impossible to keep their arrival secret; and it will also be harmful for us, when every one hears about such a foolish act. You might easily have sent them to Veas, until the father-provincial was informed of everything, for they have not had leave to return to the house from which they were taken, having been made by the command of the provincial conventuals of Veas. I think, however, that some remedy may be found for the evil: but your Reverence is the sole cause of it, through not having mentioned how many Religious you took with you, or if you received any lay-sister: indeed, you seemed to take as little notice of the provincial, as if he had no authority whatever.

According to what he told me, and considering how matters stand at present, it will be impossible for him to come to you before the winter. God grant that the father (vicar) provincial may be able to undertake the journey, for I have just received a letter from Seville, in which the prioress tells me that he has caught the plague (which is in the city, though the public do not yet know of it): brother Bartolomi has also caught it . . . earnestly recommend them to our Lord, for their death would be a great loss to the Order. The father-vicar writes in a postscript that he is a little better, but not out of danger. The poor nuns are in great affliction, and with reason, because they suffer martyrdoms in their house, and far greater labours than the nuns in your house: and yet they do not complain so much as yours! It is not so great a torment to be confined in such a small space, as to want health and nourishment; and since you are in such high esteem with so many grandees, I cannot see why you complain: we cannot expect everything to happen just as we wish . . .

As for the nuns of Veas, it is so proper they should return, that if I were not fearful of being the occasion of your offending God by some act of disobedience, I would send an express command to your Reverence, because in everything relating to the affairs of our Discalced Carmelites, I hold the place of our provincial. In virtue, then, of my authority, I direct and command that all those who have come from Veas shall return as soon as possible, except the mother-prioress, Anna of Jesus: even though they should have a house suitable in every respect, what use would it be, unless they had a revenue sufficient to keep them from want? It is not wise to begin a foundation with such a large community; and for many other reasons it is better.

For some days I have been praying about all this (for I did not wish to answer the letters immediately), and I find it is God's will this should be done; the more repugnance you feel, the more must it be done. It is quite opposed to the spirit of our nuns to be attached to anything, even were it to their prioress, for this would always prevent them from advancing in perfection. God wishes his spouses to be attached to no one but himself. I do not want the house to start like that of Veas; for I shall never forget the letter which the sisters wrote to me from that convent, when your Reverence gave up office. Attachments are the source of rivalries and other disorders which are not perceived at first. On this account, I beg you, for the love of God, not to follow any opinion but mine on this occasion; when you are more securely established, and the nuns more detached, then they may return, if it seems expedient.

I don't really know who exactly followed you there, for you kept this a secret from me and your father (provincial). I did not think your Reverence would have taken so great a number with you; but they were those who were very attached to your Reverence . . . You are bringing up souls to be the brides of our crucified Saviour; for this reason you ought to mortify their wills, so that they are not attached to trifles. Remember that you are beginning a foundation in a kingdom newly conquered from the Moors, and that your Reverence and all the other sisters are obliged to advance the more in perfection, not as weak and timid women, but like strong and valiant men.

What does it matter, my mother, whether the father-provincial calls you president, or prioress, or call you by your name, Anna of Jesus? It is certain that if you were not at the head of the community, people would no more apply to you than to another, for there have been prioresses like yourself. As you have so seldom written, it is no wonder they are ignorant whether you have been elected or not. I assure you, I am quite grieved to see the Discalced Carmelites become attached so soon to such mean trifles, and that they should even make them the subject of conversation, and above all, that Mother Maria de Christo, whom I sent from Avila to Granada, should take great notice of such things! This seems so strange to me, that I believe either her imperfections have affected her head, or the devil has been using all his arts to infect the Order with diabolical principles.

After all, your Reverence is praised for being very courageous, as if submission would take away your courage! May God give my Discalced daughters the grace to be humble and obedient and submissive; for courage *without* these virtues is nothing but the source of numerous imperfections . . .

I can easily believe your Reverence must have many troubles when starting this foundation. Do not, however, be astonished at this, for so important a work cannot be done without problems, since the reward (they say) is very great. God grant that the imperfections with which such works are performed, may not deserve punishment rather than rewards: this thought always makes me fearful.

I will write to the Prioress of Veas to ask her to contribute something towards the expenses of the journey, for which we have such slender means. I shall tell her, that if Avila were as near (as Veas) I should be very glad to take back my nuns. This may be done in time, by the help of our Lord, and so your Reverence may tell them that as soon as the foundation is finished, and you have a sufficient number of nuns to take their place, they must return to their own house . . .

I quite forgot to mention that I am informed that the nuns of Veas, even after the chapter was held, have been leaving their house to see to the church. I cannot understand how this is possible, because not even the provincial himself can give them leave to do that, since the Pope, by a *motu proprio*, has especially forbidden it under pain of excommunication: besides, our own constitutions expressly forbid it. When the Order began, this was difficult for us, but now I am very glad it is the rule. Now we are not allowed to go so far as to shut the gate. The sisters of Avila know very well that anything like that is forbidden: I cannot imagine why they did not tell you so. See to this, for the love of God, for I am sure God will provide someone to look after the church: there are always ways to get things done.

I feel quite grieved every time I think how you are crowding Don Luis and his sister. I told you the other day to use every possible exertion in order to find a house, even though it might not be convenient in every respect; for whatever inconvenience you might suffer yourself, it is not proper *they* should suffer when they have done so much for you . . .

If you desire anything from our father, remember you have not written to him: and, as I told you before, it will be very late before I can send your letters to him; however, I will send them as soon as I can. He will have to go from Villanueva to Daimiel, in order to inaugurate the monastery, and then he will go to Malagon and Toledo, and afterwards to Salamanca and Alva. When these visitations have all been made, he will have I know not how many prioresses to elect. He told me when leaving that he did not think he would be at Toledo before the month of August. I am quite grieved to think of the long journeys he has to make in such hot places. Pray for him, and persuade your friends to do everything possible to buy another house for you.

The sisters I spoke of may stay till you have informed his Reverence of everything, and he will do what he thinks for the best . . . May God ever guide your Reverence.

Your Servant,

TERESA OF JESUS.

Obras de Santa Teresa de Jesus, P. Silverio, ed. (Burgos, 1915–24), *carta* lxv; *The Letters of St Teresa of Avila*, John Dalton, ed. & tr. (London, 1902), adapted; cf. *The Letters of Saint Teresa of Jesus*, E. Allison Peers, tr. & ed., vol. 2 (London, 1951), pp. 935–42.

SR ANNE DE MARQUETS

One of the most skilled devotional poets of the sixteenth century, Anne de Marquets was known for her ability to express divine truths, but also for the unusually sharp and pithy sonnets in which she rebuked those who wished to denigrate the capabilities of women. The following are examples of these two main types of verse for which she is now increasingly celebrated.

The soul

Like a delicate flower born to
Blossom in the right soil, so often
Refreshed by rain and dew, my soul,
Watered well with the sweet virtue of
The Holy Spirit, grows and flourishes,
But, once it loses that divine grace,
Languishes and finds its beauty fades,
Like any flower born in dry soil when
Suddenly bereft of the vital rain or dew
That first raised and nourished it.

Anne de Marquets, 'L'âme', in: A. Séché, *Les Muses Françaises: Anthologie des Femmes Poètes (1200–1891)* (Paris, 1908), p. 90

* * *

Hurt us no longer, proud lords and masters

Hurt us no longer, proud lords and masters.
Harsh-hearted and unfeeling men, we know
You have heard that God in heaven loves us,
Who made us women as he made you men.

Yes, many of you are wise and gracious,
Yet many women have their own virtues,
For we are all cased in the same flesh,
And similar desires plague both sexes.

Recall how women not men were honoured
As the first to see the risen Lord, kiss
His feet and tell men how he conquered death.

We need no pedestal or empty praises,
Stay content with what is best in you and
Forget your envy of our special graces.

Anne de Marquets, 'Ne jetez plus sur nous d'injures si grands sommes', in: *Sonets spirituels, de feue tres-vertueuse et tres-docte Dame Sr Anne de Marquets, Religieuse de Poissi* (Paris, 1605), p. 193.

SR JUANA INES DE LA CRUZ (Sor Juana Inés de la Cruz)

In this extract from her Autodefensa Espiritual *of 1681 (her* Letter of Spiritual Self-justification to her Confessor*), the poet, nun and proto-feminist Juana, who lived in Mexico during the Spanish colonial period, defends her right and freedom to read and study even though she is a woman. She also asserts a woman's right to education and intellectual attainments in her* Reply to Sister Philothea *of 1691 ('Sor Philotea' was actually a bishop whose sermon Juana had already criticized, and who published Juana's attack together with his counter-criticism, seemingly the commentary of a well-informed nun).*

Spiritual Self-justification

Who, pray, has forbidden women to study privately, or, in fact, anything in particular? Surely women possess minds that are just as rational as the minds of men. As far as I can see, there is no reason why those rational female minds cannot enjoy the same privilege of literary exposition as rational male minds. You must admit that the female intellect and spirit is as open to divine grace and glory as yours. In that case, it must be capable of assimilating as much information and knowledge as yours or any man's. Tell me what divine revelation, what declaration of the Church, or what rational argument has decreed that women should be subject to so harsh a law ... Why is it held to be improper for me to prefer to study rather than to peer out of the window prattling away, or be stuck in a cell murmuring about whatever trumpery things might be afoot inside or outside the house, or be arguing with someone like myself, or reproving some unfortunate servant, or be wondering what might be happening here and there throughout the world? As far as I can see, the question is especially relevant since I am aware that God has given me the capacity for knowledge, literature and the arts, and this does not seem to contravene his most holy Law, or to offend against the obligations of my state of life. I am certainly drawn to learning. If there is anything wrong about this, well, I didn't make myself a rational being. That is how I was born and that is how I shall die . . . I repeat yet again that I am merely trying to beg your Reverence that if you do not wish to favour me, you should not think of me at all unless to recommend me to the Lord, which I believe you will certainly do of your infinite kindness.

The education of women

An immense amount of harm would be avoided in this country if older women were as learned as Laeta (the daughter in law of Paula, who consulted St Jerome on the education of her daughter), and if they knew how to teach as St Paul and my Father St Jerome advise. But instead of that, if fathers want to educate their daughters beyond the usual extent, the lack of trained older women and the great negligence from which women unfortunately have to suffer because there are no well-educated older women, force them to engage men as teachers for their daughters, to show them how to read, write and count, how to play music and acquire other skills. This is most injurious, as we hear every day, with regard to so many instances of unsuitable matches. Unsurprisingly, the ease of meeting and close association over so long a period of time lead to quite unlooked-for results. Consequently, many fathers prefer to leave their daughters in a barbaric, uncultivated state rather than expose them to the obvious dangers they will encounter in the close company of men . . .

I was a slow learner though very anxious to acquire knowledge. Nevertheless, my hair grew rapidly. Therefore I decided to scissor off my hair to punish my head for its ignorance. I thought it most improper that a head so bereft of knowledge should be

adorned with hair. Clearly, knowledge is a more desirable head-
dress than hair.

*Fama, y Obras Posthumas de Fenix de Mexico, decima musa, poetisa
Americana, Sor Juana Inés de la Cruz* (Madrid, 1700), *passim.*

MOTHER MARIE DE L'INCARNATION (Marie Guyard)

---

*Mother Marie writes to her son from Quebec to describe the
vicissitudes of missionary life in Canada. She tells of the burning
of the Monastery and the extreme poverty to which the Sisters
have been reduced. She has been advised to rebuild the Monastery and is working at it. This extraordinarily graphic account is
superbly composed to bring the various stages of the event to life,
from preamble to resolution, so that the recipient forgets the way
in which the letter is delivered, the time it has taken to reach him,
the fact that the building has been replaced by now, and even
that his mother is actually an enclosed nun, for he is suddenly
plunged into the noise, tumult and terror of the mission's experiences as if they were his own.*

---

3 September 1651

My dear Son,

This is the third means which we are using to spread awareness
in France of the distress the Lord has decided to send us. The first
was by way of New England, and the second by the fisherman. I
think that these are uncertain channels, because we have had to
depend on individuals who came here in canoes separated from
their big ships. They have to pass through obvious dangers as do
the packets entrusted to them. Nevertheless, I have resorted to
them to take every opportunity of letting you have our news, and
I am trying this third method so that you can learn how God's
mighty hand has touched us. On 30 December last, which was
the octave of our Lord's birth, he decided to share the suffering

and impoverishment of his crib with us, as I shall now relate. A good Sister who was about to bake bread next day was preparing her dough, and because it was so very cold put hot coals into the kneading trough to heat it. She had planned to take the coals out before going to bed, but because she didn't generally use fire like this, she easily forgot to remove them. The trough was firmly closed on every side, so that a Sister going into the bakery at 8 am did not see the coals. Since the fire had dried the naturally resinous wood, the fire spread without hindrance. The partitions and the ceiling caught fire, as did the stairs just under the boarding school where Mother Seraphin and the children were sleeping. She was awakened abruptly by the noise and the fire crackling. She leaped out of her bed, thinking somebody was saying: 'Get up! Save the children or they will be burned alive!' In fact the floor was already burning and the fire was blazing in the dormitory. Mother Seraphin was so scared that she called out to the children: 'Save yourselves! You must save yourselves!' She went to the dormitory to awaken the community, and her voice was so loud that they all leaped out of their beds. One Sister rang the big bell to summon help. The others got ready to fight the fire, but instead I ran there and told the Sisters to abandon everything, for there was no way of putting it out. I tried to reach the place where I stored cloth and other provisions for the community. I threw them from my cell window together with whatever came to hand. I was on my own in the building, still thinking of my original plan, for I was aware that Sisters had escaped half-naked and needed some kind of covering. I tried to get to our little store-room, but the dormitory was already alight. The fire was consuming not only the spot I wished to reach, but was running along the roof of the house and had penetrated the downstairs rooms. I was stuck between two fires, and a third one was in hot pursuit. I was not afraid of the flames but almost choking because of the fumes. I had to go under the bell to save my life, and thus run the risk of being overcome in the fountain.

Mother Assistant and Sister St Lawrence had broken the grille, which was only made of wood, in order to save herself and some children who had returned to the dormitory. Only the bigger ones had escaped: the little ones were still in danger. Sister St Ignatius wondered whether in all conscience she should give her life to save these little innocents, because the cloisters were already on fire. She risked her life by entering the room and did save them, although the floor was already crumbling.

I was still in the dormitory. Realizing that there was nothing I could do and that I was about to die in the flames, I bowed my head to my crucifix, accepting the decisions of Divine Providence and reciting an act of abandonment to the will of God. Nevertheless, I managed to escape through the parlour at the end of the dormitory. As I came down, I met the helpers whom Father Superior had brought. They soon realized that they could do nothing upstairs, and descended to the chapel where, with difficulty, they rescued the Blessed Sacrament and the vestments and sacred vessels in the sacristy. Our Reverend Mother had gone out first to open the doors and was standing to one side. When she could see none of us anywhere near her, she suffered most agonizingly at the thought of some of us wrapped in flames. She called to us but still could not see us, and we could not hear her. She fell to her knees at the feet of our Lady and made a vow in honour of the Immaculate Conception. I can't say absolutely what effect this vow had as far as God was concerned, but I believe that it was truly miraculous that none of us was consumed in so precipitate and fierce a fire. A Huron woman, who was a very good Christian, did not wake up as quickly as the others and could think of no way of escaping apart from jumping from the window onto a road where the icy snow was doubly hard from the feet of passers-by. She was so stunned that we thought she was dead, yet she came to her senses, for God had wished to preserve her and restore her to us.

At long last, the Sisters found our Mother. She began to breathe freely but she still had not seen our French and native boarders. They were lined up quite close to her, where they almost died of cold for they were still in their chemises and all their clothes and possessions had been burned. I was most deeply affected by the discomfort suffered by our poor invalid. If she had been as strong as she was courageous, she could have saved some part of the things in the dormitory, but she was so weak that her arms failed her when she tried to move her mattress. Mine was the only one to be preserved, together with what covered me, which was just right for her. I had thrown my habits out of the window, but they got caught in the refectory grille and were burned with the rest, so I was left naked like the others, who were in the snow praying to God and watching this terrifying furnace burn. Their faces showed clearly that God was in their hearts, for they were so serene and accepting of God's will amidst the deprivation to which Providence had reduced us. We had lost all our possessions and were left as naked as Job on his dung hill, although we were in the snow and bitter cold. We were indeed reduced to the poverty of Job, but in our case our friends, French and native, were touched by great compassion, which was a boon that poor holy Job had to do without. Everyone who saw us was reduced to tears to see the distress we were in but also our serenity. One good man who could not understand how we might suffer such a calamity without any outward expression of sorrow, said aloud: 'These women are either fools or they love God immensely'. The Lord whose hand touched us knows which proposition is true, and the effect of his goodness in us at the time . . .

When the Father Superior, together with all the Fathers (since the whole Jesuit household had come to help us), realized that we were all safe, they had some of the children carried to our workmen's house, and the rest to a neighbour's house. They were wearing nothing but their chemises and were bitterly cold, so that a few of them fell very ill. The Superior led us to his own house and put us in the parlour, in spite of the state we were in. On the way there people gave us two or three pairs of shoes out of charity, for some of us were barefoot, as was our Founder. She survived with no more than an old worn tunic; like the rest of us she lost all her possessions in Canada. The Superior gave shoes to all the others who were barefoot. Only three of us still had their shoes, which they had worn to bed because it was so cold.

When the reverend Mothers of the hospital learned that we

were in the Fathers' house, and were to go to the fort, they invited us to their house. The Father Superior thought this was more appropriate and took us there himself. These good Mothers, with whom we have always been closely united, were more distressed by our condition than we were ourselves. They clothed us in their grey habits and also gave all fifteen of us linen and other things we needed desperately. We shared their life, sat at the same table, and followed the same holy exercises. We lived in their house as if we were their sisters.

The day after the fire, the Father Superior and the Governor led us to see the sad ruins, or rather the dread furnace which no one dared approach too closely. All the chimneys had collapsed, the partition walls were down, and the main walls were cracked and burned to the foundations. It seemed as if these ruins could never be restored. Anyway, all our foundation funds would never have been enough to do it. We were far from thinking of repairing our buildings, for we were without the necessities of life until the ships arrived. All this made people think that we must intend to go back to France, but each of us willingly accepted God's will for us. No one wished to return to the motherland. Moreover, this country offered many opportunities to teach French girls as well as natives, and we were unanimous in deciding to remain here.

After staying three weeks with our good and generous hosts, we were taken to the little building which our founder had constructed for herself some time before but gave to us later on. It was truly comforting to experience the love and affection among us in such a cramped space. Our dear hosts not only had the expense of looking after us but lent us five hundred livres' worth of all kinds of supplies, both for ourselves and for the workmen. Then there were the Fathers, who helped us as far as they were able, and even sent us the cloth they had kept back for their own cassocks. They also sent us provisions, linen and bedclothes. Their Brothers and workmen laboured for us day after day. We would have died of cold and hunger without their great charity. Governor d'Ailleboust and his wife were of great assistance to us. All our friends showed us compassion and charity.

Even the poorest offered us a towel and another a chemise, and yet another a cloak. One gave us a hen, another a few eggs, and others surrendered other things. You know how poor the country is, but its charity is even greater. Nevertheless, only almighty God could compensate us for the loss of all our goods, which were valued at 50,000 livres, the estimated cost of our monastery and the furniture.

We were all together in our tiny house, suffering the inconvenience, deprivation and lack of space, but nothing was being done to redress the situation. The Governor, the Father Superior and a few friends discussed what should happen. They decided that we would have to rebuild on the original foundations without any delay. Because our bad luck had not eroded out courage, our vocations were as strong as ever, and anyway the local girls, both French and native, needed our help. We were told the decision and approved it all the more readily when they promised to lend us the money to cover expenses.

And so we started work on a second building. Initially, the Fathers lent us 8000 livres but at the time of writing this letter we still owe them a good 15,000 livres. Before the building is ready we shall owe them 20,000 livres, not counting the work inside and the furniture. We have to depend on Providence to pay our debts and for all the other things we need. The same Lord placed us in our previous state, and he will build us up again, through the prayers of our Lady. We are so certain of her assistance that we live in peace. Whatever she decides not to do herself she finds friends to carry out, and in this way she will do everything. She has already worked very hard, so that the building is already up to the roof and we shall soon be able to live in it. Everyone who sees it is full of admiration and says: 'It is as if it were building itself and God's own finger was at work on it!' The whole country rejoices to see us about to take up our teaching again, which we have been able to do on a very small scale in a bark cabin.

As you know, Mother St Athanasius' term has come to an end, and our Lord has put me in charge of this little community. This is an onerous task considering my weakness and our circumstances here. I already had charge of our buildings, which made me very tired during the winter and until now. The new duties are no easier but, after all, I have chosen the cross. Ask Jesus to enable me to bear it for his glory and to give me the grace to die attached to it as he was.

The Iroquois are still raiding among us. They captured a French woman from Montreal after killing her husband. This settlement has suffered immensely, as has Three Rivers. The barbarians have defeated the neutral nation, which makes them more proud and insolent towards us. Nevertheless, peace reigns in Quebec.

Goodbye, my very dear son.

Lettres de la Révérende Mère Marie de l'Incarnation, L'Abbé Richaudeau, ed. (Paris, 1876), pp. 439–48 (Lettre lxii)

ST THERESE OF LISIEUX

'The lack of a fire in winter caused her the greatest physical suffering, and it is easy to understand how a delicate constitution such as hers would be tried by the long Norman winters and the damp climate of Lisieux. When the temperature was lower than usual and she had spent the day half-frozen with cold, she would go to the community-room in the evening, after Matins, to warm herself for a few minutes. To get from there to her cell, she had to walk some sixty yards in the open air, under the cloisters, then, after climbing the staircase, make her way down a long icy corridor, so that by the time she reached her room the little heat she had so grudgingly allowed herself to gain was utterly lost. As she lay on her straw mattress, with two thin blankets for covering, sleep came to her only in snatches. Sometimes she would pass the entire night shivering without ever falling asleep. If, from the beginning, she had told the Novice Mistress about this, the situation would have been remedied immediately, but she preferred

to accept this stern penance without uttering a complaint. It was only on her deathbed that she revealed it, in these expressive words: "Throughout my religious life the cold has caused me more physical pain than anything else – I have suffered from cold until I almost died of it".' (Story of a Soul, adapted, T. N. Taylor, ed. & tr. [London, 1912], p. 218). In spite of this excessive self-denial, which was not uncommon in religious communities in the past, Thérèse was always concerned for the other Sisters.

Convent life

Before Sister St Peter became quite helpless, someone had to leave the evening meditation at ten minutes to six and take her to the refectory. Aware of the difficulty, or rather the impossibility, of pleasing the poor invalid, it cost me a great effort to offer my services. I was unwilling, however, to lose such a golden opportunity, remembering our Lord's own words: 'As long as you did it to one of these, the least of my brethren, you did it to me'.

I therefore humbly offered my help, which was accepted, though only after considerable persuasion. Every evening, when I saw her shake the sand in her hour-glass to measure the time, I knew it was the sign to start.

Summoning up all my courage I rose, and quite a ceremony commenced. First her stool had to be moved and carried in a particular way, without the least hurry, and then began the journey. Supporting the poor old Sister by her girdle, I tried to acquit myself of the task as gently as I could; if by some misfortune she stumbled, I was told I was going too fast and that she would certainly fall; when I tried to lead her more slowly she would say: 'Where are you? . . . I don't feel your hand . . . You are letting go your hold . . . I am going to fall! . . . I was right when I said you were too young to take care of me'.

At last we reached the refectory without any further accident, but there fresh difficulties awaited me. Taking every care not to hurt the poor invalid, I had to install her, with some manoeuvring, in her place; that done, I had to turn back her sleeves

– according to her own special style – and then I was free to go. Noticing, however, that she cut her bread with extreme difficulty, I would not leave her until I had rendered this last little service. As she had never expressed any wish that I should do so, the unexpected kindness touched her greatly. Through it – as I learnt later – and still more by giving her my 'sweetest smile' at the end of my task, I won her entire confidence . . .

For a long time my place at meditation was near a Sister who behaved very oddly. . . . As soon as she arrived she would make a weird little noise like someone rubbing two sea-shells together. Possibly I alone heard her because of my very sensitive ear (rather too sensitive sometimes), but I cannot tell you to what an extent I was tried by the irritating noise. I was strongly tempted to turn round and with one glance to silence the offender, who of course was not aware of her tic; yet in my heart I knew I ought to bear with her patiently, for the love of God first of all, and also to avoid causing her pain. I therefore remained quiet, but the effort cost me so much that sometimes I started to sweat, and my meditation consisted merely of the prayer of suffering. Finally I sought a way of gaining peace, in my inmost heart at least, and so I tried to find pleasure in the disagreeable noise. Instead of vainly attempting not to hear it, I made myself listen attentively as though it was delightful music, and my meditation (which was not the prayer of 'quiet') was spent in offering this music to our Lord.

On another occasion when I was engaged in the laundry, the Sister opposite to me, who was washing handkerchiefs, kept splashing me continually with dirty water. My first impulse was to draw back and wipe my face in order to show her that I wanted her to be more careful. The next moment, however, I saw the folly of refusing benefits that were offered so generously, and I carefully stopped myself from showing that I was annoyed in any way. On the contrary, I made such efforts to welcome the shower of dirty water that at the end of half an hour I had taken quite a fancy to this novel kind of aspersion. In fact I decided to return as often as possible to the place where such precious treasures were freely bestowed.

Adapted from: Thérèse of Lisieux, *Story of a Soul*, T.N. Taylor, ed. & tr. (London, 1912), pp. 184–7; cf. *Oeuvres Complètes* (Paris, 2001), pp. 274–6.

JESSICA POWERS (Sr Miriam of the Holy Spirit)

Jessica Powers' poem is a statement of compassion, sympathy and understanding for the inadequate, marginalized and excluded.

The Uninvited

There is a city that through time shall lie
in a fixed darkness of the earth and sky;
and many dwell therein this very hour.
It is a city without seed or flower,
estranged from every bird and butterfly.

Who walked these streets of night? I know them well.
Those who come out of life's sequestered places:
the lonely, the unloved, the weak and shy,
the broken-winged who piteously would fly,
the poor who still have starlight in their faces.

They are the outcast ones, the last, the least,
whom earth has not invited to her feast,
and who, were they invited in the end,
finding their wedding clothes too frayed to mend,
would not attend.

From: *The Selected Poetry of Jessica Powers*, Regina Siegfried & Robert Morneau, eds, p. 10 (published by ICS publications, Washington, D.C., 1999) or: Jessica Powers, *The House at Rest* (published by Carmelite Monastery, Pewaukee, WI). Used with permission.

MOTHER MARIBEL OF WANTAGE

During her visits to her Community's houses in Africa and India, Mother Maribel constantly showed her ability to empathize with all sorts and conditions of humanity and with the country's profound religious traditions and their emphasis on so many of the aspects of Christian faith and practice stressed at Wantage. Indeed, her devout aphorisms often have the quality of the quotations from the sages of Eastern religions that encapsulate great wisdom, such as her insistence that 'Silence is not a thing we make; it is something into which we enter . . . Silence is precious for it is of God . . . In silence alone can his voice be heard and his word spoken.' Her last letter to the Sisters for Lent 1935 was written from Poona while she was visiting the Indian Province, and in it she describes her encounter with an old Hindu holy man.

As we talked it was difficult to remember that he was not a Christian. He had a very great love of our Lord and the Saints, especially St Francis. He was deeply distressed by the godlessness and materialism he found in the West, seeing in Christian Religious Communities the chief hope both for the West and for the East, so increasingly influenced by the impact of Western materialism. He asked me to deliver you this message, a message from a Hindu Sadhu to Christian Religious: 'It is not your good works and your activities which India needs. It is your prayer and your life of union with God. Do not be afraid to speak of God and the inner life. Indians expect it of you. They understand'. When I spoke of our British reserve, he said, 'Yes, I know. But it does not really matter whether you speak with your lips. Your inner life betrays itself. Your eyes speak, your expression, your whole bearing. We know; you cannot hide it from us. We are not ungrateful for your works of mercy, but it is hearts aflame with the love of God we need'. What can we do to poke up our dying embers once more till we become flaming souls for love of him?

We do not know what the future holds, but probably the Sadhu is right; we shall be wanted less and less for work and activities, and more and more for witness – everywhere.

Sister Janet CSMV, *Mother Maribel of Wantage* (London, 1972), pp. 65, 70.

SR SANDRA SCHNEIDERS

'The bad news . . . was that by the mid-1960s very few Catholic girls considered religious life and even fewer entered. The good news is that the only real reason, now, for a young woman to enter was that she really felt called by God to a life of consecrated celibacy lived with others who shared this vocation and expressed in a total commitment to the service of God's people . . .'.

Why we stay(ed)

Beginning in the late 1960s and on into the 1980s there was a massive exodus of women from religious life. There were certainly some who left in bitterness and anger at what they considered an alienating and oppressive life of uniformity and repression in which they had somehow become trapped. But the vast majority, many of whom continue to this day to maintain warm relationships with their former Orders and convent classmates, left because they came to realize that they were not called to religious life. Many realized that they were called to marriage and that celibacy was not required for holiness or for engagement in ministry, which was, for many, the main reason they had entered. Others wanted careers, financial independence, or personal autonomy incompatible with religious poverty, obedience, and community. The new theology of vocation and moral freedom and responsibility encouraged by the Council made the once 'unthinkable' (i.e. change of state of life) thinkable. The stigma attached to 'leaving the convent' largely vanished, making the change culturally acceptable. These women, part of the great influx of the 1950s and 1960s, were now in their twenties, thirties, or forties, generally well-educated and professionally prepared for a world and Church that now had much more room for lay women in many areas. Many of the thousands of women who left religious life within a couple decades of entering remain to this day profoundly grateful for the psychological, spiritual, and professional formation they received in religious life. They are not sorry they entered and do not consider their convent experience a 'mistake' or those years 'wasted'. But they are also glad that they realized in time that they were not called to that life and that it was possible for them to follow peacefully God's will in leaving as they had followed that will, as they understood it, when they entered.

The combination of many departures and few entrants has created a 'gap' between age 20 and ages 50–90 in most Orders. This creates problems for women entering today who have few peers and few Religious immediately ahead of them. No one underestimates the seriousness of this situation, and efforts like 'Giving Voice' (a cross-congregational association of younger Religious) and inter-congregational formation programmes are trying to address it. But it is important to realize that neither the exodus from religious life nor the decline in numbers entering was due to a sudden deterioration in the quality of religious life. The change in demographics, in the sociology of the Catholic sub-culture, in theology of states of life and vocation, in roles of women in Church and society, and many other factors we cannot delve into here created the situation with which we are contending today.

That situation, in my opinion and that of most Religious I know, is indeed challenging but not desperate. Nor will it be rectified by a reversion to pre-Conciliar convent lifestyles or disciplinary initiatives of Vatican authorities. The response, which is and will continue to be arduous, lies with those who have stayed.

The ones who stayed

A far more interesting question than who left and why is: 'Why did the ones who stayed, stay?' These are the women who, today, compose the largest cohort in religious life, the 60–80 year olds. This is not only the largest but also the most vibrant group in religious life, flanked at one end with a small number of wonderfully courageous new entrants in their late twenties to forties and, at the other end, by a still numerous group of women in their nineties and beyond who continue to witness with stunning beauty to the joy and fruitfulness of a life totally given to God and God's people. The members of this largest cohort are examples of '80 being the new 60'. Generally in vigorous mental, psychological, and physical health, they have to take time off from full-time ministries to celebrate their 50th and 60th anniversaries in religious life. They are carrying the responsibilities of leadership in their Orders and supporting with indomitable hope and courage the Church-wide but beleaguered effort to keep the spirit and substance of Vatican II from succumbing to the tides of restorationism. These Religious are not hankering for the 'good old days,' for a return to special clothes and titles, instant recognition and elite status in Church and society, and someone to support them, think for them, and keep their life in order in a turbulent world. The real question is, who are these 'stayers' and why did/do they stay?

These women are the contemporaries of those who left in the exodus of the 1970s and 1980s. Like those who left, they were young (twenties to forties), perhaps the best educated group of women in America at the time, professionally precocious, theologically well-grounded, and becoming increasingly interdependently autonomous as women in the Church and world. These Religious were eminently well positioned to leave and had every reason (but one) to do so. They watched in aguish as increasing numbers of their friends made that choice. Religious life had little to offer them, humanly or materially speaking. Orders were losing their big institutions; financial insecurity was becoming a major concern; few were entering. The institutional

Church was repudiating feminism in all its forms; the papacy was engaged in vigorous restorationism; many in and outside the Church, including some in religious life, had resigned themselves to (or rejoiced in) what they saw as 'the death of the Council' or the end of 'renewal.' The exciting theologies of liberation and lay ministerial empowerment in the Church were being repressed in favour of a renewed clericalism and centralization of power. From a strictly human standpoint it was a bleak time for those who had come of age in the joyous, Spirit-filled enthusiasm of the Council when community, equality of discipleship in the Church, commitment to the building of a better world, deepening spirituality, inter-religious dialogue, feminist empowerment were the very air they breathed. From every angle hope was being crushed and old-world narrowness, neo-orthodoxy, and Vatican re-centralization were replacing the Spirit-filled, world-affirming, humane spirit of John XXIII and the Council.

In this crucible the ones who stayed were tested by fire. Elsewhere I have referred to and described in more detail this period as a corporate 'dark night of sense and spirit' for women Religious. They were experiencing a deep purification of any sense of spiritual superiority (to say nothing of arrogant certainty), of elitism, of corporate power and influence, of 'most favoured status' or mysterious specialness in the Church. Their faith was being battered by profound theological tensions raised by the clash between what they most deeply, if obscurely, knew was true and what was happening in the Church and world. They had to find the taproot of their vocation, not in peer-group euphoria, social status, or preferential treatment by the hierarchy, but in the core of their spirituality, face to face with the One to whom they had given their lives in celibate love, in the emptiness of a poverty that was spiritual as well as material, and in an obedience unto the death of everything they cherished, except the God in whom they believed. They found out experientially why Jesus withdrew to the mountains or the desert in the middle of the night and before dawn to pray – not to 'set a good example' for the less spiritual but because he desperately needed God to make it through one more day.

As this cohort of women Religious made its way through the 1990s toward the new millennium, and even as financial and ecclesiastical problems multiplied, a serenity began to surface from the darkness. Even secular sociologists, but especially the laity who associate with these Religious and those they serve, have recognized that the joy and counter-intuitive confidence, the capacity for work and suffering, the whole-hearted commitment to their own spiritual lives and to the people to whom they minister, the unity and solidarity in community that is evident in most women's religious Congregations – given the enormity of the challenges they confront – must be rooted in something, Someone, much deeper and more central to their lives than anything temporal or material.

Some Congregations have had to face their imminent demise and have begun to prepare, not to be passively wiped out by circumstances beyond their control, but, like Archbishop Oscar Romero of El Salvador, to die into Christ's resurrection leaving a legacy that will somehow rise in those they have loved and served. Many Congregations have reconfigured their corporate lives by consolidation or merging or re-founding and are launched into new adventures in a still strange land. Others, though diminished in size and resources, have decided that they can and will make it together into the future and have undertaken vigorous, faith-based strategic planning, including vocation work, to make that happen. But the important thing for our purposes here is that these women are still 'staying' because, in the very core of their being, they do not just 'belong to a religious Order'; they *are* Religious. Hopefully, the present investigation will make evident to those whose concerns gave rise to it the meaning of religious life as it is being envisioned, lived, and handed on today in Congregations renewed in and by that Pentecostal outpouring of the Spirit called the Second Vatican Council.

From: Sandra M. Schneiders, 'Why we stayed', in *Ministries in the Church, Concilium*, 2010, No. 1, pp. 126–30. The article first appeared in the *National Catholic Reporter* and is reprinted by permission.

SR MARTHA ZECHMEISTER-MACHHART

Professor Zechmeister-Machhart tells us that, when she was a young woman, a little book on the religious life by the German theologian of hope and liberation, Johann Baptist Metz, led her to enter the Order to which she still belongs. It also aroused her desire to take the risk of engaging in an evangelically radical way of life, and to commit herself to the dual mystical and political recommendations of the Christian Gospel.

In 1999 I set out for El Salvador for the first time. I was to spend a year there as a teacher and student at the José Simeón Cañas University of Central America (UCA). That is the university where the military murdered six Jesuits and two women on 16 November 1989 because of their commitment to justice and peace . . .

I introduced a sizeable group of theology students, especially young Central American members of men's religious Orders, to the work of Johann Baptist Metz. Although I was inexperienced as far as the real nature of conditions in Latin America was concerned, and my linguistic competence was still very inadequate, it was not long before the students asked me: 'How is it that you understand us and our situation so well even though you are a European, and a woman?' I was faced with this question on several occasions, and tried to get to the bottom of it myself. I came to the conclusion that there was no reason to think that this capacity was attributable to an unusual gift of empathy on my part. I realized that it was actually the basic hermeneutical principles of Metz's theology that made understanding and a meeting of minds possible.

Recognizing the traces of God in the very otherness of other people in spite of any hermeneutics of comprehension or adaptation was certainly the primary and most important aim that made me include Johann Baptist Metz in my intellectual baggage for the visit to El Salvador. When I got there I began to see that if I tried to come to terms with other people, with people of other countries, only on the basis of what I knew already or from other sources, my conception of them would be null and void, and I would do no more than bring myself and my preconceptions to the encounter. But really opening myself up to the unknown, to what was alien and outlandish, definitely called for a fundamental shock and convulsion. It had to be 'dangerous' in Metz's sense. The image that has never left me since that moment of realization is based on geologists' explanation of the origin of earthquakes. It is not at all imaginative but relies on a very real environment. El Salvador is a volcanic region constantly menaced by earthquakes. It was there that I found out for the first time what it feels like when the ground under your feet really starts to quiver threateningly. Experts tell us that the ground is convulsed to this extent when the continental plates collide in the depths of the ocean. That was exactly what happened to me, and I shall never forget it. The result is an immensely powerful and shattering collision of totally different worlds in the depths of one's consciousness, to such a degree that a lot of things collapse that beforehand seemed to guarantee shelter and security. Yet precisely when the first crack appeared in my superficial convictions and assurance, and I realized how vulnerable I was, my experience of authentic encounter began. It is in such moments, I would say, that I begin to sense something of the mystery of God and encounter the 'totally Other' who so affects me in my meeting with those others who are my fellow humans, and in my discovery of another world that is so different from the one I knew before . . .

I remember the *via crucis*, the way of the cross on Good Friday in 'Maria de los pobres', a parish where civil-war refugees were stranded on the periphery of the city in the 1980s. For three hours in the throbbing heat we stumbled rather than walked through this area. The 'main highway' there is a railway line where a goods train thunders directly past people's living quarters twice a day, and regularly claims its victims. If you don't live right by the railway you will be housed where the 'river' descends, and by that I mean the *'agua negra'*, the sewage of the entire city, which stinks so unspeakably as it flows by.

That night there were more than three hundred there, many of them children and young people, praying and singing together, not to forget the dogs who accompanied us loyally all the way to the closing devotions in the church. As those hot and sweaty hours of prayer continued I recalled earlier occasions when I had made the stations of the cross or meditated on the passion during spiritual exercises under others' or my own direction. But what I remembered was an experience of profound individual meditation in an aesthetic environment and peaceful ambiance where I could listen to Bach and contemplate a painting by Grünewald. The contrast between those times and what I was living through in El Salvador could not have been more acute. The stench and noise around me, and all that dust and heat – the more they affected me the more I became aware that if I did not realize under these conditions that Jesus' cross and these people's crosses were related, I was lost. If I couldn't recognize Jesus' cross in the crosses these people had to bear, then its redemptive power was lost on me.

Excerpted from: Martha Zechmeister-Machhart, 'Theology and Biography: a Woman Political Theologian in El Salvador – Evil Today and Struggles to be Human', *Concilium* (London, 2009/1), 39–43.

SR HELEN PREJEAN

Among the humane causes for which Sister Prejean has worked over the years, the most prominent and best-known is that of opposition to the death sentence, primarily in the USA. Her poems, such as 'More is required', assert the importance of the individual responsibility demanded by love. Her letter to Mr Timothy Lockwood is an example of her practical writing on behalf of a specific cause.

More is required

More is required than being swept along –
All the currents pulling me,
Easy and wide in a long, slow drift –
Without rudder, floating backwards, now to the side.
What can one person do against a sucking tide?

I coil like a bow;
I gather like a fist;
I forge like a rudder,
And I lean into the wide, slow drift.

I tack and veer by God's own will.
I raise my voice against the silence.
My voice alone until a chorus joins.

* * *

Make the torture and killing transparent

A Letter about Proposed Amendments to the Lethal Injection
Protocol in California
26 June 2009
To: Mr. Timothy Lockwood, Chief of CDCR Regulation and
Policy Management
From: Sister Helen Prejean, CSJ, 3009 Grand Rt St John #5,
New Orleans, LA

*Public Hearing regarding proposed amendments to Title 15,
Article 7.5, Sections 3349*

Dear Mr Lockwood,

All of my remarks about the proposed amendments to the
lethal injection protocol centre around this theme: KEEP THE
WINDOW OPEN, MAKE THE TORTURE AND KILLING
TRANSPARENT.

Sadly, it is the personal experience I have had of accompanying six human beings to their deaths at the hand of the state that urges me to give this testimony.

KEEP THE WINDOW OPEN as the execution team goes about strapping down the person to be killed and as they insert the intravenous lines, including cut downs that may be necessary if there is difficulty in finding a suitable vein.

KEEP THE WINDOW OPEN during the administration of the poisonous chemicals and as the person is dying, as well as after the person has been killed, as the medical professional verifies the death and as the corpse is put into a body bag and removed. Do not conceal any part of the killing process, and do not hide the identity of the personnel who carry out the killing, including the medical personnel. If we feel no need to protect the identity of legislators who have enacted death as punishment on the statute books or district attorneys who seek and secure death sentences, or juries who sentence people to die or judges who pronounce sentence, why do we hide the identity of those who carry out the killing, including those who concoct and administer the lethal chemicals and the medical personnel who supervise the proceedings?

KEEP THE WINDOW OPEN TO THE MEDIA so the citizens can witness the killings done in their name and which, perhaps, they themselves have called for. Through media coverage, let legislators see the killings they have desired and mandated into law, and require district attorneys who procured the death sentences to witness the killing they sought.

DO NOT KEEP OUR EYES FROM SEEING THE DEATH AGONY of the person being killed by use of a paralytic drug. Are you aware that in hearings about lethal injection, veterinarians have testified that in the euthanasia of animals they no longer use paralytic agents because such drugs prevent them from seeing if the animal is in distress as they are dying? Use of a paralytic agent in the killing of a human being may be the most cowardly act of all. Its sole purpose is to hide the death agony from the eyes of those who witness the death. What if, for whatever reason, the sleeping barbiturate does not take effect? What if those being killed at our hands are fully conscious but, because of paralysis, are unable to move a finger or cry out as the potassium chloride burns through their veins and convulses their heart? If these killings are legitimate and legal, why do we take such pains to shield ourselves from seeing the agony they necessarily entail? The curtain that must be removed is not only the curtain on the window of the execution chamber at San Quentin, it is the curtain masking our own hearts toward these killings of our citizens, which we claim to want, yet are so reluctant to face.

I wrote the books, *Dead Man Walking* and *The Death of Innocents,* and give talks around this nation to bring people face to face with state-sanctioned killing and what it does to us all. May my testimony advance the day when the great state of California will forever consign to a museum the instruments and policies and protocols of state killing that we address today.

From Sister Prejean's website. Used with permission.

SR MARIAN O'SULLIVAN

Sister Marian describes an exemplary, committed individual and communal project to protect a threatened earth.

An Ecology Centre

An Tairseach is a project of the Irish Dominican Congregation, established in Wicklow, Ireland, in 1997. It is an Ecology Centre within the setting of an organic/biodynamic farm and conservation area for wildlife. Its purpose is to educate young and old about life on this beautiful planet that is in danger of extinction ... The name *An Tairseach* (the threshold) implies a hope that we are on the brink of a new era when humans will realize that, while we are intimately connected to the earth, we cannot control earth's processes. We are participants in her life rather than lords of creation.

As Dominicans committed to the search for truth, we have come to believe that we should be raising our awareness about our intimate connection to the earth, about our responsibility to care for this planet, that we should be challenging destructive practices, both of our own and those of others, including the large corporations.

Further challenged by Pope John Paul II's exhortation that, 'Christians in particular [should] realize that their responsibility within creation and their duty towards nature and the Creator are an essential part of their faith' . . . at their 1992 General Chapter the Sisters committed themselves, individually and as a community, to 'support and advance the call to protect the earth' by deepening their own understanding and, by using their skills as educators as well as their resources, to promote this awareness in the wider community. Out of this decision *An Tairseach* was born. The convent in Wicklow, with its seventy-acre farm, offered the ideal location . . .

The first phase involved clearing the land of chemicals (a two-year effort) and conversion to an organic farm system.

To promote thoughtful and life-giving immersion in these surroundings, a programme of activities and rituals was developed to assist people in both mind and heart to be more in tune with the natural rhythm of the seasons. Though we may think that in our modern life we can have warmth and light at the flick of a switch, it is important to realize that we are using up the non-renewable resources of the planet at an alarming rate and that we are utterly dependent on the solar system and particularly our planet Earth for our life, our sustenance, and our health . . . We share the insights of twentieth-century prophets such as Teilhard de Chardin in the West and Sri Aurobindo in the East, who saw the unfolding of the universe is both a physical and spiritual evolution.

To involve the whole body and to engage the deeper aesthetic senses, we use ritual, art, music, and movement to help us internalize our questions and our experience. For example there is the 'cosmic garden', which marks the major moments in the epic of evolution on a spiral on the ground. We invite people to 'walk' this spiral path, to gain some sense of the vastness of the time it took the earth to create first the stars, then the planets including planet Earth, and finally, to burst forth into life itself.

Embracing and suffusing all of these aspects of our programme at *An Tairseach* is the wisdom of the mystics. We reflect upon the insights of Pierre Teilhard de Chardin, Hildegard of Bingen and Julian of Norwich, and with Meister Eckhart, who, echoing Thomas Aquinas, insisted that 'All creatures are the utterance of God'. Nor are these mystical insights foreign to the traditions of our Celtic forebears; they too came to a knowledge of the divine through their intimacy with nature long before God became incarnate in Jesus. In fact, because of this awareness of God's presence in the whole of creation, Irish churches in the early Christian period were very small since worship normally took place out of doors in the presence of nature in spite of inclement weather.

Marian O'Sullivan, '*An Tairseach*: a Dominican Response to Ecological Awareness', *Concilium* (2009/3), issue on eco-theology, 114–8.

Biographies and Bibliographies

ANGELA OF FOLIGNO, Bd (1248–1309)

Italian mystic and Franciscan.

She was born into a rich family, married young and lived luxuriously. In 1285, after her husband's death, she changed her life to one of austerity and devotion, and eventually became a third-order Franciscan. She experienced intense visions, especially of Christ's sufferings. Brother Arnold, her Franciscan confessor, recorded her religious insights and teachings as she dictated them. In her *Book of Divine Consolation,* a masterpiece of early Franciscan piety, Angela describes God's summons to the soul and its ultimately successful quest for him, and stresses the importance of Christ's saving work and eucharistic presence in that progress towards God.

Angela of Foligno, *Liber visionum et instructionum* (Alcalá, 1502); *The Book of Divine Consolation of the Blessed Angela of Foligno,* Mary G. Steegman, tr. (London, 1908–9); *Le Livre des Visions de Sainte Angèle de Foligno,* M.J. Ferré & L. Baudry, eds & tr. (Paris, 1927); *Angela of Foligno, Complete Works,* Paul Lachance, tr. (New York, 1993); L. Leclève, *Sainte Angèle de Foligno* (Paris, 1936).

ANGELIQUE DE SAINT-JEAN ARNAULD D'ANDILLY, Mother (1624–1684)

French nun of Port Royal des Champs, writer, chronicler and autobiographer.

She was a member of the Jansenist Arnauld family. When six years old she was treated as 'already in religion' and was committed to the care of her aunts at Port Royal des Champs. She entered the novitiate in 1641 and took her final vows on 25 January 1644. She was novice-mistress for almost 20 years. In 1652 she began to write secret memoirs of all she could discover about Port Royal and its personalities. She was notably influenced by Pascal and wrote a considerable number of subtly-argued 'conferences' and other works on fundamental and moral theology in the neo-Augustinian tradition, which are now seen as among the most important products of the Port Royal school of thought. She was appointed sub-prioress in 1653. She and her four sisters were strongly opposed to the official formulary imposed on the supposed heretics of Port Royal. She was arrested in August 1664 and held at the convent of the Annonciades until 1665. Angélique wrote an account of her captivity, which was published in 1711 and became a classic of prison and protest literature by women. She refused the sacraments until the Clementine peace of 1669, and was appointed abbess in 1678.

Angélique de Saint-Jean Arnauld d'Andilly, *Aux portes des ténèbres: Relation de captivité*, preface by Sébastien Lapaque, notes by Louis Cognet (Paris [1711], 2005); *Mémoires pour servir à l'histoire de Port Royal; et à la vie de la Révérende Mère Marie Angélique de Sainte Magdeleine Arnauld, Réformatrice de ce Monastère* (Utrecht, 1742); *Lettres de la mère Angélique de S. Jean à Mr. Arnaud, écrites depuis que la communauté fut transférée à Port-Royal des Champs jusqu'à la paix de l'Église* (n.p., 1600–99); *Les Ecrivains de Port-Royal*, Maurice Catel, ed. (Paris, 1962).

ANNA KATHARINA EMMERICK (Anne Catherine Emmerich), Bd (1774–1824)

German nun, mystic, mystical muse and stigmatic.

She was born into a big family in the farming community of Flamsche, Coesfeld, Germany. She helped in the house and on the farm, and later for three years on a neighbouring farm. She received very little education yet would seem to have learned a great deal about religion and was exceptionally devout from an early age. She wanted to enter a convent, and applied to many religious houses, but was rejected, usually because she had no dowry. Finally the Poor Clares of Münster accepted her on condition that she learned to play the organ. The local organist agreed to train her but her family's poverty made this impossible. Eventually, in 1802, Anna and her friend Klara Söntgen entered the Agnetenberg convent in Dülmen and she took her religious vows in 1803. Her fellow-nuns had no respect for her peasant background, enthusiasm and willingness to work hard. She was often in pain from an obscure illness. The convent was secularized in 1811. Anna became a priest's housekeeper but was soon so sick that she was confined to bed and her younger sister took over the housekeeping. The fact that she had had the stigmata (or bleeding replicas of the wounds of Christ) on her body for some time was now revealed. The young Dr Franz Wesener was impressed by her and became a faithful friend for 11 years during which he kept a diary about his meetings with Anna. She welcomed visitors, many of them well-known people of the day, whom she often encouraged spiritually. She had an almost hypnotic power to engage the devotion of certain people. The Romantic poet, dramatist, writer of tales and novelist Clemens Brentano (1778–1842) stayed in Dülmen for five years and appointed himself soul-companion and amanuensis to Anna. He gave up creative writing to record Anna's visions, which she related in the Westphalian dialect. Brentano's transcriptions into standard German eventually amounted to 40 volumes. Some were published without Brentano's name during his lifetime, and others, duly ascribed to him, after his death. Anna grew much weaker in 1823 and died in February 1824. Brentano said: 'She stands like a cross by the wayside'. He produced no more work after her death. The theologian Hans Urs von Balthasar said: 'She brought her friendship with God to bear in solidarity with humankind.' She was beatified by Pope John Paul II on 3 October 2004. The physical particularity of her visions of, e.g., Christ's suffering or Mary's house, has always been controversial and delayed her beatification for many years. Anna and, more especially, Brentano have been accused of anti-Semitism. Her extraordinarily graphic visions are popular with traditionalist and, some would say, fundamentalist Catholics.

Clemens Brentano, *Das bittere Leiden unseres Herrn Jesu Christi. Nach den Betrachtungen der gottseligen Anna Katharina Emmerich* (Regensburg,

1833); Anna Catherine Emmerich, *The Dolorous Passion of Our Lord Jesus Christ* (Rockford, Ill., 1983); id., *The Life of the Blessed Virgin Mary: From the Visions of Anna Catherine Emmerich* (Rockford, Ill., 1970); id., *The Bitter Passion and the Life of Mary: From the Visions of Anna Catherine Emmerich: As Recorded in the Journals of Clemens Brentano* (Fresno, Calif., 1954); Thomas Wegener, *Life of Sister Anna Katherina Emmerich* (New York, 1898); Karl Schmoger, *Life of Anna Katherina Emmerich* (Rockford, Ill., 1974); Hartwig Schulz, *Clemens Brentano* (Stuttgart, 1999).

ANNA VAN SCHURMAN (1607–1678)

German-Dutch thinker, commentator, writer, artist and sister in, and joint inspiration of, a pioneering religious community.

Anna van Schurman was born into a wealthy family in Cologne, Germany. After her father's death in 1613, she moved to Utrecht, the Netherlands, with her mother. In 1636 she was the first woman to study at Utrecht University but had to hide behind a curtain lest male students should see her. She graduated in law. She practised engraving, sculpture, wax modelling, and ivory and wood carving, and painted portraits. She was a singularly well-educated and devout Protestant who wrote about education for women and defended their right to develop their knowledge and intellect. She was visited and consulted by Queen Christina of Sweden and corresponded with other eminent religious and political figures. In the course of her self-education she went through various phases of mystical speculation. She was neither a Catholic nor a professed nun but, towards the end of her life, joined a contemplative religious sect founded by the former Jesuit Jean de Labadie, who gave his name to 'Labadism', a quasi-mystical offshoot of Catholicism that preached the importance of communal property. For some time, the Labadist communities of brothers and sisters which Anna joined under the guidance of the master himself, and which eventually benefited from her own powerful influence, were of great interest to prominent Quakers as their practice seemed to complement their own. She defended her decision to join Labadie in *Eucleria*, an autobiographical, theological and philosophical treatise in Latin and Greek. The group went to Amsterdam, then to Altona

(Denmark, now Germany), where Jean de Labadie died in 1674, then to Wiewerd, Friesland, where Anna died.

Anna van Schurman, *Nobiliss. virginis Annae Mariae à Schurman Opuscula Hebraea, Graeca, Latina, Gallica: prosaica & metrica* (Trajecti ad Rhenum [Utrecht 3rd ed.], 1648, ³1652); id., *De Vitae Humanae Termino* (medical ethics textbook) (1639); id., *The Learned Maid or Whether a Maid may be a Scholar (or Whether the study of letters is Fitting for a Christian Woman)*. *A logick exercise* (London, 1641, 1659); id., *Opuscula* (correspondence) (1642); id., *Eukleria seu Melioris partis electio: Tractatus brevem vitae eius delineationem exhibens* (Altonae ad Albim [Altona], 1673); *Whether a Christian Woman Should Be Educated and Other Writings from Her Intellectual Circle*, Anna Maria van Schurman, Joyce Irwin, ed. & tr. (Chicago, 1999); *Choosing the Better Part. Anna Maria van Schurman (1607–1678)*, Mirjam de Baar *et al.*, eds (Dordrecht, Boston & London, 1996).

ANNE DE MARQUETS (*c*.1533–1586)

French Dominican nun, poet and spiritual writer.

She was born into a noble Norman family in the Comté d'Eu. When nine or ten she entered the prestigious royal monastery at Poissy, where she was taught by the humanist printer and publisher Henri Estienne. She was unusually well educated for a girl of the time, and had fluent Greek and Latin. She took final vows in 1548–9, remained cloistered until her death, and became an accomplished writer of largely devotional and polemical, i.e. pro-Catholic and essentially anti-Hugenot, verse showing the influence of Counter-Reformation theology and meditation techniques, mainly in the vernacular, including several hundred sonnets. She met and possibly corresponded with Ronsard and other eminent poets. Her poetry shows her considerable knowledge of Scripture, the liturgy and theology, but also her far from submissive attitude to male cultural dominance. She has been called a proto-feminist. She lost her sight later in life and dictated many poems. Her works were first circulated in manuscript versions. Some were published in various editions in her lifetime (her first collection was *Sonets, prières et devises*, 1562, dedicated to Charles, Cardinal of Lorraine), including translations of Marc Antonio Flaminio's neo-Latin verse. Some of her most original creations were published by her sister after Anne's death.

Because she was a woman and a nun, the qualities and importance of her poems were not acknowledged for many years.

Anne de Marquets, *Sonets spirituels, de feue tres-vertueuse et tres-docte Dame Sr. Anne des Marquets, Religieuse de Poissi* (Paris, 1605); id., *Sonets spirituels*, Gary Ferguson, ed. (Geneva, 1997); Sister Mary Hilarine Seiler, *Anne de Marquets, poétesse religieuse du XVIe* (Washington, DC, 1931); Terence Cave, *Devotional Poetry in France c. 1570–1613* (London, 1969); Russell Ganim, 'Variations on the Virgin: Anne de Marquets's Depiction of Mary in the *Sonets Spirituels*,' in R.G. Hodgson, ed., *La femme au XVIIe siècle* (Tübingen, 2002), 407–17.

ANNE OF ST BARTHOLOMEW, Bd (Ana Garcia) (1549–1626)

Spanish Carmelite nun born at Almendral, Castille.

She was the child of peasants who died when she was ten. She was a shepherdess until she was 20. She resisted the pressure put on her to marry by her brothers and in 1572 made her profession as the first lay sister of the Reformed Carmelites under St Teresa, at St Joseph's, Avila, the saint's first reformed Carmel, to which she had been admitted in 1570. From 1575 to 1582 she accompanied Teresa on most of her journeys, learned to read and write to act as Teresa's secretary, and later became her nurse. After Teresa's death Anne remained at Avila for six years but in 1588 she went with the saint's successor, Sister Anne. of Jesus, and four others to establish a Discalced Carmelite house in Paris. She started to prepare meals but was persuaded to become a choir nun and was eventually appointed prioress at Pontoise, then Tours, and in 1612 began her own foundation at Antwerp, now Belgium. She met with many difficulties often arising from differences of social class between herself and other 'superior' nuns. She wrote an autobiography, was said to have protected the city when it was besieged by the forces of the Calvinist Prince of Orange, and was held in such great esteem for her holiness and her association with the great Teresa that 20,000 people came to view her body when she died in Antwerp. She was beatified by Pope Benedict XV in 1917.

Blessed Mother Anne of Saint Bartholomew, *Autobiography*, Marcel Bouis, SJ, ed., a Religious of the Carmel of St Louis, tr. (St Louis, Mo., 1916); *La Vie et les instructions de la Ven. Mère Anne de S. Barthelemy, par un solitaire de Montaigne* (Brussels, 1708; new ed., Paris, 1895).

BEATRICE (Beatrix) of Nazareth, Bd (Beatrijs van Nazareth) (1200–1268)

Dutch or Flemish Cistercian nun, prioress, contemplative and illuminator.

She was born the youngest of six children in a wealthy family near Leuven (now in Belgium). Her mother died when she was seven. She was sent to live in a community of Beguines, and was educated there and at a local school. After a year she went home and her father responded to her interest in the religious life by taking her at age ten to a Cistercian monastery at Bloemendaal/Florival. When 16, she became a novice there and was professed in 1216. She learned how to write manuscripts and choir-books at La Ramée monastery and directed work on the still extant 'Beatrice of Nazareth Choir-Book'. After meeting the Cistercian mystic Ida of Nivelles, Beatrice developed her spiritual life and codified her mystical experiences. She moved to a monastery at Maagdendal and then, accompanied by her own sisters, to Our Lady of Nazareth near Lier in Brabant. Here she became prioress and wrote a spiritual journal and then *The Seven Ways of Divine Love (Seven Manieren van Heilige Minnen; De septem modis sancti amoris)*, originally composed in the Dutch vernacular, about the soul's journey of purification and transformation on its way back to God who made it, and with a clear debt of inspiration (if not exposition) to Bernard of Clairvaux, as well as (it is said) other devotional help-books drawn from her own intense experience of stages and growth in the inward life. She is said to have practised such physical austerities as wearing a girdle of thorns, and to have received a form of stigmata during Mass. Beatrice was not a Beguine, although she has been classified as one, along with Hadewijch of Brabant, Mechthild of Magdeburg, and similar medieval contemplatives.

Beatrijs van Nazareth, *Seven manieren van minne*, R. Faesen, ed. (Kapellen, 1999); id., *Vita Beatricis/The Life of Beatrice of Nazareth*, Roger De Ganck, ed. & tr. (Kalamazoo, Mich., 1991); Chrysostomus Henriquez, *Lilia Cistercii* (Douai, 1633); E. A. Petroff, *Medieval Women's Visionary Literature* (Oxford, 1986), esp. pp. 200–6; F. Bowie, *Beguine Spirituality* (London, 1989); Michael Casey, *Sacred Reading: The ancient art of lectio divina* (Liguori, Miss., 1996).

BERNADETTE of Lourdes, St (1844–79)

French nun and visionary.

Bernadette Soubirous was a poor, minimally-educated miller's daughter, born at Lourdes in the Hautes-Pyrénées region of France. On several occasions in 1858, while she was tending sheep on the mountainside, our Lady appeared and talked to her. Among other 'instructions,' Mary told Bernadette to strike a certain spot where water began to gush out. The water apparently had great healing power and miracles were acclaimed. At first there was great excitement but also much scepticism at Bernadette's revelations. An enquiry was held, which resulted in Rome declaring that the apparitions were genuine. Bernadette became a sister of Notre Dame in 1866 and lived a life of pious obscurity. Her reports and the apparitions inspired a movement of intense devotion, prayer and pilgrimage that spread throughout France, Europe and the world. Although this particular kind of piety faded gradually from World War I onwards, Bernadette was beatified and canonized, and Lourdes remains one of the world's great healing shrines and centres of pilgrimage.

Lourdes, Documents authentiques, R. Laurentin, B. Billet & P. Galland, eds (Paris, 1958ff); *Les Ecrits de Sainte Bernadette et sa voie spirituelle*, A. Ravier, SJ, ed. (Paris, 1961); *Logia de Bernadette*, vols I, II, III, R. Laurentin & M.-T. Bourgeade, eds (Paris, 1971); F.P. Keyes, *Bernadette of Lourdes* (London, 1953); Francis Trochu, *Sainte Bernadette Soubirous* (London, 1957); L.J.M. Cros & P.M. Olphe-Galliard SJ, *Lourdes 1858* (Paris, 1957); R. Laurentin, *Bernadette of Lourdes* (London, 1979); A. Ravier, *Bernadette Soubirous* (Paris, 1979); Ruth Harris, *Lourdes* (London, 1999).

CATHERINE DEI RICCI, St (Alessandra Lucrezia Romola de'Ricci) (1522–90)

Italian nun, stigmatist and ecstatic mystic.

She was born into a prominent family in Florence and entered the Dominican convent of St Vincent at Prado (where her uncle was director) at the age of 13. While still very young she became novice-mistress, then sub-prioress, and was elected prioress in 1552. She became famous for her extraordinary mystical experiences, particularly for the series of ecstatic trances, renewed weekly for 12 years (1542–54), during which she watched and enacted scenes from the Lord's Passion. Crowds of people came to see these manifestations and she asked the nuns to pray that they would stop, which eventually happened. She received the stigmata, and was also said to have been given a ring that some claimed was placed upon her left forefinger by Christ as evidence of her spiritual marriage. St Philip Neri, among others, was convinced that she was capable of bilocation. Obviously she was so impressive and intense an individual that a letter or thought of hers could seem like her presence. In everyday affairs she was a capable administrator, and exercised a wide and beneficent influence all around her. She was a superbly optimistic and helpful correspondent.

F.M. Capes, *St Catherine dei Ricci: her Life, her Letters, her Community* (London, 1905); J. Petrie, *St Catherine de'Ricci: Sources* (London, 1985).

CATHERINE of Siena, St (1347–80)

Italian Dominican tertiary and Doctor of the Church.

Caterina Benincasa was born in Siena as the 23rd of a wealthy dyer's 25 children. She made a vow of perpetual virginity for Jesus' sake when she was 12. When 16, she became a Dominican lay sister. After three years of seclusion at home, she decided to devote herself, together with a 'family' of men and women, clerics and lay folk, to looking after the sick and poor and converting sinners. She was an extraordinarily effective and assertive woman in an age when women had little scope for self-expression. She was soon asked to mediate in disputes between local groups, and even Florence and the Holy See. Members of her 'family' travelled with her on her diplomatic missions. She dictated an immense number of letters on behaviour and public affairs, such as a crusade against the Turks and the Great Schism, of which 383 survive. Major topics of her writings are the unity of the Church and the crucified Christ, especially the concept of his Blood, which she presented as the main sign of God's love and the reason for our own reciprocation of it. She helped to persuade Pope Gregory XI to move the papacy from Avignon to Rome in 1377, indeed, demanded that he should return to Rome. She died on 29 April 1380, aged 33. Many commentators say this was a result of the agony she suffered over the Great Schism.

S. Catherine of Siena, *Dialogo,* G. Cavallini, ed. (Rome, 1968); id., *La Verità dell'Amore* [sel. letters], G. Cavallini, ed. (Rome, 1978); *I, Catherine,* K. Foster, OP & M.J. Ronayne, OP tr. & ed. (London, 1980) *The Letters of St Catherine of Siena,* S. Noffke, OP tr. & ed. (New York, 1988).

CECILE Bruyère, Mother (Jeanne-Henriette Bruyère [Jenny]) (1845–1909)

French abbess, founder and spiritual instructor.

She was born into a wealthy Parisian family; her grandfather was the architect of the Madeleine church. In 1870, under the guidance of Dom Prosper Guéranger, founder of Solesmes Abbey and responsible for reviving the French Benedictine tradition, she established the first women's community in his Congregation. She became the first abbess of St Cecilia's Abbey, Solesmes, where the nuns learned Latin and Gregorian chant. In the early twentieth century, the Government's onslaught on religious orders sent them into exile at St Cecilia's Abbey, Ryde, Isle of Wight, where she died. The nuns were allowed to return to France in 1921, and her body was reburied in Solesmes. In her *Spiritual Life and Prayer in accordance with Scripture and Monastic Tradition*, she combines Guéranger's and patristic teaching with her own spiritual thought in a scheme of instruction for nuns seeking perfection in the Benedictine way that stresses tradition, the sacraments, the liturgy and the role of the Church.

Mère Cécile Bruyère, *La vie spirituelle et l'oraison, d'après la Sainte Ecriture et la tradition monastique* (Solesmes, 1899).

CLARE of Assisi, St (1193–1253)

Italian Franciscan and founder.

Clare was born into what was probably a rich family in an aggressive world of people on the make. She resisted pressures to marry early in life. When 18, she was inspired by the preaching of St Francis and his message of ardent love for God and the transfiguration of all creation by divine radiance, adoption of radical poverty, and contempt for a world of power and glory. She ran away from home, abandoned all her possessions to become a nun, and was housed temporarily in a Benedictine convent. Her friends and relations tried to drag her away but she resisted and was taken to another nunnery, where her sister joined her. She became superior of a new convent near the church of San Damiano, on the outskirts of Assisi. She was joined there by her mother and others. St Francis wrote a first Rule for the nuns, who led a remarkably austere life of extreme self-denial. Within a few years Poor Clare monasteries were founded in several countries, among them Bohemia, where Blessed Agnes of Prague took the habit and received letters from Clare. Clare was the first woman to write a Rule for other women. The Pope tried to reduce the degree of poverty of Clare's nuns, but eventually some houses were allowed to live by alms alone. Clare governed her convent for 40 years and is said never to have left it. She was celebrated as a great saint in her own lifetime and was canonized in 1255.

H. Roggen, *L'Esprit de Sainte Claire* (Paris, 1969); M. Bartoli, *Clare of Assisi* (London, 1994); *The Legend and Writings of St Clare of Assisi* (St Bonaventure, NY, 1953); *Francis and Clare: the complete works*, J. Armstrong & I. Brady, eds & trs (New York, 1982); M. D. Lambert, *Franciscan Poverty* (London, 1961); id., *Medieval Heresy* (London, 1992).

EGERIA of Spain (late fourth century AD)

Religious superior, pilgrim and devotional travel writer.

Egeria (or Etheria) was a devout woman of the late fourth century or early fifth century who is generally supposed to have been a nun, and was most probably the superior of a community of women religious in Spain or Gaul. She made a pilgrimage in 381–4 to the Holy Land, Egypt, Asia Minor and Constantinople, identified several sites associated with major events described in the Old Testament, and visited churches built on or close to the presumed sites of important New Testament events, such as the finding of the Cross. She wrote a *Peregrinatio*, or account of her pilgrimage, presumably for the edification of her community, and included details not only of these holy places, but of her reception by local churchpeople and of various liturgical practices. The (eleventh-century) manuscript in an unusual Latin dialect was discovered at Arezzo in 1884. Eventually, the author was identified with some degree of probability as the Egeria (or Etheria) already known from the work of the seventh-century northern Spanish monk Valerius. The text is written with the authority, concern and intelligence proper to an *amma* or spiritual guide and 'mother' that allow us to classify Egeria as a 'desert mother'.

The Pilgrimage of Etheria, M.I. McClure & C.L. Feltoe, eds (London, 1919); *Pilgrimage of Egeria*, J. Wilkinson, ed. & tr. (Jerusalem & Warminster, 1981); H. Sivan, 'Who was Egeria? Pilgrimage and Piety in the Age of Gratian', *Harvard Theological Review*, 81 (1988), 59–72; Mary Forman, *Praying with the Desert Mothers* (Collegeville, Minn., 2005).

ELIZABETH A. JOHNSON, CSJ, Sr (1941–)

American nun, teacher, author, editor, lecturer.

She is a member of the Sisters of St Joseph of Brentwood, New York, a public lecturer in theology, a former president of the Catholic Theological Society of America and of the ecumenical American Theological Society, and a member of the editorial boards of *Theological Studies, Horizons: Journal of the College Theology Society*, and *Theoforum*. She has received numerous awards including: the annual *U.S. Catholic Award* for promoting the cause of women in the Church, 1994; the Sacred Universe Award of the environmental group SpiritEarth for promoting care for the Earth, 1999; the Monika Hellwig Award for promoting the intellectual life of Catholics, 2006; the Myser Award for promoting Catholic identity, 2008; the Sophia Award for excellence in theology at the service of ministry.

She has written many books and articles. Her *She Who Is: The Mystery of God in Feminist Theological Discourse* was given the Grawemeyer Award in Religion, 1992, and other citations, and her books include: *Friends of God and Prophets: A Feminist Reading of the Communion of Saints,* which received an American Academy of Religion Award for Excellence in the Study of Religion, 1999; *The Church Women Want, Truly Our Sister: A Theology of Mary in the Communion of Saints,* and *Quest for the Living God: Mapping Frontiers in the Theology of God,* all of which received awards and citations.

EMMANUELLE, Sr (born Madeleine Cinquin) (1908–2008)

French nun, writer, humanitarian and social missionary.

A member of the Congregation of Notre-Dame of Sion. Born in Brussels, the daughter of a family of lingerie manufacturers. When she was six she saw her father drown. In 1980 she founded the Asmae-Association Sœur Emmanuelle, to fight poverty and homelessness in a number of countries including Egypt, Sudan, the Philippines and India. Sœur Emmanuelle became a very popular figure with the French public because of her humanitarianism, her frank and outspoken views and her vibrant personality.

Sœur Emmanuelle, *Chiffonnière avec les chiffonniers* (1977); *La Foi des chiffonniers* (1988); *Le Paradis, c'est les autres, entretiens avec Marlène Tuininga* (1995); *Jésus tel que je le connais,* with Marlène Tuininga (1996); *Yalla, en avant les jeunes!,* with Philippe Asso (1997); *Richesse de la pauvreté,* with Philippe Asso (2001); *Vivre, à quoi ça sert?,* with Philippe Asso (2004); *Confessions d'une religieuse* (2008).

ESTHER, Sr (born Emma Caroline Silcock) (1858–1931)

Australian Anglican nun, social pioneer and founder.

Sister (as she was generally known, but more properly Mother) Esther was the daughter of a Norfolk shopkeeper. She was baptized an Anglican in 1877 and joined the Community of St Mary the Virgin, Wantage, in 1884, worked for a year in the London slums, damaged her back, and was sent to Australia to recover. She joined a Church of England 'Mission to the Streets and Lanes' of the terrible slums concealed behind the facades of the wealthy city of Melbourne and gradually built a community of women initially centred on a rat-infested house opposite a brothel. They visited homes, factories, prisons and hospitals, and cared for drunk and drugged women of the streets. In spite of much opposition, Emma eventually founded the Community of the Holy Name as a genuinely Australian Order which fed hundreds of poor people, worked indefatigably among all sorts and conditions of folk, ran schools and free dispensaries, built children's and babies' homes and hospitals and, by the time of Mother Esther's death, had nine community houses in two States. She and her nuns did much to enhance the novel reputation of the Anglican Church in Australia as a body with classless concerns that belied its perceived status as the official church of the middle and upper classes.

Sister Elizabeth, *Esther, Mother Founder of the Community of the Holy Name* (Melbourne, 1949); L. Strachan, *Out of the Silence* (Melbourne, 1988); John W. Stewart, 'Sister Esther: An Anglican Saint', in *The Melbourne Anglican* (September, 2001); Peter Joliffe, 'Silcock, Emma Caroline (1858–1931)', *Australian Dictionary of Biography*, vol. 11 (Melbourne, 1988), pp. 606–7.

GENEVIEVE Gallois, Mother (1888–1962)

French Benedictine nun, painter, engraver, and stained-glass designer.

She studied art at the Académie des Beaux-Arts in Paris. In 1917, although known for her anti-clerical views, she astonished her friends by abandoning a promising artistic career to join an order of Benedictine nuns at Saint-Louis-du-Temple, 20 rue Monsieur, Paris, where she produced figurative religious drawings and engravings but above all stained glass of great originality. Admirers of her work have classed it alongside that of Rouault for intensity of vision and colouration based on years of close observation of people and thought about the nature of the human condition.

Sœur Geneviève Gallois, *The Life of Little Saint Placid* (New York, 1956); Noël Alexandre, *Mère Geneviève Gallois: Bénédictine, peintre, graveur, verrier* (Brussels, 1999).

GERTRUDE of Helfta, St (St Gertude the Great) (1256–1301/2)

German prioress, visionary, mystic and devotional writer

She was born in Eisleben, Upper Saxony. When she was five she was placed with the nuns to whom she was 'offered' in the Benedictine abbey of Rodarsdorf, Thuringia (which moved to Helfta later). She was a diligent and scholarly student with very good Latin, studied philosophy and theology, and came under the influence of the abbess's sister, St Mechthild. She reported privileged revelations of Jesus Christ from her twenty-sixth year. Her first visions were of Jesus as a boy of 16 reproaching her for neglecting prayer in favour of study. For the most part, her mystical experiences occurred during divine worship; their language was influenced by liturgical offices, and by the Song of Songs and St John the Divine. Of the five books entitled the *Insinuations of the Divine Goodness (Legate of Divine Love* or *Revelations of St Gertrude)*, the second was written by Gertrude herself and the first, third and fourth were compiled by Helfta nuns on the basis of manuscripts which Gertrude was said to have written following God's instructions. The fifth contains accounts of her last illness and death, and of other associated events. She wrote a popular book of prayers and described intense devotions to the Sacred Heart of Jesus and to our Lady. Gertrude's works had an immense influence on many mystics and religious writers, such as St Teresa of Avila and St Francis of Sales. She was elected prioress in 1294 and held the position for 40 years. She was canonized by 'acclamation' but her feast was officially authorized.

The Exercises of St Gertrude, Virgin and Abbess, of the Order of St Benedict (London, 1863); *Gertrude of Helfta. The Herald of Divine Love*, Margaret Winkworth, ed. (New York, 1993).

HADEWIJCH (fl.1230–50)

Flemish poet, mystic and visionary.

Hadewijch lived in the Duchy of Brabant in the second quarter of the thirteenth century and wrote in the local dialect. Her *Visions* and letters seem to show that she was a Beguine. She was well-educated, and knew the Latin Bible, theology, and some French romantic works. She writes for those (presumably Beguines) who wish to know how to unite their souls with a loving God who is greater than all possibilities of possession and union. Her letters were cited by Ruysbroeck in the fourteenth century and were translated into High German. Some manuscripts were definitively ascribed to her in the early nineteenth century. The authorship of some poems formerly (and some still) attributed to her is uncertain. She described the main figures in the contemporary religious development of most interest to her, and provided a list of 138 perfect models of the love of God. These were anchorites and anchoresses from the area between Paris and Saxony.

Het Visionenboek van Hadewijch, P.H. Vekeman, ed. (Nijmegen & Bruges, 1979); Hadewich, *Lettres spirituelles* (Geneva, 1971); Hadewijch, *The Complete Works*, Mother Columba Hart OSB, tr. & ed. (New York & London, 1980); J. B. Porion, *Hadewijch d'Anvers* (Paris, 1954).

HELEN PREJEAN CSJ, Sr (1939–)

American nun, teacher, adviser and activist.

She is a member of the Sisters of St Joseph of Medaille. A teacher and educationalist, she is also a spiritual adviser to condemned criminals, author, campaigner, speaker and a leading advocate for the abolition of the death penalty in the USA. She founded 'Survive', an organization dedicated to counselling the families of victims of violence. She has received numerous honorary doctorates and awards including the Pax Christi USA Pope Paul VI Teacher of Peace Award (1996) and the World Methodist Peace Award (2008). She is the author of *Dead Man Walking*, an autobiographical account of her relationship with Sonnier and other inmates on death row, and *The Death of Innocents: An Eyewitness Account of Wrongful Executions* (2004).

HILDEGARD of Bingen (1098–1179)

German abbess, healer, counsellor, poet, theologian and mystic prophetess.

When she was eight, Hildegard was dedicated to the religious life, and entered a small Benedictine monastery close to her home. She proved to be a ready learner and assimilated a vast amount of Scripture, theology, natural science, cosmology, and medical and natural lore which gradually bore fruit in the form of practical, theoretical and mystico-literary works. She was an influential nun and her sisters elected her abbess in 1136. Eventually she moved her community to Rupertsberg near Bingen, where she built a much larger convent. She became a religious adviser to powerful people and a counsellor to all sorts and conditions of men and women. Her writing covers an immense variety of subjects from hagiography, through sermons, medicine, marital and sexual recommendations, to natural history. She was a fine poet and composed liturgical music. She is mainly celebrated for her visionary works.

The Life and Visions of St. Hildegarde, Francisca Maria Steele, ed. & tr. (London, 1914); Heinrich Schipperges, *The World of Hildegard of Bingen: Her Life, Times and Visions*, J. Cumming, tr. (London, 1997); Renate Craine, *Hildegard, Prophet of the Cosmic Christ* (New York, 1997).

HROSWITHA (or Hrosvit) of Gandersheim (*c.*935–*c.*1000)

German poet, dramatist, hagiographer and moralist.

Hroswitha was born to a noble Christian family early in the tenth century. She was probably very young when she entered the highly selective and prestigious abbey at Gandersheim, in

Saxony, which was reserved for aristocrats' daughters. Eventually, she became a canoness, having taken vows of celibacy and obedience, but not poverty. Gandersheim was a much-respected abbey with a strong reputation for education and the devotional life, and Hroswitha's writings show a wide-ranging knowledge of Latin classics and Scripture, and an ability to manipulate literary genres and formal structures. Gandersheim maintained an army and a court for legal disputes, and produced its own coinage. Hroswitha cherished her writing ability, which she devoted to morally improving yet stylistically and structurally interesting verse, dramas and tales, in which firmly upheld chastity was a recurrent topic.

Hroswitha of Gandersheim, *Plays*, Katharina M. Wilson, ed. & tr. (Saskatoon, 1986; rev. ed., New York & London, 1989); A.L. Haight, ed. *Hroswitha of Gandersheim* (New York, 1965); Peter Dronke, *Women Writers of the Middle Ages* (Cambridge, 1984); K.M. Wilson, *Hroswitha of Gandersheim* (Leiden, 1988).

JEANNE-FRANÇOISE DE CHANTAL, St (Jeanne-Françoise Frémyot de Chantal; Jane Frances de Chantal) (1572–1641)

French founder and spiritual writer.

She was born into an aristocratic family in Dijon, France. In 1592 her father married her to Christophe de Rabutin, Baron de Chantal. She had four children. She came into contact with the main trends of mysticism that developed in French Catholicism after the Tridentine reforms. After the Baron's death in a hunting accident in 1601, with the help of St. Francis de Sales, Bishop of Geneva (her spiritual director from 1604), she established the Order of the Visitation of the Virgin Mary at Annecy in 1610. In spite of much opposition, she founded 87 convents in her own lifetime. The Order welcomed widows and women whom other Orders rejected because of ill-health. St Jeanne experienced periods of mystical dryness and spiritual anxiety which increased on the death of Francis de Sales in 1622, when she sought the help of St Vincent de Paul and later that of Saint-Cyran. Jeanne was a very sensitive person who led a mystical prayer-life which she was reluctant to describe in great detail. She was an influential spiritual director, encouraged mental prayer, and discouraged excessive demonstrations of mystical experience. She was suspected for a time of Jansenist sympathies and Quietism. She was a constant practitioner of her charitable ideals and ensured that the needs of her Order were met. She was beatified in 1751 and canonized in 1767.

Sainte J.F. Frémyot de Chantal: Sa vie et ses oeuvres, F.-M. de Chaugy, ed., 8 vols (Paris, 1874–9); *The Spirit of St Jane de Chantal*, Sisters of the Visitation, tr. (London, 1933), E. Stopp, *Saint Jane Frances de Chantal* (London, 1962); R.P. Mezard, *Doctrine spirituelle de Sainte Jeanne-Françoise de Chantal* (Paris, 1980); A. Ravier, *Jeanne-Françoise Frémyot, baronne de Chantal* (Paris, 1983); Marie-Claire Bussat-Enevoldsen, *Le voile et la plume – Jeanne de Chantal – François de Sales* (Paris, 2010).

JEANNE de Jussie (1503–61)

Swiss Poor Clare, chronicler and perceptive commentator on religio-historical events.

She was born into a noble family and entered the Poor Clare (Franciscan) convent in Geneva when she was 18. She was appointed scribe to the convent with responsibility for written relations with the city and the world outside the enclosed community. Her chronicle of the clash between Protestantism and Catholicism in sixteenth-century Geneva, and then its transition from rule by the Duke of Savoy to a Protestant republic in 1535 (leading to Calvin's takeover in 1536), was not published until 1611. Jeanne was an acute observer of extra-religious political and social unrest as well as of the psychological effects of severe events (such as the iconoclasts' destruction of religious art and artefacts before the nuns' eyes, threats of brutality, enforced marriage, rape and cruel expulsion) on the larger and on her own special community, but also on different emotional types within them. She had a journalist's sense of the dramatic, and sometimes an appreciation of the incongruous and ridiculous that approaches modernist narrative techniques, yet is always controlled by her far from superficial, if understandably partisan, comprehension of the theological and ethical questions involved. Her descriptions imply a distinction between psychological and

spiritual aspects of group and individual reactions to external
events that is rarely met with in the writings of nuns schooled in
narrative restraint.

*Le Levain du Calvinisme, ou commencement de l'héresie de Genève, faict par
Reuerende Soeur Ieanne de Iussie, suivi de notes justificatives et d'une notice
sur l'Ordre religieux de Sainte-Claire et sur la communauté des Clarisses à
Genève*, Ad.-C. Grivel, ed. (Geneva, 1865); Jeanne de Jussie, *Petite Chro-
nique. Einleitung, Edition, Kommentar*, Helmut Feld, ed. (Mainz, 1996);
*Jeanne de Jussie: The Short Chronicle. A Poor Clare's Account of the Ref-
ormation of Geneva*, Carrie F. Klaus, tr. (Chicago & London, 2006); *The
Cloister and the World: Early Modern Convent Voices*, T.M. Carr Jr, ed.
(Charlottesville, Va., 2007).

JESSICA POWERS (Sr Miriam of the Holy Spirit)
(1905–1988)

American Carmelite nun, poet and mystic.

Jessica was born in Mauston, Wisconsin, USA. While still in grade
school she was encouraged by one of her teachers, a Dominican Sister, to write poetry. Later she was enrolled in the school
of journalism at Marquette University in Milwaukee, WI. She
began to publish her poems in various journals. Her first book of
poetry was published by Clifford Laube, suburban editor of *The
New York Times* and associate editor of *Spirit*. She was received
into the Milwaukee Community of the Carmel of the Mother of
God in 1941 and was clothed in 1942 as Sister Miriam of the
Holy Spirit. She made her first profession of vows in 1943 and
her perpetual profession in 1946. Her second book of poetry
was published in 1946. She was elected prioress in 1955. When
the Carmelites moved to a new Carmel in Pewaukee, Wisconsin
in 1958, she began a second term as prioress, and then a third
term in 1964. After the publication of other volumes of verse, in
1988 she approved the manuscript of selected poetry assembled
by Sister Regina Siegfried and Bishop Robert Morneau. She is
one of the most acclaimed religious poets in modern American
literature.

Regina Siegfried & Robert Morneau, eds., The *Selected Poetry of Jessica
Powers* (published by ICS Publications, Washington, DC, 1999); Jessica
Powers, *The House at Rest*, published by Carmelite Monastery, Pewaukee,

WI; Delores R. Leckey, *Winter Music: A life of Jessica Powers: Poet, nun, woman of the 20th century* (New York, 1992); Marcianne Kappes, *Track of the Mystic: the Spirituality of Jessica Powers* (New York, 1994)

JOAN CHITTISTER, Sr (1936–)

American Benedictine, spiritual adviser, founder, peacebuilder, theologian, spiritual author, speaker and social commentator.

Sister Joan D. Chittister, OSB, is a member of the Benedictine Sisters of Erie, Pennsylvania, USA, where she was prioress for 12 years. She is one of the most influential and respected women religious in the USA and has received a vast number of honorary degrees and awards. She has campaigned for, and lectured and written on, peace, justice, the religion of the heart, spirituality, a novel future for religious life, women as friends, women's issues in Church and society and the ordination of women in the Roman Catholic Church (in defiance of Pope John-Paul's and rigorous traditional Catholic opposition to it, as recorded especially in *Ordinatio sacerdotalis* [*Priestly Ordination*]). She is Co-Chair of the Global Peace Institute of Women Religious and Spiritual Leaders, President of the Leadership Conference of Women Religious, executive director of Benetvision, a resource and research centre for contemporary spirituality, and a director of many other organizations. She has written more than 40 books, including *The Breath of the Soul* (2009) and *The Liturgical Year* (2010). She has contributed a weekly column entitled 'From where I Stand' to the *National Catholic Reporter*.

JUANA INÉS DE LA CRUZ, Sr (Sor Juana Inés de la Cruz de Asbaje y Ramirez) (1648–1695)

Mexican nun, poet and feminist during Mexico's colonial period. She was known as the Tenth Muse of America.

Juana was born in a village near Mexico City. She was illegitimate and raised by her mother's parents. She was sent to a girls' school when three, and studied in her grandfather's library for many years, although she made a vain attempt to persuade her mother to send her to the university disguised as a boy. She was given Latin lessons, wrote a dramatic poem on the Holy Sacrament when young, and gained a reputation for prodigious learning. From age 16, she spent five years at the vice-regal court, and became an acclaimed controversialist and occasional poet. In 1667 she spent some months as a Discalced Carmelite but left because of the Order's rigorous Rule. In 1669 she entered the far from austere Convent of the Order of St Jerome and remained there under the protection of the vice-regents, which ceased in 1688. She had elaborate living quarters, with her own library and servants. She could study, write and receive friends and acquaintances in what amounted to a cultural salon. She wrote carols, secular plays, and lyrical and other verse. In 1689 an anthology of her poems was published in Spain. In 1690, she addressed a critique of a famous Jesuit sermon to the Bishop of Puebla, who published it together with a refutation under the pseudonym 'Sister Philothea de la Cruz'. In 1691 Juana replied with an apologia for her intellectual history and a defence of women's right to education in *Reply to Sister Philothea*. Juana came under pressure to stop writing, and in 1693 said she repented of 'having lived so long without religion in a religious community.' She wrote no more and in 1695 died of plague caught while nursing her fellow-nuns.

Fama, y Obras Posthumas de Fenix de Mexico, decima musa, poetisa Americana, Sor Juana Inés de la Cruz (Madrid, 1700); Sor Juana de la Cruz, *A Sor Juana Anthology*, Alan S. Trueblood, tr. (Cambridge, Mass., 1988); Gerard Flynn, *Sor Juana Inés De La Cruz* (New York, 1971); Mary Christine Morkovsky, 'Sor Juana Inés de la Cruz' in: *A History of Women Philosophers: Modern Women Philosophers, 1600–1900*, Mary Ellen Waithe, ed. (Boston, 1991); *Sor Juana: Poet, Nun, Feminist*, Alicia Zavala Galván, ed. & tr. [in Spanish and English] (Mexico, 1998).

JULIAN of Norwich (1342–c.1416)
English hermit and spiritual writer.

Probably an anchoress (living in considerable physical restriction) near the church of St Julian the Hospitaller in Norwich and author of the first book in English certainly written by a woman.

This work, *Sixteen Revelations of Divine Love*, has come down to us as two texts, one short, one long, in later manuscript versions. It was based on her mystical visions in 1373, and has one essential theme: the nature and irresistible power of the love of God. Julian is convinced that God means love; that this love keeps everything in being; and that, ultimately, everything in the universe will be for the best. Her description of the Trinity as Father, Mother and Lord leads into her presentation of divine love as motherly, and of Christ's suffering on the cross as the pains of a woman in childbirth. This aspect of her work has proved especially attractive to modern, and above all feminist, theologians.

Julian of Norwich, *Revelations of Divine Love*, Grace Warrack, tr. (London, 1901); id., *Revelations of Divine Love*, R. Hudleston, tr. (London, 1927); id., *Revelations of Divine Love*, C. Wolters, tr. (Harmondsworth, 1966); id., *Showings*, E. Colledge OSA & J. Walsh SJ, ed. & tr. (London, 1978); Paul Molinari, *Julian of Norwich* (London, 1958); Matthew Fox, *Original Blessing* (Santa Fe, NM, 1983); Grace M. Jantzen, *Julian of Norwich: Mystic and Theologian* (London, 1987); Frodo Okulam, *The Julian Mystique* (Mystic, CT, 1998).

KATHLEEN BRYANT RSC, Sr

American Sister of Charity and spiritual author.

Sr Kathleen Bryant was born and raised in Los Angeles. She became a Religious Sister of Charity in 1967. She has a Master's degree in spirituality from the University of San Francisco, and a Doctor of ministry degree from the Graduate Theological Foundation in Indiana. Sr Kathy has worked and lived in Africa, Ireland and California. She was Vocation Director for the Archdiocese of Los Angeles for twenty-one years, has given workshops internationally and has published works in the field of spirituality. Currently she still gives retreats and conducts workshops and is a spiritual director. Her Order fights for the abolition of human trafficking, the new slavery.

Vocations Anonymous: A Handbook for Adults Discerning Priesthood and Religious Life (Illinois, 1997); *On the Way to Priesthood: A Journal and Reflection Guide for Men Discerning the Priesthood* (Illinois, 2000); *All for Love: A Discernment Journal* (Illinois, 2002).

LOUISE de Marillac, St (1591–1660)

French wife, mother, widow, nun and co-founder with Saint Vincent de Paul of the Daughters of Charity.

She was born into the ancient Marillac family, but out of wedlock. Her mother died soon afterwards. Her father's new wife refused to look after Louise, who was well educated at the royal convent, where her aunt was a Dominican sister. Louise repressed a youthful desire to become a Capuchin nun, and at the age of 22 married the ambitious Anthony Le Gras, secretary to Marie de Medici; he soon became bed-ridden with a lingering illness that lasted 12 years. When her husband died, Louise vowed to devote herself to God's service. St Vincent de Paul became her spiritual director for many years and when he tried to organize his 'Confraternities of Charity' to supplement his existing, though inadequate, Ladies of Charity, he found that Madame Le Gras was a ready and extremely well-organized helper in caring for the horribly neglected sick, poor and destitute people of France. In 1633 Louise turned her house into a training centre for the first candidates of the internationally famous Institute of the Sisters of Charity of St Vincent de Paul, whom she advised to: 'Love the poor and honour them as you would honour Christ himself.' She told them always to ask: 'What would Jesus do in this situation?' Her Daughters gradually expanded their scope from the central hospital in Paris to one in Angers, and soon after to hospitals, orphanages, institutions for the elderly and mentally ill. They visited prisons and schools. Their integrated contemplation and activity made their work highly successful. For centuries, the grey-blue habit and white cornette of St Louise's daughters was found where people were sick or poor, children were hungry and uneducated, and families needed help. Louise's only child, a son, disappointed his mother's hopes, but under St Vincent's instruction the boy lived responsibly, married, and was with his mother when she died on 15 March 1660, six months before the 80-year-old St Vincent de Paul. She was beatified by Pope Benedict XV on 9 May 1920 and canonized by Pope Pius XI on 11 March 1934.

Sainte Louise de Marillac: Ses Ecrits (Paris, 1961); *Spiritual Writings of Louise de Marillac: Correspondence and Thoughts*, Louise Sullivan, ed. & tr. (New York, 1996).

LUCIE CHRISTINE (Mathilde Boutlé, née Mathilde Bertrand) (1844–1908)

French spiritual diarist, mystic and married tertiary.

Mathilde Bertrand was born into a cultured Parisian family. Seven out of eight first cousins became religious. She was an early practitioner of what might be called introspective mysticism and recorded her developing religious experiences in a journal which she was encouraged to keep by her spiritual adviser, the respected writer on mysticism, Fr A. Poulain. She married Thomas Boutlé, of English descent, had five children, and suffered from her husband's improvidence, weak character, and violence. The nuns of Adoration Réparatrice, founded by the forward-looking Mother Marie Thérèse, started a semi-secular 'tertiary' order in the world. They had an immense influence on Mathilde who, like the other members, followed the Order's ethos of prayer and adoration while pursuing her secular vocation. For Mathilde this was her work as wife and mother, which she recorded in her journal alongside her intense and evolving relationship with God, which passed from an intellectual to a positively imaginative phase. She was widowed when she was 45 and after her death her journals were given to the nuns, but all family references were excluded. Fr Poulain published an attenuated version under the pseudonym 'Lucie Christine' (or 'Light of Christ'). The author's identity was disclosed only in recent years.

Lucie Christine, *Journal spirituel (1870–1910)*, A. Poulain SJ, ed. (Paris, 1910); A. Poulain, *The Spiritual Journal of Lucie Christine* (London, 1915; New York, 1920); Evelyn Underhill, *Mystics of the Church* (London & New York, 1964), p. 244; Astrid O'Brien, 'Lucie Christine: Nineteenth-century Wife, Mother and Mystic', in *Mapping the Catholic Cultural Landscape*, Sr Paula Miller & R. Fossey, eds (Lanham, Maryland, 2004), 145–56; id., *A Mysticism of Kindness: The Lucie Christine Story* (Scranton, 2010).

MARGUERITE PORETE (died 1310)

French theologian, religious writer and probable Beguine who was burnt as a heretic.

Very little is known about Marguerite Porete, the author of *Le Miroeur des simples âmes*, who is presumed to have belonged to the quasi-Franciscan movement known as the Brethren of the Free Spirit. She was probably a native of Hainaut. She was burnt at the stake in Paris on 1 June 1310 for continuing to circulate copies of her book, which had already been condemned as heretical. After the unfortunate author's death, Latin, (Middle) English and Italian translations of the book, presented as versions of an anonymous minor Christian classic, were published for centuries in Roman Catholic and other environments, and the authorship and the book's 'heretical' nature were re-established only in recent years. It is a major classic of the school of 'Freedom of the Spirit' (because most such works were destroyed).

A Mirror for Simple Souls, C. Crawford, ed. & tr. (London & New York, 1981); P. Dronke, *Women Writers of the Middle Ages* (London, 1981).

MARIA CELESTE, Sr (Maria Celeste [Virginia or Polissena] Galilei) (1600–1634)

Italian Poor Clare nun and indefatigable correspondent.

Virginia, Galileo's first child, was born the daughter of his housekeeper, Maria Gamba, when Galileo was Professor of Mathematics in Padua. Galileo took Virginia and her sister Livia to Florence in 1610 and left his son, Vincenzio, with his mother for some years. In 1613, a few years after moving to Florence, having obtained a dispensation because of their youth, Galileo succeeded in placing Virginia and Livia in St Matthew's Convent in Arcetri. Virginia was clothed in 1616 as Sister Maria Celeste. More than a hundred of Celeste's letters to her father, starting in 1623, have been preserved and are the only real source for information about her. She was always concerned for her father's health and happiness and was clearly distressed by his unjust censure by the ecclesiastical authorites for a dissertation on solar spots, inferences regarding the sun's rotation, and advocacy of the Copernican system, which ran counter to the cosmology approved by the pope and Church. Later he was tried and imprisoned and forced to deny the truth of his observations. Celeste's letters are a valuable source of descriptions of contemporary convent life by a humane and perceptive observer.

Mary Allan-Olney, *The Private Life of Galileo, compiled principally from his correspondence and that of his eldest daughter, Sister Maria Celeste* (London, 1870); Stillman Drake, *Galileo* (Oxford, 1980); Dava Sobel, *Galileo's Daughter: a drama of science, faith and love* (London, 1999); David Wootton, *Galileo* (New York & London, 2010); J.L. Heilbron, *Galileo* (Oxford, 2010).

MARIA ELIZABETTA (Mary Elizabeth) HESSELBLAD, Bd (1870–1957)

Swedish nun, founder, humanitarian and ecumenist.

Mary Elizabeth Hesselblad was born to Lutheran parents at Faglavik, Sweden. From infancy she asked why there were so many Christian churches and this interest developed into her later passionate concern to promote ecumenism. After her father's bankruptcy she had to work to help the family. She emigrated to the USA when she was 18 to become a student nurse in a Catholic hospital in New York. She nursed a Catholic nun, made Catholic friends and was received into the Church in 1902. She dreamed of bringing Sweden back to Catholicism and of restoring the religious Order founded by St Bridget of Sweden. In 1904 she asked the Carmelite nuns occupying St Bridget's convent on the Piazza Farnese in Rome if she could enter their novitiate. She visited the four remaining Brigittine houses in 1908–11, won two postulants for her plan, and with papal approval reestablished the Brigittine Order in Rome in 1911. After more than 12 years she founded two convents in Sweden itself, and eventually there were 36 houses throughout the world. Elizabeth also became a pioneer of ecumenism. During World War II, in her little Roman convent Mother Elizabeth sheltered without discrimination not only Communists, Socialists and other political refugees from the Fascist regime but Jews fleeing Italian and German persecution and certain death in German extermination camps. After the foundation of the State of Israel she was recognized as one of the few just Gentiles who had helped their Jewish fellow-humans during the Nazi years from 1933 to 1945 at the risk of their own lives. In 2004 she received one of the world's most honourable accolades when she was declared one of the Righteous among the Nations at Yad Vashem. Her friends came from many walks of life and ranged from the film star Ingrid Bergman to the Chef Rabbi of Rome. In 1945 she gave the ecumenical Unitas Association a headquarters in her convent and asked her nuns everywhere to devote themselves permanently to the cause of Christian unity. She was beatified by Pope John Paul II in 2000.

Maria Elisabetta Hesselblad. The most extraordinary woman in Rome, a 60-minute film produced by Nova-t (Turin, 2000).

MARIA SKOBTSOVA, St (Mother Maria Skobtsova; Elizaveta Pilenko) (1891–1945)

Orthodox nun, theologian, spiritual writer, and humanitarian.

Mother Maria was born Elizaveta Pilenko to devout Orthodox Christians in Riga, then Russia. As a child she wished to become a nun or a pilgrim. In St Petersburg she was a popular member of avant-garde literary and political circles that included the apocalyptic symbolist poet, Blok. She wrote and published verse. She was 18 and a social idealist when she married a Bolshevik. After an atheistic phase she was admitted as the only woman to the Theological Academy of the Alexander Nevsky Monastery. Just before World War I her marriage broke up. She passed from physical asceticism to a developing social Christianity. After serving as a deputy mayor she married a White Russian and fled the country, reaching Paris in 1923. After her daughter's death she became a 'mother for all who need motherly help, care and protection' and worked for the Russian Student Christian Movement. She came under the influence of the theologian Bulgakov, published religious and literary works and evolved an intense social spiritual practice and philosophy, while looking for a new kind of monasticism that would combine the religious life with service to those in need. Her husband agreed to her becoming a nun and she was professed by the Metropolitan in 1932. She studied conventional monasticism in Latvia and Estonia, which she found indifferent to the fact that the world was 'on fire'. She decided that a religious life sharing that of the destitute was her vocation. With the bishop's help she opened a house of hospitality in a derelict building. She founded hostels and a sanatorium, and fed the needy with food she collected. Other nuns and a priest joined her in helping the poor, unemployed, mentally sick, addicts, the elderly, and hopeless cases. For her, sharing in God's mercy was the sole route to heaven. She saw Nazism as the 'new paganism' and during the German occupation she and Father Dmitri issued baptismal certificates to Jews threatened with deportation. During the mass arrests of Jews in 1942 she worked for three days in the terrible conditions of the Sports Stadium where people of all ages were largely without food and water. She contacted the dustmen and smuggled children out in rubbish bins. She, the priest, her son and a helper were arrested, sent to a prison and then concentration camps. Mother Maria was murdered in a gas chamber at Ravensbrück in 1945. In 2002 she was declared a saint by the Metropolitan of Constantinople (Istanbul).

Mat' Maria (Skobtsova), *Vospominaniya, stat'i, ocherki*, vols I & II (Paris, 1992); *Mother Maria Skobtsova: Essential Writings*, Helene Klepinin Arjakovsky, ed., Richard Pevear & Larissa Volokhonsky, trs (New York, 2000); Sergei Hackel, *Love of Great Price. The Life of Mother Maria Skobtsova, Martyr of Ravensbrück* (London, 1965).

MARIAN O'SULLIVAN, Sr OP

Irish Dominican teacher, egalitarian and social and environmental conscientizer.

An educator and school principal for many years in South Africa, she participated in negotiations during the apartheid regime to open Catholic schools to all races. As elected Prioress of her Congregation (1986–98), her involvement in education spanned many countries. She is currently Marian Director of the ecology centre *An Tairseach* at Wicklow, Ireland.

MARIBEL, Mother (Mary Isabella Rough [Toussa]) (1887–1970)

Anglican nun, sculptor and artist.

She was born into a devout High-Church military family in Weymouth. She studied at the Slade School of Art, and became an accomplished artist and sculptress. She entered the community of St Mary the Virgin (CSMV) in Wantage, a Church of England religious Order founded in 1848 by William John Butler, vicar of Wantage. After some time as an art teacher, she set up a studio at the convent and started a flourishing enterprise producing figures for cribs, religious statues and numerous other commissioned works that were sent all over the world. She was elected Mother General of the Community during the London Blitz of 1940. She visited the Community's houses in South Africa and India. She was a charismatic and much loved friend and adviser who encouraged many lasting vocations and whose life exemplified the deep truths conveyed through her holiness and simplicity and in her many pithy sayings, such as 'If Christ lives in us, then he prays in us, and our chief concern should be to provide him a place where he can pray' or 'It is not God's intention that we should be adequate. Until our human strength fails, we cannot use his.'

Sister Janet, CSMV, *Mother Maribel of Wantage* (London, 1973).

MARIE COUDERC. See: THERESE COUDERC

MARIE DE LA PASSION, Bd (Mother Mary of the Passion [Hélène de Chappotin]) (1839–1904)

Founder of the Missionary Institute of the Franciscan Missionaries of Mary.

Hélène de Chappotin was born in Nantes into a family with a vast property outside the town. Initially she wished to devote herself to a contemplative life but by age 28 she was Provincial of the Sœurs réparatrices (Reparation Sisters) working for widows and young women in India. She and her sister disagreed with their unadventurous Superior and left the Reparation Sisters. Mother Marie became one of the great missionary nuns and founders of the nineteenth century and, as Mother Mary of the Passion, established a religious congregation in the tradition of Franciscan spirituality in 1877. She was a devout yet very lively child whose mother fiercely opposed her desire to be a nun. From infancy the future founder grew used to fighting for her objectives. In spite of the many obstacles in the way of women's advancement in the Church, an unjust dismissal and a triumphant reinstatement, Mother Marie was an immensely original, daring and astute nun who placed her new missionary institute under the direct protection of the Holy See as the Franciscan Missionary Sisters of Mary, devoted to the service of the poor of all nations. Within the constraints of the time, Hélène de Chappotin adapted her nuns' missionary work to their particular environment, from Ceylon (Sri Lanka) to Tunisia, from China to the Belgian Congo (Democratic Republic of the Congo), from Canada to Chile, and was a pioneer of what is now known as inculturation. She tried to give each community as international a composition as possible. She was an active advocate of professional schools and training and a just wage for women. At her death her congregation already numbered almost 3000 nuns in 86 foundations on four continents. She was beatified by Pope John Paul II in 2002.

Georges Goyau, *Mère Marie de la Passion et les Franciscaines Missionaires de Marie* (Paris, 1935); Marcel Launay, *Hélène de Chappotin (1839–1904) et les Franciscaines Missionaires de Marie* (Paris, 2001).

MARIE DE LA TRINITE, Sr (Paule de Mulatier)
(1903–1980)

French Dominican nun, mystic and spiritual writer.

She was born as the seventh child into a family of wealthy industrialists in Lyons. She was often ill. From infancy she wished to become a nun and in 1930 entered a new branch of the Dominicans founded by Mother Saint Jean (and unacknowledged officially for some time) specializing in local missionary work in the Jura. She was clothed in 1932 and was appointed to various duties, including those of novice mistress. She became well versed in modern and ancient languages, including Hebrew. She published many articles and a popular guide to reading Scripture. From 1929 she experienced intense spiritual revelations and states of mind. In 1940 she met Father Antonin Motte, who advised her to start what became her major spiritual and literary work, the 3250 pages of her *Carnets* (or Journals), which she continued until 1945. For ten years she suffered severe bouts of clinical depression and consulted various specialists, including the controversial Jacques Lacan (from 1950 to 1953), who drew on her thinking and experience for his own work on mysticism and psychology. He retained the volume of her journals devoted to her course of therapy. In 1953, she recovered, after psychoanalysis, rigorous chemical (including insulin) therapy, and a sleep cure. In 1955 she trained as a psychotherapist and practised at the Vaugirard Hospital in Paris under Professeur Cornelia Quarti, and won a considerable reputation, but was recalled to the headquarters of her Order at Flavigny to assist Mother Saint Jean, with whom she established a close spiritual understanding. She remained there as a hermit when the congregation moved to Luzarches. She died of cancer. The gradual publication of her works since 1980 has increased her spiritual influence. The theologian Hans Urs von Balthasar admired her writings and translated an anthology into German.

Paule de Mulatier (known as Marie de la Trinité), *Le Petit Livre des Grâces*; *Consens à n'être rien*; *Entre dans ma Gloire*; *De l'angoisse à la paix*; *Paule dite Marie*; *Je te veux auprès de Moi*; *Le Silence de Joseph* (Paris, 1986–2010).

MARIE DE L'INCARNATION, Bd (Mary of the Incarnation; Madame Barbe (Avrillot) Acarie) (1566–1618)

French Carmelite, founder and devotional writer.

She became an important figure in the renewal of spirituality in France, although she was born into an aristocratic family obdurately opposed to her wish to become a nun. She was only 16 when they married her to Pierre Acarie, Seigneur de Montbrost and de Ronceray, a counsellor to the Treasury, and a leading member of the League opposed to the succession of the Huguenot Prince Henri to the throne of France. She had six children. When the League was dissolved after Henri's abjuration of his religion, her husband left Paris, her house was ransacked, and she was reduced to abject poverty. Even her relations refused to help her and advised her to apprentice her children to a shoemaker. She had a riding accident and was so crippled that she had to use crutches for the rest of her life. During the siege of Paris in 1590 she cared for the sick and for victims of the plague. Her house, Hotel Acarie, became a centre of Catholic spiritual revival. Her three daughters had already become nuns. She had two visions of St Teresa of Avila asking her to establish the reformed Carmelites in France, which she did with the help of her cousin Pierre de Bérulle. The first French Carmel was set up in the faubourg Saint-Jacques in 1604 and she created a small community, the Congregation of Saint Geneviève, to teach the novices. Later, in 1610, she also established the Ursulines in Paris. After her husband's death she entered the Carmel of Amiens as a lay sister called Marie de l'Incarnation in religion. She was forced to carry out menial tasks in the kitchen and was not allowed to give spiritual direction. She was beatified by Pope Pius VI in 1791.

Marguerite Acarie, *Lettres spirituelles* (Paris, 1993); Madame Acarie, *Ecrits spirituels* (Orbey, 2004).

MARIE DE L'INCARNATION, Bd (Mary of the Incarnation; Marie Guyard) (1599–1672)

French-Canadian mother, widow and Ursuline nun, missionary and founder.

She was born in Tours, France; her father was a master-baker. She married, had a child (Claude, who later became a Benedictine monk and wrote the first biography of his mother), and was widowed by the age of 19. She had always wanted to be a nun and, in spite of her family's opposition, she entered the Ursuline Order in 1631, leaving her 11-year-old son in her sister's care, and then with the Jesuits. She wished to become a missionary and a dream revealed Canada as her destination. In 1639 she left for 'New France' to set up the first women's monastery there. She was the first French missionary sister to go to America, and has been called 'Mother of the Catholic Church in Canada'. The Ursuline convents and schools supported the work of the Jesuit missionaries. Although the Ursulines were enclosed, Marie was remarkably resilient in the face of many difficulties, including the loss of her monastery in a fire in 1650 and the Iroquois resistance to the French from 1653 to 1663. She had extraordinary energy. Her schools were very successful. She not only acted as Superior and novice mistress, but as bursar. She mastered four indigenous spoken languages; wrote dictionaries, text books, and an account of her spiritual development; and carried on an immense correspondence which is both spiritually instructive and of great historical value; took part in the education of children and adults; and shared in housekeeping. She led a physically austere penitential life beyond the limits of the severe self-punishment not uncommon among religious at the time. She developed a liver disease in 1645, from which she recovered, although she suffered from its effects until her death. Her spirituality was founded on that of St Teresa of Avila and on St Francis of Sales' *Introduction to a Devout Life* and other eminent sources. Though celebrated as a saint at her death, the official fear of Jansenist tendencies in French mystics delayed her beatification until 1980.

Marie de l'Incarnation, *Ecrits spirituels et historiques,* Dom Claude Martin, ed. (Tours, 1681; Paris, 1876); Claude Martin, *La Vie de la Vénérable Mère Marie de l'Incarnation* (Paris, 1677; Solesmes, 1981); Marie de l'Incarnation, *Ecrits Spirituels et Historiques,* A. Jamet, ed., vols 1–4 (Paris, 1929–39; Solesmes, 1985); *The Autobiography of Venerable Marie of the Incarnation,* J.J. Sullivan, ed. & tr. (London, 1964); *Marie of the Incarnation: Selected Writings,* Irene Mahoney, ed. (New York, 1997); Natalie Zemon Davis, *Women on the Margins: Three Seventeenth-century Lives* (Cambridge, Mass. & London, 1995).

MARIE-LOUISE HARTZER, Mother (1837–1908)

Mother, widow, founder and superior-general.

Born in Wissembourg, Alsace. Her father was a Dutch physician and her mother came from a wealthy brewing family. Her father died when she was 17, and she took charge of her sick mother and two sisters. In 1858 she married an inspector of prisons, but her husband became progressively paralyzed and died in 1869. She took her two young sons to Strasbourg, where she looked after her ailing mother and one remaining sister. The Franco-Prussian war caused them to take refuge in France. Later her sons joined the Society of Missionaries of the Sacred Heart. When visiting them in Issoudun, she met the founder, Father Chevalier, and learned that he had also founded a congregation called the Daughters of Our Lady of the Sacred Heart. After her mother's death and her sons' ordination, she entered aged 45 and was professed in 1884. Although initially reluctant ('All I know is how to run a home'), she was appointed first Superior General of the Order which, in any real sense, she founded, for she expanded it most successfully until it spread to 28 countries, with many houses in Australasia, Oceania and even Papua-New Guinea. She could not visit them all, but she was an exceedingly competent director of this vast community and was much respected. In 1902 the new French anti-clerical laws forced her to move to Belgium, where she established a house in Thuin. She died there aged 71. Many lively correspondents throughout her empire, such as Sister Marie-Madeline in Oceania, kept her in effective touch with its achievements and problems.

Fernand & Léopold Hartzer, *La Révérende Mère Marie-Louise Hartzer, Fondatrice des Filles de Notre-Dame du Sacré-Cœur et les Missions d'Océanie* (Issoudun, Thuin & Paris, 1913); Fernand & Leopold Hartzer, *Force upon the Earth: the Life of Mother Marie-Louise Hartzer, Foundress of the Daughters of Our Lady of the Sacred Heart, and the Missions in Oceania*, E.J. Dwyer, tr. (Sydney, 1948).

MARIE-LOUISE TRICHET, Bd (Marie-Louise de Jésus) (1684–1759)

Nun, teacher and founder (with St Louis-Marie Grignion de Montfort) of the Daughters of Wisdom (Filles de la Sagesse).

She was born into a very devout family in Poitiers, France. Her parents did not wish her to leave their comfortable home in 1703 to live in the unappetizing general hospital as advised by Louis de Montfort. He was chaplain to the institution, which housed beggars and down-and-outs. Their numbers in the country and in the hospital rapidly increased when a law prohibiting begging was passed. There was one bed for every two or three inmates in the same room, coarse bread, a stew of indeterminate origin, and a rough grey uniform. Marie-Louise worked there for ten years and eventually was given charge of the place. In 1715 Marie-Louise and Catherine Brunet started a school in La Rochelle to teach children and care for the poor. Marie-Louise Trichet became the superior of the new Order, the Daughters of Wisdom. There were only four sisters in the community when Louis Marie de Montfort died in 1716 and Marie-Louise was in sole charge of his foundation. In 1719 the sisters returned to Poitiers. In 1720 they started a Mother House at Saint-Laurent-sur-Sèvre which is now a museum devoted to Marie-Louise's life and to the Daughters of Wisdom. By 1729 Marie-Louise had established thirty new charitable communities where the Daughters of Wisdom visited the poor, nursed the sick and taught children without payment, but were supported by benefactors or parishioners. When she was 66, Marie-Louise made a long journey on horseback to visit all her communities under the watchword 'Your real Superior is Mary. I am only her servant.' When she died from an accidental fall, the congregation comprised 174 sisters in 36 communities and the Mother House. Marie-Louise was beatified by Pope John Paul II.

Laurentin René, *Petite vie de Marie-Louise Trichet* (Paris, 1993).

MARIE-MADELEINE, Sr, of the Daughters of Our Lady of the Sacred Heart. See: Marie-Louise Hartzer, Mother

MARTHA ZECHMEISTER-MACHHART, Sr (1956–)

Austrian nun, university teacher and author.

She is a member of the Congregatio Jesu, an Order of women religious. She studied theology in Vienna and in 1997 was awarded a higher degree entitling her to teach at professorial level. Since 1999 she has been Professor of fundamental theology in the faculty of Catholic theology at Passau University. She is currently on leave of absence as Professor at the Central American University at San Salvador, El Salvador. She is a stalwart defender of the right to theological freedom of thought and expression. Her publications include: *Mystik und Sendung, Ignatius von Loyola erfährt Gott* (Würzburg, 1986) (on St Ignatius of Loyola's experience of God); *Gottes-Nacht. Erich Przywaras Weg Negativer Theologie* (Münster, 2000).

MARY OF THE CROSS, St (Mary Helen MacKillop) (1842–1909)

Founder, teacher, pioneer feminist and Australia's first saint.

Mary's parents were emigrant Scots. Alexander MacKillop, who had studied for the priesthood in Rome, met and married Flora McDonald in 1840. He was an unsuccessful businessman and had to teach his eight children at home. When 14, the unusually well-educated Mary started work in a shop and later became a governess for her uncle's children in South Australia. There she met Father Julian Woods, who became her spiritual mentor and co-founder of the Australian Sisters of St Joseph, a teaching order for poor children. Mary took her final vows in 1869. The order was praised for exceptional charitable work among people of all faiths and backgrounds, and for sustained austerity. It grew and sisters were recruited in Britain. Two disturbed pseudo-mystic sisters and clerical factions working to control education and major mission areas caused dissension. Local priests were humiliated when the congregation reported a Father Keating to the vicar-general for child abuse and he was sent back to Ireland. For five months Mary was excommunicated for 'disobedience and rebellion' by Bishop Shiel of Adelaide, a martinet and alcoholic who tried to control the congregation and dispensed 47 nuns from their vows. She was publicly vilified and forced into hiding but, knowing the sentence was unjust, continued to receive communion. In 1872, on his deathbed, Shiel apologized and reinstated Mary. A Roman delegation led the Vatican to support MacKillop and her nuns against local bishops. Mary became superior-general in 1875. In 1885 the congregation was attacked again, but was supported by the Holy See, which nevertheless decided that Mary had been in charge too long. A Mother Bernard served as superior-general from 1888 to 1898. On her death, Mary once again became superior-general until her own death. The congregation is still at the forefront of the Catholic education of girls in Australia. Mary was beatified by Pope John Paul II in Australia in 1995 and raised to sainthood by Pope Benedict XVI in 2010.

Mary MacKillop, *Julian Tenison Woods: A Life*, Margaret Press, RSJ, ed. (Sydney, 1997); *Correspondence between Mary MacKillop and her mother Flora McDonald MacKillop*, Sheila McCreanor, RSJ, ed. (Sydney, 2004); id., *Mary MacKillop in Challenging Times – 1883–1899* (Sydney, 2006); William Modystack, *Mary MacKillop: A Woman Before Her Time* (Adelaide, 1982); A Sister of St Joseph (Sr Chanel O'Loughlin), *Life and Letters of Mother Mary, Foundress of the Sisterhood of St Joseph of the Sacred Heart* (Sydney, 1916); Paul Gardiner SJ, *Mary MacKillop–An Extraordinary Australian* (Sydney, [1993] 2007); Bernadette Doyle, *El-Hage, Lila and The Story of Mary MacKillop* (Sydney, 2010); [Sisters of St Joseph, 1925–26], *Memories of Mary by those who knew her* (Sydney, 2010).

MARY WARD (1585–1645)

English founder, teacher and spiritual guide.

Mary Ward was born in Yorkshire and baptized a Catholic. She became an 'out-sister' of the Poor Clares of St Omer in 1606, and set up a daughter-house in Gravelines. After three years she left the convent, recruited five other women in England, went back to St Omer, and founded what became the Institute of the Blessed

Virgin Mary, the first unenclosed Catholic order for active rather than contemplative women, without enclosure or choir offices. Similar houses were established in Liège, Cologne, Rome, and other places. Ward's Institute was subject directly to the Pope, not to a bishop. The authorities sensed the dangers of such near-autonomy, suppressed the Institute in 1631, and confined Ward to the Convent of the Poor Clares in Munich. Eventually she was freed and went to Rome to obtain papal permission for her Institute to operate informally. In 1639 she returned to England and died near York. Her organization has led a chequered life but persists as three Institutes with three General Superiors.

Mary C. E. Chambers, *The Life of Mary Ward, 1585–1645*, 2 vols., Henry James Coleridge, ed. (London, 1882–5); Mother M. Salome, *Mary Ward: A Founder of the 17th Century* (London, 1901); *Till God Will: Mary Ward through her writings*, Emmanuel Orchard, IBVM, ed. (London, 1985).

MECHTHILD of Magdeburg (*c.*1208–82/97)

German Beguine and visionary.

Mechthild was born into a wealthy aristocratic family and was well-educated although she never studied Latin or theology. She became a nun while young and was granted mystical experiences from the age of 12, but for some 30 years remained silent about them. In about 1250 her Dominican confessor persuaded her to dictate vivid accounts of her visions. She took notes after each mystical encounter. In 1270 she joined the Cistercian monastery of Helfta. Her work is said to have influenced Dante and was very influential among the Dominicans until the beginning of the sixteenth century.

Offenbarungen der Schwester M.v.M. oder das fliessende Licht der Gottheit, G. Morel, ed. (Regensburg, 1869; Darmstadt, 1976); *Das fliessende Licht der Gottheit*, M. Schmidt, ed. (Einsiedeln, Zurich, Cologne, 1955); Mechthild de Magdebourg, *La lumière de la divinité. Révélations* (Paris, 1878); *Revelations of Mechthild of Magdeburg or the flowing light of the Godhead*, Lucy Menzies, tr. (London, 1953).

PHILIPPINE DUCHESNE, St (Rose Philippine Duchesne) (1769–1852)

Franco-American nun, founder, missionary and frontierswoman.

She was born at Grenoble, France, into a prosperous commercial family. When 17, she joined the Visitandine nuns who had educated her, but the outbreak of the Revolution prevented her profession, and when the nuns were expelled in 1781, Philippine returned home. After the Concordat of 1801 she acquired her old convent, and tried to rebuild it and re-establish a community of Visitandines. This proved hopeless, so she offered the site to Mother Barat, who had recently set up her first house at Amiens. In 1805 Philippine Duchesne was professed as a member of the newly-founded Society of the Sacred Heart. She developed a longing to become a missionary. In March 1818, after much preparation by Mother Barat, Mother Duchesne was sent to New Orleans as the head of a party of five religious. In a log cabin, at St Charles near St Louis, Missouri, she established the first house of the Society in the New World. In 1820 she opened the first American free school west of the Mississippi. By 1828 she had already founded six houses. In 1840, at the age of 71, she resigned as superior and started a school for Native Americans at Sugar Creek, Kansas. In spite of many trials and difficulties, she established the Society on firm and lasting foundations in the New World. She died aged 83. She was beatified in 1940 and canonized by Pope John Paul II in 1988.

Majorie Erskine, *Mother Philippine Duchesne* (London, 1926); Catherine M. Mooney, *Philippine Duchesne: A Woman with the Poor* (New York, 1990).

PIA BUXTON, Sr CJ (Judith Buxton) (1932–2010)

English Provincial Superior, Ignatian spiritual director, writer, counsellor and retreat leader, co-founder of the Cambridge Spiritual Direction Course.

She spent 20 years at St Mary's School, Ascot, England, where she taught geography and later became novice mistress. She had a lifelong devotion to Mary Ward and to St Ignatius. She worked within the Church for the rights of women. In a talk given to a gathering of women contemplatives in 1986, she said: 'To follow Christ as women today we may have to be prophetic in order to be loyal, and get hurt and sometimes disturbed.' 'She not only challenged other people to be prophetic, but challenged herself to be so as well. In another talk she referred to something that was ever closer to her heart: the role of women in the world and in the Church, and the continuation of the place of women as a second-class citizenry in the Church in particular. She described herself, absolutely truthfully, as "a loyal and loving member of the Roman Catholic Church" and said that it was "because of my love and concern for the Church that I say what I say". We . . . acknowledge her concern for the Church and for the effects of its overwhelmingly masculine, patriarchal and clerical organization, as seen in its authority structure, in its liturgical expression and in its failure to value and harness the power of the feminine . . . Her life-long interest in geography possibly helped her to understand that the Kingdom was not a Kingdom confined to Church-goers (of any Church) or to followers of any of the great Abrahamic religions, but a Kingdom absolutely open to all those seeking meaning and purpose' (From the funeral address by Sister Jane Livesey CJ).

RADEGUND, St (Radegunde) (518–587)

Thuringian Princess, Frankish Queen, nun, founder and poet.

Radegund was the daughter of the pagan Prince Berthaire, and born in Erfurt (now Germany). At age 12 (c. 531), she was taken prisoner by raiding Franks, and at 18 she was forced to marry the nominally Christian King Clothaire of the Neustrian Franks, who was possibly already married five times. She became a Christian then, or was perhaps already baptized at her father's court. She fell out of favour with her violent husband because she seemed barren. She founded a leper hospital and pleaded with the bishop to make her a nun. Eventually he allowed her to become a deaconess. She founded a monastery for men at Tours and a monastery for men and women at Poitiers, adopting the

Rule of St Caesarius of Arles, and settled there in about 561. After many appeals from Radegund, St Germanus of Paris persuaded Clothaire to cease persecuting her. The monastery finally took the name 'Holy Cross'. Radegund made her friend Agnes abbess, and assembled a group of cultivated and devout women from royal and aristocratic families who made Holy Cross a centre of intellectual life and refinement. Poitiers became the home of the poet-priest and hymn-writer St Venantius Fortunatus. He was soon Radegund's confidant and chaplain to the community. He exchanged many elegant and often moving verse letters with Radegund and Agnes. Radegund was completely secluded for the closing years of her life and was celebrated as a miracle-worker. A number of her letters, many in verse, survive.

Acta Sanctorum (Amsterdam, 1642), Aug. 3, cc 66–92; *Monumenta Germaniae Historiae, Scriptores Rerum Merovingicarum* (Hanover, 1839–1921), 2, cc. 358–95; F. Brittain, *St Radegund, Patroness of Jesus College Cambridge* (Cambridge, 1925); J.M. Wallace-Hadrill, *The Frankish Church* (London, 1983).

SANDRA SCHNEIDERS, Sr

Sandra M. Schneiders is a member of the religious Congregation of the Sisters, Servants of the Immaculate Heart of Mary (IHM) of Monroe, Michigan, USA. She is Professor Emerita of New Testament Studies and Spirituality at the Jesuit School of Theology of Santa Clara University and the Graduate Theological Union in Berkeley, California. Her writings have been in the areas of New Testament, especially Johannine studies, hermeneutics, Roman Catholic religious life, Christian feminism, and spirituality as an academic discipline.

TERESA of Avila, St (1515–82)

Spanish Carmelite, superior, mystic, autobiographer, spiritual writer and Doctor of the Church.

St Teresa was born in Avila, Spain. In about 1535, she became a nun in the Carmelite Convent of the Incarnation as Teresa de Jesús. She came to believe that the order's discipline ought to be reformed in accordance with her notions of primitive observance. In 1562, in spite of long periods of illness and much opposition from powerful enemies, including the Inquisition, she founded a new convent, and later 16 others, in Spain. Together with St John of the Cross she was responsible for similar reforms among the friars. She was an extremely perceptive and responsible governor of, and provider for, her houses. She was also a great mystic able to convey her extremely varied experiences in subtly composed literary works that are profound, strict, tender, amusing, realistic, psychologically acute, and sublimely ecstatic, as the occasion or circumstance demands. They include one of the world's great autobiographies and a multitude of letters. Like many original works they aroused much suspicion among the dull, authoritarian and small-minded.

The Letters of Saint Teresa of Avila, E. Allison Peers, tr. & ed. (London, 1951); St Teresa of Avila, *The Way of Perfection*, A Benedictine of Stanbrook, tr., rev. B. Zimmerman, OCD (London, 1961); St Teresa of Avila, 'The Interior Castle', in *The Complete Works of St Teresa of Jesus*, E. Allison Peers, tr. & ed. (London, 1963*); The Life of St Teresa of Avila by Herself*, D. Lewis, tr., D. Knowles, ed. (London, 1962); E. Sackville-West, *The Eagle and the Dove* (London, 1943); E. W. Trueman Dicken, *The Crucible of Love* (London, 1963); S. Clissold, *St Teresa of Avila* (London, 1978).

TERESA, Bd Mother (Bd Teresa of Calcutta) (Agnes Gonxha Bojaxhiu) (1910–1997)

Nun, teacher and founder.

She was born in Skopje, Macedonia, into a family of Albanian descent. Even at age 12, she was convinced of her vocation to become a nun. She joined the Loreto Sisters, an Irish Community of Sisters in India, where she worked as a teacher. She founded the Missionaries of Charity in Calcutta in 1950. Her Order's primary task was to love and care for despised, destitute, marginal, abandoned, orphaned, crippled, and dying adults and infants, and those suffering from HIV/AIDS, leprosy, tuberculosis and so on, whom no one else was prepared to look after. As her fame and accounts of the work of her nuns spread far and wide, hospices and homes of her Order and similar enterprises were opened in many countries. She extended her work to radiation and disaster victims in other countries, and founded a number of ancillary organisations, including those for sympathetic priests and even non-Catholic laypeople. She received numerous honours and accolades, such as the Pope John XXIII Peace Prize in 1971 and the Nobel Peace Prize in 1979. In the latter instance, she refused the customary banquet and asked that the money be given to the poor in India instead. India awarded her the Bharat Ratna in 1980. She took the name 'Teresa' in homage to the memory of St Thérèse of Lisieux, and lived her life in the spirit of St Francis. She achieved celebrity status and was universally admired, but also had her share of critics, especially for her unflinching opposition to contraception as well as abortion, but also for what seemed to be her praise of poverty. Adverse comments were sometimes expressed about the alleged uncertain allocation of the vast funds raised on behalf of her organization. Mother Teresa also passed through periods of intense religious doubt and depression which she did not try to conceal. Nevertheless, in 2003 Pope John Paul II beatified Mother Teresa as Blessed Teresa of Calcutta. At the time of her death, Mother Teresa's Order numbered more than 4,000 sisters as well as many brothers and various associates.

Kathryn Spink, *Mother Teresa: A complete authorized biography* (New York, 1997); Navin Chawla, *Mother Teresa: The Authorized Biography* (London, 1992; Louise Slavicek, *Mother Teresa* (New York, 2007).

THÉRÈSE COUDERC, St (Marie Victoire Thérèse Couderc) (1805–1885)

French founder and spiritual writer.

She was born at Le Mas de Sablières in the Ardèche. She joined the Sisters of Saint Regis and became a novice mistress and house Superior in Lalouvesc, and eventually Superior General of her Order. Fr Stephen Terme, a diocesan missionary, pilgrimage chaplain and parish priest in a poor and minimally-educated area, asked her and two other nuns to run a mountain hostel for women pilgrims making pilgrimages to the tomb of St Regis. She found that many of the pilgrims had scant knowledge of their faith, and in 1826, to repair this deficiency as best as possible, founded, together with Fr Terme, the Congregation of Our Lady of the Retreat in the Cenacle, an Order dedicated to running retreats based initially on the Spiritual Exercises of St Ignatius of Loyola. From 1878 lay members could join the congregation. The Order now has about 600 nuns in 16 countries. Thérèse suffered from severe illnesses, was falsely accused of diversion of funds, was for a time separated from the Order, then humiliated by direction to menial tasks, but was eventually rehabilitated. She went through periods of great spiritual dryness, yet developed an authentic spirituality of hope and endurance in which she did not flinch from recognition of her difficulties. This example still helps and inspires those who pass through similar states of mind and spirit. She was beatified in 1851 and canonized by Pope Paul VI in 2006.

Hélène Caumeil & Chantal de la Forge, *Prier 15 jours avec Thérèse Couderc* (Paris, 2005).

THÉRÈSE of Lisieux, St (1873–97)

French nun, autobiographer, poet and dramatist. Doctor of the Church.

Thérèse Martin was born into an intensely religious Norman family. She was the last of nine children, of whom five girls survived; all became nuns. Thérèse's mother died when she was just four years old. At fifteen Thérèse became a Carmelite nun in the convent at Lisieux and took the name 'of the Child Jesus' to which she later added 'and the Holy Face.' She was made novice-mistress of her convent but suffered from extreme ill-health. In spite of the obscurity of her short life, her 'little way' and her approach to the execution of everyday tasks and duties with care and humility were soon immensely influential among all sorts and conditions of people. She was asked to write her autobiography by her Mother Superior. She died of tuberculosis aged 24. Her *Journal of a Soul* (at first heavily edited and only recently published as written) became extremely popular and has had a universal influence.

Thérèse de l'Enfant-Jésus et de La Sainte Face, *Histoire d'une Âme* (Lisieux 1898; id., *Oeuvres Complètes* (Paris, 2001); *St Thérèse of Lisieux, Story of a Soul*, J. Clarke, tr. (Washington DC, 1975); *Poems of St Thérèse of the Child Jesus*, Carmelites of Santa Clara, tr. (London, 1925); *Lettres de Sainte Thérèse de Lisieux de l'Enfant Jésus*, A. Combes, ed. (Paris, 1948); *Collected Letters of Saint Thérèse of Lisieux*, F. J. Sheed, tr. (London & New York, 1949); Ida Görres, *The Hidden Face* (London, 1959); Felicity Leng, *Smiles of God: the Flowers of St Thérèse of Lisieux* (London, 2003).

WALBURG SCHEFFLERIN VON EICHSTÄTT, Mother (d. 1528)

German Brigittine prioress and chronicler.

Mother Walburg kept a 'Salbuch', in which she wrote a detailed account of the achievements and characters of 76 sisters and 32 brothers of the Unterlinden Convent in Nuremberg in the early sixteenth century and during the Peasant Wars that devastated the area. Her short lives of the religious there complement the details of convent life that appear in the 60 or so surviving letters of Sister Katharina Lemlin (or Katharina Lemmel), a well-to-do widow who became a founder-nun there.

Georg Grupp, 'Maihinger Brigitterinnen aus Nürnberg,' *Mitteilungen des Vereins für die Geschichte der Stadt Nürnberg*, 13 (1896), 79–97; Johan Kamann, 'Briefe aus dem Birgittenkloster: Maihingen im Ries 1516–1522', *Zeitschrift für Kulturgeschichte*, 6 (1899), 249–327, 385–410; 7 (1900), 170–99.

WENDY BECKETT, Sr (1930–)

English nun, teacher, writer, consecrated virgin.

She was born in South Africa and brought up in Edinburgh. In 1946 she entered the convent of the Sisters of Notre Dame de Namur. After taking a degree at Oxford, she taught English and Latin in the Notre Dame convent school in South Africa. When the Order closed she returned to Britain and obtained papal permission to become a consecrated virgin. She lives in a caravan in the grounds of a Carmelite convent in Norfolk where she spends much of the time in contemplative silence and prayer. She allows herself two hours work a day. She has written numerous books and made several television documentaries on art (initially on contemporary art but later on many aspects of the subject).

Sister Wendy Beckett, *Sister Wendy Contemplates Saint Paul in Art* (London, 2008); id., *Encounters with God: In Quest of the Ancient Icons of Mary* (London, 2009). Television documentaries: *Sister Wendy's Odyssey* (1992); *Sister Wendy's Grand Tour* (1997).

YVETTE OF HUY, Bd (Ivetta of Huy; Juette of Huy; Jutta of Huy) (1158–1228)

Mother, nun and visionary of the Low Countries.

A thirteenth-century anchoress known to us from the *Life* by John of Magdeburg (who also wrote a biography of Margaret the Lame of Magdeburg), but above all from the Latin biography by the Premonstratensian Hugh of Floreffe, who relays to us her own accounts of her visions and the people who came to consult her. She was born into a wealthy family at Huy, near Liège, now Belgium. Her father (whom she converted in later life) forced her to marry when she was only 12 or 13. She had three children and was widowed before she was 18. From then on she shunned various suitors and ordinary secular life, and chose to labour in a hospital for lepers for ten years. Then she asked to be walled up as a recluse in a room next to the lepers, and lived there for another ten years, experiencing occasions of vivid and privileged enlightenment while enraptured. She claimed to have been granted a special gift of discernment of minds and souls, and even of foreknowledge, which enabled her to help many of those who came to her for psychotherapy, and to rescue or chasten priests and religious who tried to seduce others or were in danger of offending against their vows in various ways. One of her sons became a Cistercian and abbot of Orval.

Chrysostomus Henriques, *Lilia Cistercii sive sacrarum virginum Cisterciencium origo, instituta et res gestae* (Douai, 1633); Hugh of Floreffe, *Acta Sanctorum*, 13 January; id., *The Life of Yvette of Huy*, Jo Ann McNamara, tr. & ed. (Toronto, 2000); Jennifer Carpenter, 'Juette of Huy: Mother and Recluse', in Jennifer Carpenter & Sally-Beth MacLean, eds, *Power of the Weak: Studies on Medieval Women* (Champaign, 1995); Isabelle Cochelin, 'Evolution de la sainteté laïque: L'exemple de Juette de Huy (1158–1228)', *Le Moyen Age*, 95 (1989), 397–417.

General Works on Women Religious

Arenal, Electa & Stacey Schlau, eds, *Untold sisters: Hispanic Nuns in their Own Works*, USA 1989.

Carr, Thomas M., guest editor, Anne L. Birberick and Russell Ganim, eds. *Studies in Early Modern France, Vol. 11, The Cloister and the World: Early Modern Convent Voices*, USA 2007.

Choudhury, Mita, *Convents and Nuns in Eighteenth-Century French Politics and Culture*, USA 2004.

Dauge-Roth, Katherine, *Nuns, Demons and Exorcisms: Ventriloquism and the Voice of Authority in Provence (1609–1611)*, USA 2008.

Dauzet, Dominique-Marie, *La Mystique Bien Tempérée: écriture feminine de l'expérience spirituelle XIXe – XXe siècle*, Paris 2006.

Diefendorf, Barbara B., *From Penitence to Charity: Pious Women and the Catholic Reformation in Paris*, Oxford 2004.

Evangelisti, Silvia, *Nuns: A History of Convent Life*, Oxford 2007.

Flinders, Carol Lee, *Enduring Grace: Living Portraits of Seven Women Mystics*, London 1993.

Fremantle, Anne, ed., *The Protestant Mystics: an Anthology of Spiritual Experience from Martin Luther to T.S. Eliot*, USA 1964.

McNamara, Jo Ann Kay, *Sisters in Arms: Catholic Nuns Through Two Millennia*, USA 1996.

Myers, Kathleen A, & Amanda Powell eds. *A Wild Country Out in the Garden: The Spiritual Journals of a Colonial Mexican Nun*, USA 1999.

Rapley, Elizabeth, *The Dévotes: Women and Church in Seventeenth Century France*, USA 1990.

—— *A Social History of the Cloister: Daily Life in the Teaching Monasteries of the Old Regime*, Canada 2001.

Ranft, Patricia, *Woman's Way: The Forgotten History of Women Spiritual Directors*, USA 2000.

Russell, Rinaldini, ed., *Sister Maria Celeste's Letters to Her Father, Galileo*, USA 2000.

Sobel, Dava, *Galileo's Daughter: A Historical Memoir*, USA 1996.

Acknowledgements

The author and publisher gratefully acknowledge the kind permission of the following to reprint and/or adapt extracts from published and unpublished works:

A passage from *Mother Maria Skobtsova: Essential Writings*. English edition copyright © 2003 by Orbis Books. Published in 2003 by Orbis Books, Maryknoll, New York 10545. Used by permission of the publisher.

An excerpt from the Nobel Prize Acceptance Speech of Bd Mother Teresa of Calcutta, copyright: The Nobel Foundation, used with permission.

Sister Helen Prejean CSJ, for the poem 'More is Required' and an extract from a letter to Mr Timothy Lockwood on proposed amendments to the lethal injection protocol in California, both copyright © 2011 Sister Helen Prejean, used with permission.

The Discalced Carmelite nuns of the Carmel of the Mother of God, Pewaukee, Wisconsin, USA, for poems by Jessica Powers (Sister Miriam of the Holy Spirit) from: *The Selected Poetry of Jessica Powers*, Regina Siegfried & Robert Morneau, eds (published by ICS publications, Washington, D.C., 1999) or: Jessica Powers, *The House at Rest* (published by Carmelite Monastery, Pewaukee, WI). Used with permission.

The Congregation of Jesus and the estate of Judith Buxton for an excerpt from a talk entitled 'Light from the Buddha', by Sister Pia Buxton CJ, published originally in the *Tablet*, London, and copyright © 2010 Judith Buxton. Used with permission.

Sister Sandra Schneiders IHM, the *National Catholic Reporter*, the International Association of Conciliar Theology and SCM Press for an excerpt from an article 'Why We Stay(ed)' by Sister Sandra Schneiders that appeared in *Concilium* and originally in the *National Catholic Reporter*, copyright © 2010 Sandra Schneiders, used with permission.

ACKNOWLEDGEMENTS

John Griffiths and Charles Crawford for translations of extracts from the writings of St Catherine of Siena in *The Cell of Self-Knowledge*, ed. J. Griffiths (Dublin & New York, 1981), copyright © 1981 John Griffiths & Charles Crawford.

Sources of quotations are acknowledged after extracts throughout this book, and occasionally after the short biographies in the final section. Every effort has been made to trace copyright holders. If any copyright has been left unacknowledged and has been unknowingly infringed, apology is made for this and full acknowledgement will be made in future editions of this work. All otherwise unreferenced translations, adaptations and modernizations are the work of the author and copyright © 2011 by Felicity Leng.

Index